D0793499

DAMN THE TORPEDOES

Other Books by the Same Author

Agenda: A Plan for Action (1971)
Exit Inflation (1981)
Jobs for All: Capitalism on Trial (1984)
Canada at the Crossroads (1990)

DAMN THE TORPEDOES

My Fight To Unify
Canada's Armed Forces

Paul Hellyer

May 15, 1990

To: Matthew McBride
In appreciation of an excellent
interview and with many best wish

Paul T. Hellyer

M&S

For my family and extended family

Canadian Cataloguing in Publication Data

Hellyer, Paul, 1923-
  Damn the torpedoes

Includes bibliographical references.
ISBN 0-7710-4061-X

1. Hellyer, Paul, 1923-   . 2. Canada – Politics
and government – 1963-1968.* 3. Canada – Military
policy.   4. Canada. Canadian Armed Forces –
Organization – History.   5. Cabinet ministe Forces –
Organization – History.   5. Cabinet ministers –
Canada – Biography.* I. Title.

FC621.H44A3 1990   971.064'3'092   C90-093414-X
F1034.3.H44A3 1990

Printed and bound in Canada. The paper used in this book is acid free.

McClelland & Stewart Inc.
The Canadian Publishers
481 University Avenue
Toronto, Ontario
M5G 2E9

CONTENTS

ACKNOWLEDGEMENTS

Many people and organizations have been helpful in the preparation of this book. I am indebted to the National Defence Historical Section for access to Defence Council minutes; to Laurie Farrington and Thelma Nicholson of the Access to Information Office for providing me with every comfort while reviewing cabinet minutes; to Dacre P. Cole, Historical Section, Department of External Affairs, for searching out records; and to the Public Archives for exceptional cooperation. John Smith in Ottawa, as well as Charles Dwarka and Bryan Davis in Toronto, deserve special thanks for arranging to have many of my records shipped to Toronto for convenient access. This saved much time and expense.

I am also very grateful to those who read part or all of the manuscript: former Deputy Ministers Elgin Armstrong and John Baldwin; my friend from political days, former Chief Judge Colin Bennett; my long-suffering and faithful former private secretary, Margaret Bulger; my executive assistant and right arm throughout the difficult unification days, Bill Lee; independent critics Bill Bussiere and James Maclean; ex-cabinet colleagues Walter Harris and Jack Pickersgill; my sister, Hazel Race; and last, but by no means least, my former military aides Marc Favreau and Reg Weeks. Some of them knew much of the story first-hand and consequently were able to point out numerous errors and omissions. Those that slipped through the net are my responsibility alone.

Darcea Hiltz deserves special mention for countless hours spent doing research and verifying facts and for then patiently recording the narrative chapter by chapter.

I am grateful to Pat Kennedy for her careful and inspired editing and, finally, to Avie Bennett and Douglas Gibson of McClelland & Stewart for their conviction that the story should be told. Without them it would just be gathering dust.

INTRODUCTION

"It is difficult to quote Hellyer in cold type without making him look conceited; whereas unembarrassed objectivity would be a better description." This quotation from an article by David Willock that appeared in the *Montreal Standard* at the outset of my political career, came to mind as I began to write this book. I dislike the first person singular to the point that I sometimes use the "royal we", to which my wife invariably objects when it is not precise. Consequently, after only a few pages, I abandoned any attempt to fudge the issue or feign false modesty. I simply tell the story the way I remember it.

This is not a political history and no attempt has been made to include the achievements of other players on the political field. It is simply part of my story, which includes diverse encounters and interactions with myriad others. In many cases their roles are not adequately recognized, and this is especially true of my long-suffering family; my private secretary, Marg Bulger, whose responsibilities extended far beyond those normally associated with the office; and my special assistant, Bill Lee. Without Bill's extraordinary expertise and effort I could not possibly have accomplished as much. He was always at my side, counselling and encouraging his minister at every step along the stormy path. I acknowledge this debt at the outset, along with my gratitude to the literally hundreds of friends, relatives, and political supporters whose names are not mentioned at all. They have been shortchanged by the severe limitations of space and context.

Two further notes of explanation. I have not attempted to use non-specific terms when it comes to a distinction by gender; and although I quote extensively from my diary, it will be obvious that it was originally written without thought of publication. I include numerous quotes from it because they provide a more accurate reflection of how I felt at the time than I would be capable of achieving in retrospect – and without the filter of hindsight. I should also mention that I use the military titles and abbreviations that were used at the time the events occurred.

The unification of the armed forces forms the principal part of the narrative. A number of books have been written by opponents of unification and they contain much that I consider unfairly biased. The most damaging allegation is that the whole reorganization was politically motivated. This is an absolute falsehood! The Royal Canadian Navy, Canadian Army, and Royal Canadian Air Force were combined to form a single Canadian Armed Force because the Government of Canada and I thought it was the right thing to do, and I still think so.

Changes of such sweeping magnitude do not come either automatically or easily, however, and for that reason I have written the central part of the story more or less chronologically, as a case study in political process. Inevitably this means the inclusion of much that is trivial and the exclusion of other material of greater substance. My hope is that people interested in politics may gain a deeper insight into the day-by-day activities of men and women in public life – their family tensions, changing roles, and the mood-altering events to which they are exposed. In this context the necessity of coping with the massive inertia of the bureaucratic system may help explain why it is easy for politicians to promise radical change, and then find it extremely difficult to deliver. That was the case with unification.

Frequently I am asked if, given the opportunity to turn the clock back, I would still champion unification. The answer is an unequivocal yes. Three separate services today is as out of date as a horse-drawn cart on Highway 401. A case could be made for two services in countries as large as the United States and the U.S.S.R. – a navy and an army each with its own air corps – although I personally think one service would be preferable. But for countries with the population of Britain, France, Australia, Canada, and others, no case can be made for more than one. The existence of three is an anachronism – a legacy from a different technological era. Naturally I would do some things differently a second time, with the advantage of a blueprint, though these would be primarily differences of style. On questions of substance, we were amazingly close the first time around.

The gun-blazing opposition that I faced was anticipated. No one can tamper with respected symbols without attracting substantial and sustained fire. Yet though we were on opposite sides of the trench, I would not want to give the impression that I lacked respect for my opponents. On the contrary, my regard for

Air Chief Marshal Frank Miller was deep and not without affection. The same held true, in varying degrees, for many of the other senior officers. Even the controversial Rear-Admiral William Landymore gets a high mark in my book because he was one of the few who really believed that I would do exactly what I said. I sometimes wonder, had history been different, and had my career been in the navy, if I might have been the Landymore. I like to think that, had he been the minister, he would have reached an entirely different conclusion than the one he held so strongly.

Perhaps it was inevitable that there would be some regression in the twenty years since unification became law. The establishment of Air Command, as a de facto air force headquarters, was a big step backward, and quite inconsistent with the RCAF philosophy of functional commands. A few senior officers, nostalgia-bound, couldn't accept the fact that an air force isolated from sea and land forces doesn't make sense, and they insisted they should have a "headquarters" of their own. Pity!

The hybrid civil and military armed forces "headquarters" in Ottawa was not part of my plan for unification. It came later, when Donald Macdonald was minister. He set up a Management Review Group, which recommended the merger. I have not studied the new system in depth and am not qualified to comment on its efficacy.

The return to separate uniforms under the Mulroney government, while popular with many World War II veterans and a minority of servicemen and women, was not well thought out and recreates some of the problems we faced at the time. In a unified force, in which fifty percent or more of personnel do not "belong" to navy, army, or air force, which uniform do the doctors, dentists, lawyers, communicators, and pay and supply people wear? The choice we had to make was for four uniforms or one, and the dilemma remains. The Mulroney government's emotion-driven backward march has already resulted in some unnecessary layers of "fat". More can be expected as illogic is pursued.

Certainly the time has come when it is possible to return to traditional colours. For several years I have been recommending navy blue for winter, khaki for summer, and white for ceremonial or "showing the flag" in foreign ports. For both psychological and practical reasons, however, the same uniform should be worn by all, with caps and badges used to identify trades, corps, and commands.

Finally it is no doubt unfortunate that the immediate post-unification years coincided with drastic cut-backs in military expenditures. This permitted both opponents and armchair analysts to attribute cause and effect. Of course unification is not responsible. Had those same years been a period of increased budgets and augmented personnel and equipment, the perception of unification might have benefited unfairly from the positive circumstances. The concept is valid because it permits the most efficient use of available resources. Not everyone will be convinced by the contents of this book, though I hope all readers will have a better understanding of the reasons for unification and why I believe that its implementation established Canada as a world leader in military organization.

CHAPTER 1

EARLY DAYS
AND POLITICS

A ugust 6, 1923, was a beastly hot summer day. Late in the afternoon my mother, Lulla Maude, asked that my father, Audrey Samuel, be summoned from the fields to fetch a doctor. Soon, as the exhausted and dust-covered threshers were washing up for supper, a cry from the front bedroom announced my arrival.

Home for the next seventeen years was Mont Clair View, a handsome though somewhat austere brick farm house, protected from the livestock by a fence heavy with hanging roses. It stood on the west side of the Cockshutt Road, which connected Brantford with Port Dover. We were two miles due east of Waterford, and the view from the back window included Mont Clair, the farm's original house, where my Uncle Russell and Aunt Lillian lived with their four children – Shirley, Mildred, Walter, and Editha. Father made his living from the land, and although he and Uncle Russell were classed as general farmers, their specialty and number-one crop was ginseng which, in 1715, had become one of Canada's earliest exports to the Orient.

My school life began at S.S. No. 15, just a field away from home, and continued at Waterford High about two and a half miles away. I was never a great student, but when Ken Richardson took over as principal, his personal interest produced some positive results without discouraging my participation in drama, music, and sports. After four years, I gained a graduation diploma.

I had a passion for aeronautics, which I considered a tremendously important field for a large, sparcely-populated country like Canada, and on graduation I got a bee in my bonnet and decided to take a course in aeronautical engineering at one of the American schools specializing in the subject. My choice was Curtiss-Wright Technical Institute of Aeronautics in Glendale, California. Its curriculum included all the basic requirements of engineering, without "wasting" any time on languages, history, or philosophy. That seemed like a great idea to me at the time, because I confess that I had not yet developed a genuine appreciation of the liberal arts.

Following graduation from Curtiss-Wright, I accepted a job at Fleet Aircraft Limited, Fort Erie, Ontario, which had a contract to build the Cornell primary trainer for the RCAF. It was an interesting assignment and my promotion was swift; but when production goals had been met and the company began to retool for the manufacture of Lancaster wings, I decided it was time to go, and early in the spring of 1944 I enlisted in the air force, which had always been my first love. I was tempted to apply for a commission as an engineer, with the idea of remustering to aircrew later, as several of my colleagues from Curtiss-Wright had done, but with my penchant for doing things the hard way, I finally opted to start at the bottom as aircrew-in-training.

This decision turned out to be as educational as it was frustrating. A year earlier the RCAF hadn't taken anyone who didn't agree to be a pilot, but it was subsequently determined that estimates of aircrew losses had been considerably overstated and this led to a dramatic reversal of policy. So much had the policy changed that, when it came time for specific assignments, only three out of three hundred enlistees were chosen as potential pilots. Probably because I had taken a few flying lessons in California, I was one of them. Naturally I was in high spirits when I was posted to Camp Borden en route to Initial Flying Training School. A few weeks of useful employment, better known to airmen as "useless duties", seemed like a small price to pay for such a big step along the way. Alas, the weeks dragged into months. Trainees who had been selected as air-gunners or wireless-operators got on course. So did those navigators who needed a mathematics refresher. Everyone got on course except the three potential pilots and twenty-four navigators who had been chosen as pilots and navigators and who had qualified in mathematics. Again, I was one of them.

Little did we dream that the Mackenzie King government was being shaken by an internal crisis. The Canadian Army was desperately short of reinforcements, and although a referendum had given Prime Minister Mackenzie King the authority to send conscripts overseas, he stubbornly refused for fear of offending his hard-core Liberal support in Quebec. Defence Minister J. L. Ralston resigned in disgust, precipitating a crisis that came close to toppling the regime. Part of the fallout was a decision to release 4,200 surplus aircrew, including myself, my buddy A. G. "Gibby" Allen, now Dr. Allen, and my future colleague and MP James Gillies – presumably in the hope that many of us would wind up in the army and thereby help relieve the need for reinforcements.

I was sent back to the RCAF Manning Depot in Toronto, where the confusion was so great it took nine weeks for discharge. My only consolation was the Active Service Canteen on Adelaide Street East, where one could relax or dance with carefully selected hostesses under the watchful eye of wonderfully dedicated supervisors like Irma Pattison and Peggy Jennings. It was there, during a Paul Jones, that I met an extraordinarily beautiful blonde, Ellen Ralph, who would soon play a major role in my life. When I finally got my discharge, I joined the army, where I was assigned to the Royal Canadian Artillery (Mobile), because my mathematics was above average. Shortly thereafter I was posted to "C" Troop, "D" Medium Battery, Canadian Army Training Corps, at Petawawa on the Ottawa River.

The whole indoctrination process was so absurd that I didn't know whether to laugh or cry. I received new documentation and new "dog tags". Then there was drill. When I mentioned that I was fully trained in the art of forming threes, I was told "that was air force square-bashing". Next was gas drill. The mask was the same as in the air force, but the technique was just different enough that previous experience could be contemptuously dismissed as "air force gas drill". The final indignity occurred when a doctor came by and ordered me to roll up my sleeve. The fact that I was already immunized brought a slightly scornful, "Ah yes, but those were air force shots."

I can't say that my service experience was a significant factor in the subsequent decision to unify the three forces, but it must have had an effect on the subconscious. It was of no real import that airmen slept between sheets and soldiers didn't; but I did resent soldiers being treated as second- or third-class citizens, and I abhorred the fact that, when the army overseas was desperate for reinforcements, grown men indulged in silly games that squandered valuable time. There was little effective cooperation between the services when each concentrated almost exclusively on its own interests.

On June 1, 1945, Ellen Ralph and I were married at St. Columba's United Church in Toronto. A few days later Germany surrendered, and the war in Europe was over.

As soon as I was discharged, I decided to go to university. In part it was to get even with Mackenzie King for wasting two valuable years; but more importantly, I wanted to broaden my education, which had been too narrowly technical. I decided to seek admission to the University of Toronto, but that meant living in the big city, where affordable housing was virtually non-existent. Ellen and I ploughed through the advertisements every day and scoured the city for leads, but always to no avail. Veterans had to double up with relatives or settle for a life in attics or basements.

In desperation, we considered the idea of buying a store with an apartment overhead – with a little help from my family – and spent many evenings looking at opportunities of various sorts. Finally we settled on Mari-Jane Fashions, a ladies ready-to-wear shop on Bloor Street West, which had nice living quarters above. Although we were lucky to have a roof over our heads, life was not all a bowl of cherries. We had neither icebox nor refrigerator, and storing some ham in the breadbox produced an early miracle of multiplying maggots. Ellen's washing machine was a tub with scrub board and brush. However, on the positive side she got her clothes wholesale and enjoyed the responsibility of buying for and working in the store.

By the fall of 1946 I was ready to enroll at the U. of T.'s University College. In choosing my subjects I combined my personal preferences with those subjects I needed for a proper balance. English was a must, as were political science and economics. My other courses included physics, mathematics, and psychology.

On June 26, 1947, our first child, Mary Elizabeth, was born. As a portent of things to be, I couldn't be found at the critical time, so Ellen had to take a taxi to the hospital. After she arrived she was joined by her sister-in-law, nurse Betty Ralph, who had volunteered to help. Thank goodness she did, because as things turned out, Betty was needed to assist with some tricky complications. When it was all over, Betty called to say both mother and baby daughter were doing well. I made a beeline for the hospital and that indescribable reunion that only parents will understand.

Notwithstanding the pressures of keeping up with family life, attending university, studying music, singing professionally, running the business (and rebuilding it after the store and apartment were completely gutted by fire in November 1947), my preoccupation – superimposed on all other activity – was the relentless pursuit of a Liberal nomination for the 1949 general election. On campus I had attended the meetings of all of the parties and had concluded that none of them were perfect. On balance, however, the Liberal Party seemed closest to my personal philosophy, which was quite far left, though never outright socialist. My heroes included Beland Honderich, then Financial Editor of the *Toronto Star*, and I often quoted from his editorials in my essays. Any remaining doubt about the Liberals was removed when I attended the 1948 convention that chose Louis St. Laurent as leader. The convention was in August and in September I got my card at the University of Toronto Liberal Club, where I rubbed shoulders with future notables like Keith Davey, Judy LaMarsh, Gordon Dryden, and Joe Potts. It was a dedicated group of up-and-comers.

I had already decided that I wanted to be elected to Parliament to see what I could do about my two principal concerns – housing and the economy. As Ellen and I had discovered, the early post-war housing shortage was desperate. We had made the right move when we bought Mari-Jane Fashions. The majority were less fortunate, and I was convinced that it was possible to speed up the construction of good, modest houses to meet their urgent requirements.

My concerns about the economy were related, but even more important to the future welfare of my generation. At college I was perplexed and dismayed by what I was taught. In effect, my professors accepted the destructive consequences of business cycles as natural and inevitable. They were so successful in transmitting this morbid theology to their students that, when I polled fifteen seniors as to whether they considered periodic recessions to be inevitable or not, they all gave me either a categorical or a qualified "yes". Fourteen of them quoted and the other one paraphrased the same section of the same textbook in support of their conclusion.

I would go home shaking my head in disbelief and dismissing the conventional wisdom as garbage. I was convinced that, historically, business cycles had been monetary phenomena. Influenced by the work of the great Yale Professor Irving Fisher, I concluded that the Great Depression reflected the ultimate folly of our entrenched establishment. It didn't have to happen, so, I reasoned, the post-war disaster that economists were then predicting for about 1950 could be averted with the application of a little common sense. Fearing both economic and political consequences of yet another major depression, I was driven to do everything possible to get elected, so I could do my bit to help prevent a fresh epidemic of man's inhumanity to man.

When I told Liberal stalwarts about my interest in running in the election that was expected in 1949, it was taken as something of a joke, because of my youth and inexperience. But months of persistence and a switch from one riding to another finally paid off. With the election well under way, and no other acceptable candidate in sight, my nomination in the strongly Conservative district of Davenport was unopposed. That was the easy part and simply made it possible for me to participate in what I now term "mission impossible". With five weeks to go, there were no more than a few dozen people in the riding who knew my name – and "name identification", as it's called in the trade, was a major concern, doubly important in those days before party affiliation was put on the ballot. I saturated the turf with blotters, balloons, sound trucks, and aerial banners – anything to attract voter attention.

There was such a lack of manpower that I was saddled with the jobs of publicity chairman, organization chairman, and finance chairman, in addition to that of candidate, so I hired three university students to do some of the legwork. Terry Doidge, Ray Tower, and Lewis Hertzman did a thorough door-to-door canvas, several years before Stephen Lewis was credited with inventing the idea. They faithfully reported the reactions they were getting, and it appeared we were making progress, but there was still a considerable gulf between our level of support and the victory we hoped for. With nowhere in particular to turn for help, I drafted a strong, emotional appeal in the form of a letter to electors from two-year-old daughter Mary Elizabeth. She had no backyard to play in, and other children were even less fortunate. Her Daddy wanted to get elected to do something about it.

Mary Elizabeth's letter was mailed first class in a plain envelope, so that voters would at least open it and take a peek. It was delivered the Friday before the Monday election, and overnight the canvassers could feel the impact. So, despite election-day odds of 15 to 1 against me at the local pub, when the votes were counted I had won by 955. The final score was: Hellyer (Lib.), 11,431; MacNicol (PC), 10,476; Archer (CCF), 7,366. Davenport had elected a Liberal for the first time since Confederation. Pandemonium broke loose, and it was congratulations and kisses all round as we celebrated and paraded triumphantly through the riding.

Of course this account of the story would be incomplete if I didn't point out that I was elected in a Liberal sweep. In 1949, Louis St. Laurent was a very popular father figure, and much of the ride was on his coattails. Toronto elected seven of his candidates, six more than ever before. The veteran Dave Croll was expected to win big in Spadina; J. W. G. (Jake) Hunter, Lionel Conacher, and A. J. P. (Pat) Cameron were considered possibles in Parkdale, Trinity, and High Park, respectively; Charlie Henry had been a long shot in Rosedale; and James Rooney won in St. Paul's despite "Boss" Doug McNish's disapproval. But Davenport was considered barren turf, and was consequently the biggest surprise of the seven.

A common fallacy of newly elected Members of Parliament is that they are a "Mr. or Ms. Somebody". And why not? Haven't the voters just picked them from a wide field to be their representative in Ottawa? The press contribute to this ego inflation. At twenty-five, I was the youngest MP in Canada, and the Toronto media were more than generous in their coverage. Then the *Montreal Standard*, a weekly supplement read by millions, ran a feature article on me, complete with a family portrait. It was pretty heady stuff. In Ottawa, however, the dawn of reality came quickly. No one told me what to do and, worse, no one seemed to care. Far from being a "Mr. Somebody", I was just a very, very small cog in a big impersonal machine.

Back-benchers were stacked two to an office, which is a far cry from the two- and three-room suites MPs take for granted in the eighties. My roommate, Ralph Osborne Campney, K.C., was the new member for Vancouver Centre, and the doubling up must have been quite an adjustment for one of W. L. Mackenzie King's former secretaries, who was later to become the senior partner in Campney, Owen and Cline, one of Vancouver's largest and most prestigious law firms. At fifty-five he was also old enough to be my father but, in what proved to be characteristic good humour, his opening words were, "If we are going to be cooped up in this office together, I guess we might as well use first names." That was okay with me, and this was the beginning of a comfortable relationship that was to continue through the years, as my footsteps followed his up the rungs at National Defence.

While parliamentary life was not uncongenial, I found that my political clout was just slightly above zero on a scale of one to ten, and I was often frustrated when no one was particularly interested in my economic ideas. The normal attention span of those kind enough to listen to them was less than five minutes, and my High Park colleague, Pat Cameron, finally put their reaction to me in a nutshell. "Young man, you don't remember the Great Depression," he explained, not unkindly, but in a way that made it clear that no-one my age could understand what made the world go round. As it happens, I did remember the Great Depression – well – but I was learning that in the realm of economics, everyone is an expert. Still, I continued to fuss about the ominous financial news and the new depression that had been predicted. Then, on June 27, 1950, a year to the day after my election, the Korean War began. Fear of an economic downturn quickly abated, as the same conservative financiers who lacked the wit to keep the economy afloat in peacetime "found" the money to ensure that the war effort was adequately financed.

In retrospect, the Korean conflict saw us through the period of greatest economic danger, and by the time the armistice was signed, the ideas of the great English economist, John Maynard Keynes, had penetrated the halls of academe. Then, for the first time in the more than a hundred and fifty years since the Industrial Revolution began, economic theory bore some workable relationship to the real world. Although there was another tiny thundercloud barely visible on the horizon as inflation began to inch its way upward, we were to be spared long enough to enjoy about fifteen years of unprecedented prosperity in which capital and labour both reaped handsome rewards.

I sat in the Commons almost religiously for two years, and one thing I became acutely aware of was the repetition. Many MPs, including stalwarts like Stanley Knowles, Winnipeg North Centre, and John Blackmore, Lethbridge, made basically the same speech every time their favourite subjects came up. After the first few times, when I had memorized most of the discussion, my learning curve began to drop sharply. It was suddenly revived by an accident of fate. Archie Whitelaw, who had been president of the Toronto and Yorks Young Liberals, and in that capacity helpful in my campaign, had been exposed to my housing ideas and alleged that he had clients with similar views. Would I be interested in meeting them?

Wilf Curran and Ted Hall of Curran Hall Limited, a house-building firm, entertained Archie and me at the Granite Club, which was probably my undoing. This wasn't my first glimpse of "the finer things of life", but I was still a novice, and I must have parked my brain when I parked my car. I became so intent on relating my story about the need for a General Motors of the housing business that I was oblivious to the fact that their periodic nods of agreement were perfunctory. They were desperately short of cash, and, as I found, they were interested in money rather than ideas. The upshot was that I invested my entire bundle – $4,000 – in Curran Hall. Worse, I persuaded my family to put up a comparable amount.

Not too many weeks later, after much prodding to get the facts, I realized that Curran Hall Limited was on the verge of bankruptcy. Had my investment been the only one at stake, I might have been willing to kiss it goodbye; but as Confucius undoubtedly said, "He who loses relatives' money loses face." Suddenly I found myself in the building business, plagued by material shortages, banks, bankers, and bureaucrats. It took all my spare time on weekends and holidays for eighteen months to rescue the company from the brink of oblivion and get it in the black. By then what had appeared initially to be a catastrophe was well on the way to proving a blessing in disguise. Not only was the company becoming profitable, it had provided me with a crash course in how the "real world" operates. It was very different from the theoretical world of books and classrooms.

In 1953 it was time for St. Laurent to renew his mandate, although he wisely postponed the election until August, so that it wouldn't interfere with the coronation of Queen Elizabeth II. When the election was all over, the government's majority was whittled down a bit, but it was still comfortable. I won handily in Davenport.

A big plus for the Toronto contingent was the election of two new MPs. One was Al Hollingworth, an up-and-coming lawyer from York Centre, who blotted out newspaper baron Roy Thomson. The other was York Scarborough's Frank Enfield, another fine young lawyer who was genuinely dedicated to public life. Frank, who was as easy to get along with as anyone could be, became my new office-mate and decided we should both take French lessons. The project didn't last long because of the pressures of our parliamentary schedule, but I was eternally grateful to Frank for sparking my interest in Canada's other official language.

After the election, the old subject of cabinet representation for Toronto resurfaced as a major issue. David Croll, the veteran MP for Toronto Spadina and former mayor of Windsor, appeared to be the logical choice, but the government kept stalling. Toronto MPs made representations to the Prime Minister in a concerted effort to have to have him appointed, but without success. Finally, after two years of indecision by the government, Dave was moved sideways to the Senate, and while this was a matter of keen disappointment to his friends, who had wanted to see him in the cabinet, it unlocked the previously barred door of opportunity for the rest of us. Competition was keen, and by early 1956 the Ottawa rumour mill about which Toronto MP might be chosen for promotion, was working three shifts.

On January 17, the grapevine reported that there was no decision yet, and I only wished that they would make up their minds. On February 7, Alex Hume, an Ottawa *Citizen* reporter who had the best pipeline to the PM's office, reported privately that prospects were poor for me. My heart sank. But I bounced back on February 8 when Alex advised me that my prospects were brighter and "to-morrow is critical". It was, and after cabinet met, word leaked out that all was well. At 6 p.m. the Prime Minister asked leave to read an order-in-council that named Lucien Cardin, MP for Richelieu-Verchères, as parliamentary assistant to External Affairs Minister Lester Pearson and me parliamentary assistant to Defence Minister Ralph Campney. The die was cast! I was ecstatic. At least I had my foot on the first rung, and I was delighted to be working for someone I knew and liked as well as my former roommate, who would provide me with an opportunity to prepare myself for the next step to cabinet rank.

Campney couldn't have been better! I knew in advance that the chemistry between us was right, but he really went overboard to include me in the inner circle. Briefings by the Naval Board, the Army General Staff, and the Air Staff were arranged for me, and each in turn shared with me their hopes and aspirations, right up to the "top secret" level. No doubt they were all seeking an ally to support their pet projects, but so much individual attention from so many high-ranking officers was a bit stunning.

My first assignement was less glamorous, but nonetheless useful. It was my first chance to put my business experience to work in government. I was given a four-inch-thick file on a citizen who owed the department $2,000. The man had no assets and was unlikely to ever have any – facts that had been confirmed by two or three agencies, including Dun & Bradstreet. Still, the Treasury Board wouldn't allow the sum to be written off and insisted that we sue, even though the Justice Department estimated this would cost about $10,000 in legal fees. No doubt it was my practical training, but after reading the evidence, I couldn't see any point in spending thousands of dollars to obtain a judgment that couldn't be enforced. I wrote a new and stiff submission to Treasury Board, with which they finally agreed.

December saw unexpected responsibilities loaded on my plate. Thousands of Hungarians had fled their homeland in the wake of the November uprising, and the Canadian government decided to admit a large number of them. Jack Pickersgill, as Minister of Citizenship and Immigration, was the minister in charge, but much of the action was centred in Toronto and he didn't have a parliamentary assistant of his own; I was adopted, albeit willingly, as his unofficial PA. For the next few days I was driven almost crazy by phone calls, including innumerable messages from JWP himself.

Then, before dawn on the thirteenth, in the middle of the Hungarian crisis, Ellen advised me that it was time to head for the hospital. The drive downtown through the Christmas lights was every bit as enchanting as it had been two years earlier when our second child and first son, Peter Lawrence, was born. When we arrived at Women's College Hospital, Dr. M. Yoneyama was again on hand, this time to deliver our second son, David Ralph – a good Biblical name complemented by Ellen's maiden name. It also just happened to be the same as that of my good friend and boss, Ralph Campney, so everyone was happy.

With the turn of the year we knew that 1957 would bring another election. It was to be one in which everything that could go wrong would. It would also be a continuation of the Liberal decline that dated from Mr. St. Laurent's exhausting six-week world trip in 1955. The trip left him depleted and incapable of exercising command. A relaxing summer at his country home at St. Patrick, Quebec, saw him bounce back tanned and fit, but from that point on his energy ebbed and flowed like the tide. Sometimes, as at his big seventy-fifth birthday bash in Quebec City, he radiated. At other times he was lacklustre and uninspired.

To his credit, Mr. St. Laurent wanted to quit before the 1957 election, but party activists exercised great pressure and appealed to his sense of loyalty to persuade him to stay. That decision, once made, only led to a thousand others, including the burning question of cabinet representation for Toronto on which he continued to procrastinate, even after the election was called. Walter Harris, who had succeeded C. D. Howe as the man who made political decisions for the Toronto area, consulted me on all matters relating to party fortunes in the city. On April 25, at a strategy session over lunch at the Ontario Club, he told me I would be getting a call from the Prime Minister that afternoon. A plan to bring in Edmonton's Mayor William Hawreluk had been abandoned at the last minute, but former minister Lionel Chevrier would be leaving the St. Lawrence Seaway Authority and returning to cabinet as President of the Privy Council.

When the phone rang the PM skipped the niceties and got directly to the point. "Would you like to join my colleagues and me in the cabinet as Associate Minister of National Defence?" he asked. "Yes I would, thank you very much, sir", I responded in equally business-like fashion. "Then if you will be good enough to come to Ottawa in the morning you will be sworn in at eleven," he added. There was little more except an exchange of regards to our respective wives.

The next morning, April 26, 1957, I met the PM and Chevrier at the Supreme Court building, where Chief Justice Patrick Kerwin administered the oaths. My joy knew no bounds. Toronto finally had a cabinet minister after a twenty-two-year drought. I had the further distinction of being the first Liberal minister in the history of the city. King and Mulock had been elected from the Yorks, and James Murdock, who was King's Minister of Labour and MP for Kent County, ran in High Park in 1925, but was soundly defeated. Until my appointment, no federal Liberal minister had ever represented the city proper. Press coverage was extensive and basically factual, but editorial reaction was mixed and not too complimentary. It was nothing personal, mind you, but as an antidote to years of Liberal neglect my appointment was a case of too little, too late.

My sole proposal to cabinet in those few brief weeks was an imaginative scheme for the disposal of the Long Branch Rifle Range. Although the property was surplus to Defence requirements, its disposition raised a nightmare of a problem because there were four levels of government involved and strings attached to certain parts of the land. I had begun working on the project soon after being named parliamentary assistant, and had engaged Eric Hanson, town planner, to prepare a scheme that included something for everyone. Finally I got the politicians together and hammered out a tentative agreement, with the powerful support of Metro Toronto's "Big Daddy", Fred Gardiner. After the election of 1957, the new Minister of National Defence, George Pearkes, V.C., would let the bureaucrats take over, and the former site of the rifle range, which should have become a unique beach park, became Ontario Hydro's generating plant with its "biggest coal pile in the Commonwealth".

The demands on my time increased immeasurably following my appointment, and I had to accept speaking engagements in other ridings. When I did knock on doors in Davenport, the signals were confused. Once, I did what no candidate should ever do. I spent a long time listening to a lady tell me how great I was and what a good job I was doing. Her vote appeared to be in the bag until I stepped down off the veranda and she added, in parting, "But, I can't stand C. D. Howe." I was just learning the immutable truth that "but" is the most important word in politics. You have to know the "buts" to know which way the wind is blowing.

My reading of the mood in the country was that the people weren't against the Prime Minister, although he had received a few spiteful letters from religious bigots in the West. The problem was that voters just couldn't stand the image of C. D. Howe, and the arrogance of the government as a whole, so they wanted to teach it a lesson by strengthening the Opposition. Even veteran journalists, who had urged a change, didn't expect a rout, and the respected Blair Fraser, who wrote his story in advance because *Maclean's* was going to press, said that the government had been re-elected, although it shouldn't have been.

Once the votes were counted the truth was out. When people all across the country decide to "strengthen the Opposition", the result is cumulative. The *Globe*'s early headline screamed "Harris, Howe, Hellyer Losing". In the end, Trinity's Stanley Haidasz was the only Liberal elected in Toronto. Across Canada the PCs had 112 seats to the Liberals' 105, while the CCF and Social Credit elected 25 and 19 respectively. When the military vote was in, the Prime Minister submitted his resignation and the Governor General invited John George Diefenbaker to form a government.

Back home, the change in pace was profound. Instead of "Yes, minister; no, minister", there was nothing but silence. The phone stopped ringing. The invitations stopped arriving. People would even cross the street when they saw me coming to avoid looking me in the eye – probably because they didn't know what to say. It was just like being dead. The experience put the whole "business" in perspective, and I never again took politics as seriously. For a defeated politician there is no greater blessing than a job to go to, and I was really grateful for Curran Hall Limited. Being the cautious type, I hadn't severed my connection in the few weeks after my cabinet appointment, "just in case" anything went wrong in the election. This proved to have been a wise precaution that permitted my easy transition from part-time to full-time president. I was now able to devote all my energy to the business.

In a few months, after the party had given him the signal that the time was ripe, Mr. St. Laurent announced that he was stepping down as leader. There is no doubt that Walter Harris was the former PM's choice for the succession. It is equally certain that he had majority caucus support. MPs liked and trusted him, whereas Mike Pearson, though affable, was often vague and academic and seemed uninterested in the warp and woof of partisan politics. But the pension decision had blunted Walter's edge. A $6 increase in the Old Age Pension, coming just before the election, had been an important issue and the final straw for some voters. Walter gamely took responsibility for the defeat, instead of dumping it on the collectivity as lesser men might have done. His opponents both inside and outside the party stuck him with the tag "Six-buck Harris", an epithet that jangled political nerves in Liberal circles.

Any lingering doubt about the succession was dispelled when the Nobel prizes were announced. What might have been a real race was over before it began. A committee of the Swedish Storting (Parliament) crowned LPB king of the Liberals, and the Canadian press made it official. The vote was a foregone conclusion – and in December it was made official. Although Paul Martin and Rev. Lloyd Henderson had their names on the ballot, the real vote had been taken in Stockholm weeks before.

Meanwhile, Prime Minister Diefenbaker had used the interregnum to good advantage. He had persuaded Her Majesty the Queen to open Parliament on October 14, but it wasn't the pomp and circumstance that would increase his popularity. It was the implementation of election promises between the opening of Parliament and the Christmas recess. The fiscally conservative St. Laurent government had left money in the bank, and the new Chief had no compunction about spending it. He increased veterans' pensions one day and the Old Age Pension the next. Public servants got a raise in pay. Money was made available for farm-stored wheat and the long-awaited construction of the Saskatchewan River dam was approved. Almost every day some new spending measure was introduced, and eventually almost everyone had benefited from the largesse.

Soon Diefenbaker was some kind of god to most Canadians, and in a strong position to seek a majority mandate any time the Opposition provided a reasonable excuse. By presenting his first non-confidence motion in the form of a silly suggestion that the government did not have the support of the House and the people and should therefore resign in favour of the Liberals, Pearson was more obliging than the PM could have dreamed. With the perfect scenario – the Opposition with egg on its face – Diefenbaker called an election on February 1, 1958.

I was in no mood to fight another election – especially one we had no chance of winning. Furthermore I had just contracted the mumps and felt rotten to say the least. But on February 7 my spirits were lifted by some lovely roses from my secretary Marg Bulger and her family and a call from Mike Pearson. He had heard that I was negative about running and begged me to change my mind. With diplomatic finesse he appealed to all the right instincts of loyalty to party, friends, and country. Eventually his boyish charm got to me, and I agreed to get out of my mumpy bed and stand. I put down my biography of Sir John A. Macdonald long enough to phone Marg, thank her for the flowers, let her know that I had decided to run, and ask her to turn on the switch with my supporters.

My opponent in Davenport was Doug Morton, a fellow member of Westmoreland United Church, who had beaten me handily the year before. The campaign and the result were as predicted. John Diefenbaker swept to victory with an unprecedented 208 seats – the biggest avalanche and highest proportion of the total Commons won in Canadian history. The Liberals were reduced to 49 seats and the CCF to 3. Even permanent fixtures like Stanley Knowles were swept away, and Toronto's Stan Haidasz lost his toehold in Trinity.

In August Ellen and I dedided to take a brief vacation at Arundel Lodge, in Muskoka. When we arrived, we learned that the owners, Edith and George Paish, were planning to sell. The business wasn't profitable and Edith was getting tired of cooking. We understood their problem, but it was devastating news, because we were really in love with the place. It was rustic but restful, and we always began to relax the minute we arrived. The mere thought of losing it brought tears to Mary Elizabeth's eyes. I wondered if it wouldn't be a perfect spot for a Liberal think-tank at a time when the party was in the depths. Buying it would also give Curran Hall Limited the opportunity to learn something about the tourist business, in case we decided to build a chain of motels. So, fully cognizant of the risk, the company bought Arundel.

A few days later, in early September, Keith Davey phoned to say that Ed Lockyer, the newly elected PC Member for Trinity, had died suddenly. Was I interested in running when the by-election was called? I reminded him that Stanley Haidasz had priority, but if for any reason he wasn't interested, I would be. I checked with Stan, who told me he had decided to devote his full energies to the practice of medicine – for the time being at least. Given the green light, I contacted George Ben, the riding president, who said my candidacy was okay with him, subject to the concurrence of Haidasz and Walter Harris. They probably all thought I was crazy, with the Gallup Poll showing the Tories swamping Grits by 60 percent to 30 percent. But fools rush in where angels fear to tread and, after all the pieces fell into place, I let the press know I would be seeking the nomination.

It was a campaign unlike any of the others. With volunteers drawn from all across the city, the organization was the best in my experience. It was so good that Allister Grosart, Diefenbaker's top strategist, later referred to it as a "text-book" organization. Every poll was canvassed, not just once but several times. On election day every poll was manned, inside and out, and there were plenty of reinforcements to fill any vacant spots. Midway through the afternoon, PCs George Hees and Eddie Goodman came into our committee room to say that we were winning. "The Tories are staying at home and we can't get them out to vote," they told us. My workers were sceptical and redoubled their efforts, but when the polls closed, it was clear Hees and Goodman had been telling the truth. Early results looked good, and after a few polling subdivisions had been posted on the board, an incredulous Frank Enfield turned to Keith Davey to say, "My gawd, he's winning!" Despite their hard work they hadn't really thought victory was possible. My real friends were overjoyed at my 711 vote plurality over Joe Lesniak, and none more so than Keith Davey. After years in politics, it was his first winning campaign.

The upset was grist for the press. The *Telegram* ran a cartoon of Pearson, party president Bruce Matthews, and me, dressed as prospectors panning for gold. In the pan was a nugget, labelled "Trinity". It suggested the caption: "There's gold in them there hills." The Canadian edition of *Time* magazine ran an article headed, "Old Pro at 34." The big surprise, according to the press,

was that the PCs lost the Toronto seat while retaining Springfield, Manitoba, the other by-election on the same day. The Tory
brass expected the opposite. They were confident of Trinity, but
thought they might lose Springfield, perhaps to the CCF.

The effect on the Liberal Party was electric. Heart was reborn.
Letters and telegrams poured in from all across the country –
enough to fill a whole scrapbook. On his Christmas card, Jean
Lesage wrote: "You are setting the pace for our comeback! P.S. I
am glad that *you* have recovered the seat that was lost following
my resignation." (Jean had been one of the forty-nine survivors
in the 1957 general election, but had deserted Ottawa to lead the
party in Quebec.) Veteran Liberals said the by-election was undoubtedly the turning point federally, because, until then, they
had all thought we would be out of office for twenty years.
Trinity acted as an astringent. The Liberal Party was ready to rise
and fight again.

When I got to Ottawa, Mike didn't assign me any specific
duties in the Commons, probably because he didn't want to rock
any boats. The press had already dubbed the four privy council-
lors who had been returned in the general election – Pearson,
Martin, Chevrier, and Pickersgill – the Four Horsemen of the
Apocalypse, and there was no way of crashing that august
company short of rewriting the Scriptures. I had to be content
as a supernumerary, waiting in ambush for some target of
convenience.

I didn't have long to wait. Soon after its election, the Diefenbaker government had signed the North American Air Defence
(NORAD) Treaty and approved the RCAF's proposal to locate
two Bomarc bases on Canadian soil. The latter, in particular, was
to prove a problem for the government. Almost every time the
United States Air Force sent a Bomarc aloft on a test flight, it
crashed into the Gulf of Mexico, so I felt obliged to ask the
minister why this was and whether it was wise for Canada to
place its trust in such an uncertain vehicle?

Privately, I felt sorry for the minister, General George Pearkes,
V.C. He was as honourable as he had been gallant, and it wasn't
really his fault that the Bomarcs were such duds. But politics is
politics, and it was my obvious duty to try to tag the government
with direct responsibility for each successive disaster. After I had
made several attempts in this direction, the press began referring
to me as Liberal defence critic. It wasn't long before Mary Mac-

donald, Mike Pearson's secretary, simply acknowledged any letters on defence matters addressed to the leader and said that they were being referred to the Liberal defence critic, Paul Hellyer, for a more detailed reply. That was as close as my title ever came to being "official", but it was close enough for all practical purposes. Months later Mike gave it his imprimatur by using it in public.

The cancellation of the Avro Arrow provided my first major test in the role. Mike insisted that I speak for the party in the House, which would have been fine if he had let me take a clear and unequivocal stand. I wanted to condemn the government outright. Both the Arrow airframe and its Iroquois engine were monumental, world-leading achievements, and throwing in the towel on their production was a national disgrace. But LPB would neither condemn nor condone. He wanted to keep our options open by planting one foot firmly in each camp. So for half an hour I had the dubious honour of viewing with alarm, pleading for generosity to the workers, and saying all the obvious things that fence-straddling politicians do. My Liberal colleagues seemed pleased, and the subsequent press reaction was quite favourable; but for me it was a most uncomfortable assignment.

The following spring Mike named me a member of the 1960 Canada–U.S. parliamentary-congressional group, comprised of equal numbers of senators and MPs or congressmen from each side. This pleased me, as I had been a member of the group the year before, and I thought it would be fun to visit Washington so soon after the inauguration of President John F. Kennedy. It would also provide an opportunity to renew acquaintance with Senator Church, Gerald Ford, and other friends that I had met in Montreal when the same group convened the previous year. Above all, it would give me a chance to delve more deeply into defence trends, especially during side trips to Strategic Air Command (SAC) and NORAD headquarters. For once the payoff exceeded the promise. At Colorado Springs, Air Marshal Roy Slemon, NORAD's Deputy Commander, arranged a top-secret briefing of the kind that was routine for U.S. senators and congressmen, but which was like stumbling into a diamond mine for information-impoverished Canadians.

The upshot was that when I got back to Ottawa I wrote a new defence policy for the Liberal Party. Based on the premise that the delivery of nuclear weapons was quickly shifting from manned bombers to long-range missiles, my proposal suggested that Canada should abandon its support for the SAGE-Bomarc ground-control and missile system, which would be obsolete before it was operational, cancel the purchase of the controversial F-104 "Widow-maker", and opt out of the nuclear strike role. Instead the RCAF should acquire planes for the ground-support role in Europe, where NATO should review its policy with a view to building up its conventional forces in anticipation of the day when assured mutual annihilation would render the doctrine of "massive retaliation" no longer credible. Canada's policy should aim at the provision of flexible, conventional forces and the increased airlift and sealift that would give them maximum mobility. Mike liked the plan. He liked it so much, in fact, that he adopted it as his own.

The months since the by-election had seen considerable improvement in Liberal morale. A number of successful projects had been started, and with each one Mike became more bullish. He decided to launch a risky double-barrelled policy initiative.The first shot would be a thinkers' conference, modelled on the one Vincent Massey had sponsored for Mackenzie King at Port Hope in 1934. That would be followed by a national convention in Ottawa, where any new policy would be sold to the party at large – presumably in a way that would make the rank and file think the ideas were theirs. Mitchell Sharp was asked to preside at the Kingston conclave, and Mike asked me to organize the rally.

Of the two projects, I considered Kingston a snap. There was a model for it, and academics, like politicians, love to be heard, so there would be no problem rounding up enough professors and community leaders to fill the time available. The rally was a different matter altogether. The Liberal Party hadn't had a policy meeting since the turn of the century, and it was considered unlikely that delegates could be persuaded to go to Ottawa at their own expense in the absence of an exciting leadership contest.

My reluctance to get involved was twofold. My calendar was already overbooked with political and business commitments and I really didn't have the time to do it. On top of that, the chances of failure were overwhelming. I turned to Jack Pickersgill for advice and should have anticipated his candour. "You can't win," he said. "If you turn it down, they will say the decision was based on lack of confidence in your own ability. If you accept, you run the risk of a near-certain disaster." His assessment echoed my own. Nonetheless, I mulled it over and finally decided to accept the challenge.

The Kingston affair was acclaimed as a great success. There were quite a few ideas aired that were new to the Liberal Party, though a close examination would have shown that most of them were borrowed from the Labour Party in the United Kingdom. I found the presentations fascinating, and put in my two cents' worth from time to time. On the fundamental subject of economics, however, I was keenly disappointed. The paper presented by Maurice Lamontagne, a thoughtful and likeable protégé of Walter Gordon, was basically a variation on European dirigism, a theory of centralized administration that happened to be the vogue with Quebec intellectuals at the time. From my perspective, it was a philosophy that would create as many problems as it would solve. I agreed totally with its stated goals of sustained and balanced growth, price stability, and minimum unemployment; but I categorically rejected the implication that the system of private economic initiative contains within it the seeds of prolonged depressions, massive unemployment, and "acute" insecurity. That was precisely the kind of intellectual baloney I had been fed at university. The problem didn't lie with private initiative but with the inability of governments to operate a common-sense monetary policy.

Some of my frustration must have spilled over in private conversation, and I was dismayed when reporter Harold Greer tagged me in print as being "disillusioned". When his article appeared, I wrote Mitchell Sharp to congratulate him on the excellence of the organization and to point out that the *Globe and Mail* report included "the usual amount of journalistic licence".[1] Mitchell's reply included an unexpected compliment: "It was my view," he said, "as well as [that of] others who participated, that yours was the most effective contribution of all the working politicians in attendance."[2]

After Kingston, I began to organize the three-day rally at which the new policies would be given the Liberal Party stamp of approval. As expected, it was a massive project. Even with excellent help from Paul Lafond at the National Liberal Federation, from my Ottawa secretary Beryl Naylor, from co-chairman Hédard Robichaud, and from a roster of high-powered committee chairmen, the job was all-encompassing and all-consuming.

The great conclave of 2,500 delegates got under way on January 9, 1961, and as it progressed, it proved to be a smashing success. We introduced several innovations. Pre-registration was used to avoid congestion and to shorten queues on opening day; simultaneous translation was available for the first time; a long-standing grievance was met by the provision of transportation adjustments, through which delegates from the central provinces would subsidize those who came at higher cost from greater distances; and, finally, the use of a whole series of small policy groups made it possible to give everyone a sense of participation and the chance to be heard. This technique had been used successfully at Kingston, but there was great uneasiness about transplanting it to a mass convention, which tends to be unmanageable. It worked like a charm, however, and by the time a protracted policy session ended, party members had become personally involved with the new direction that was being set.

Most important, the party attained a new sense of unity. Militants had been dissatisfied with Pearson's leadership, and there was much talk of dumping him. But after the closing dinner, when Mr. St. Laurent effected a "laying on of hands" by moving a motion of confidence in Mike, the response was an uproarious six-minute standing ovation. It was punctuated by demonstrations as diverse as pigeons of peace fluttering to the rafters and a "rain" of western wheat. The ovation took so long that Mike had to slash equal time from his speech in order to be "out" before the TV cameras switched off. It was magnificent theatre. He finished at 8:55, just as the flashing lights warned that he had less than a minute to wrap it up, thus allowing the cameras to pan out on another standing ovation. We were home free. As soon as he sat down, Mike leaned over to say, "Paul, I will never be able to thank you enough for what you have done". They were kind words that reflected the general state of euphoria.

My part in the show was ignored by the press, but not by insiders aware of the risk – Liberals both new and old. I got dozens of congratulatory letters along the lines of the following from Walter Gordon, who by then had become quite active in the party. He wrote:

You gave the impression of strength, calmness and fairness all through the piece and everyone seems to be singing your praises as they should be. ... I, for one, was very much impressed with your performance.[3]

In September, I was the keynote speaker at the Young Liberals' annual convention at Banff, Alberta. I chose as my subject "The Task of the Liberal Democratic State", which was undoubtedly a bit heavy for the occasion but comprehensive enough for my innermost thoughts. My speech was a wide-ranging discourse, which began with the nature of man as a preamble to a discussion of alternative forms of government. It concluded that liberal democracy was inherently best, but that we would have to pull up our socks to demonstrate its superiority to a sceptical world. I espoused an "equal opportunity" philosophy, including the right to work at meaningful employment in an environment free from inflation, which is a form of larceny. I argued that the twin goals of full employment and stable prices were not mutually contradictory, as most people believed, but that their achievement was being frustrated by the growth of monopoly power – including the power of unions. As I argued, "Full employment with stable prices can only – repeat, only – be achieved if a relationship is established between wage increases and the average increase in physical output per man."[4]

When I finished, Jean David, the Young Liberal president, said, "You really had to get that off your chest, didn't you?", which was very perceptive. Pearson and Walter Gordon were both furious. My emphasis on the quality as opposed to the quantity of government was not theirs, and my suggestion of treating labour unions as monopolies was anathema to them. Nor did they appreciate my preference for a "well-managed" economy over a "planned" economy, which was their deliberately vague term. I was feeling more than a little self-conscious when Maryon Pearson, Mike's wife, whose independence of mind was legend, said "Well, I liked it" in a voice loud enough to carry to the back of the room. In the end, however, my comments fell on deaf ears. Judged by subsequent standards, the inflation rate then was miniscule, and unemployment, though rising, had not yet tripped the alarm bells. Liberals were too concerned with the problems of the day to indulge in futurism.

Seven months later, on April 17, 1962, the Prime Minister announced that the next election would be June 18. The balloon was up. We said the main issue was full employment, because the breadlines, by then, had reached a post-war high. We promised to do something about it, as well as to introduce health insurance, a new pension plan, and other such measures. These were good talking points, but the public infatuation with the Conservatives had already been affected by the cancellation of the Avro Arrow, vascillation over defence policy, the Coyne affair, in which the government asked Parliament to dismiss the governor of the Bank of Canada, and a dramatic devaluation of the Canadian dollar. The bloom had gone from the Diefenbaker rose.

On election night the early results in Trinity looked good, and my ultimate plurality over PC Stanley Frolick was 3,500. The Liberals won an incredible twelve seats in Toronto and the Yorks. Perry Ryan knocked off the giant John Bassett in Spadina. Walter Gordon won easily against Doug Morton in my former riding of Davenport. Pat Cameron recaptured High Park from Dr. John Kutcherepa, and Stan Haidasz defeated the formidable Arthur Maloney in Parkdale. Donald S. Macdonald took Rosedale from David Walker, and Ian Wahn squeaked in ahead of Roland Mitchener by a slim twenty-seven votes in St. Paul's.

In the Yorks it was J. E. (Jimmy) Walker in Centre; R. B. (Ralph) Cowan in Humber; Leonard (Red) Kelly in West; John Addison in North; and Steve Otto in East. It was a strong team and a great victory, but nationally we had only 99 seats to the PC's 116. Even though we had almost doubled the size of the official Opposition and reduced the Tories to minority status, we were still a long way from forming a government. The NDP won 19 seats, but it was the Socreds, with 30 members, who held the balance of power, and it looked as though Diefenbaker was secure – for the time being at least.

In the fall of 1962 I was named as a delegate to the NATO parliamentary conference being held in Paris. It had been seven years since I had attended one, and the contrast upset me deeply. In 1955, Canadian airmen had been on top of the world because their souped-up F-86 Sabre aircraft could fly rings around the Americans. Now the government was refusing to arm the F-104s it had purchased for the strike role, and pilots were so ashamed they avoided bars frequented by their NATO colleagues. The

Canadian Army, too, was in sad shape. The infantry had no cross-country capability other than trucks; and although the artillery had received their sleek new Honest John rockets, the warheads were filled with sand – a fact no one was willing to confirm or deny.

A hastily arranged interview with General Lauris Norstad, the Supreme Allied Commander, confirmed the worst. In a forty-five-minute top-secret briefing he pulled no punches. As far as he was concerned, Canada was in default in not living up to its commitments. A subsequent chat with George Ignatieff, our Ambassador to NATO, confirmed the fact. Canada's reluctance to accept nuclear warheads was deliberately kept off the agenda of Council meetings to avoid "official" cognizance of our position.

On my return to Ottawa, I reported fully to caucus and to the leader. Caucus was impressed, but in private conversation with Mike, who listened carefully, I saw no indication that he was about to change his mind. In December I spoke out publicly to precipitate a debate and, on the last day of the year, I took another crack at trying to change the leader's mind. I reinforced my argument with a letter from defence commentator and columnist John Gellner, which said that I had persuaded him that we had no alternative but to fulfil our commitments to the Allies and later negotiate new roles more compatible with our own desires. This time it worked. On New Year's Day, Mike phoned Jack Pickersgill to say he had made up his mind, and he began to work on a speech announcing the new policy.

Meanwhile Ellen and I had taken off for Antigua and a few days' holiday. I had resigned as president of Curran Hall Limited at the end of the year and had turned the company over to Jock Ross, a bright, young Harvard MBA graduate who had been groomed as my successor. I felt good about the decision. I had rescued the company from the brink of oblivion, nursed it back to health, and helped it grow into a strong, vibrant organization. We had a strong management team that extended from the front office to field supervision, and we had become innovators on many fronts. We had won design awards five years in a row, including the National Builder of the Year Award in 1961. The time had come to pass the mantle to someone with fresh perspective and energy. So I did that, and then took time off to recover from all the emotion and extra work involved in the changeover.

As we opened the door on our return from Antigua, the phone was ringing impatiently. It was the *Toronto Star*. "Do you agree with the new defence policy Mr. Pearson set out in his speech in Scarborough last night?" I was asked.

"What did Mr. Pearson say?" I replied. "I've just returned from vacation and haven't had a chance to read the newspapers."

The reporter explained that Mr. Pearson had said he was ashamed that Canada had accepted commitments and then refused to discharge them. The government should end the evasion at once. That meant accepting nuclear warheads for those defensive tactical weapons that cannot effectively be used without them. Later we would discuss with the United States and NATO the roles that would be more realistic and effective for Canada.

"If that's what Mr. Pearson said, I agree completely," I told him, as he picked up a few quotes for his follow-up story.

A miracle had happened. LBP had come on side. I was ecstatic, but well aware that there would be powerful repercussions – especially since Mike had made the decision unilaterally, without consulting some key advisers. Walter Gordon told me he was "pretty irritated and damn nearly resigned". Finally, because he was an elected MP and chairman of the campaign committee, he felt obliged to carry on.[5] Some Montreal intellectuals must have been even more upset. Pierre Trudeau and Gérard Pelletier had considered running, but they were so disillusioned by the switch that they backed off. Trudeau wrote a scathing article in their journal, *Cité Libre*, in which he sarcastically dubbed Pearson "The Unfrocked Prince of Peace". Still, the vast majority of Liberals were as pleased as they were surprised, and quite comfortable with their leader's common-sense stand.

The fallout on the government side was even greater. As long as the Liberals were sitting on the fence, the Tories could get away with indecision. But Mike's firm stand drove a powerful wedge between the so-called hawks and doves. The former, led by Defence Minister Doug Harkness, who had taken over from Pearkes in 1960, wanted the government to sign an agreement with the United States for the provision and storage of nuclear weapons that would be under joint control. The latter, led by External Affairs Minister Howard Green, preferred to procrastinate. Diefenbaker, torn between the two factions, appeared to side with Green and stick with indecision. The sudden emergence of a clear alternative increased the pressure on him to bring things to a quick resolution.

When he didn't, Doug Harkness resigned, and, when the So-creds withdrew their support, the government soon fell on a want-of-confidence motion. An election was called, and although there were many other issues facing the nation, defence was front and centre – except in Quebec where it was a non-issue. In Ontario it was critical and tipped the balance in Mike's favour. When the votes were counted, we had won 129 seats, with gains in most provinces. It wasn't the majority we had hoped for, but it was enough for us to know that Mike would soon be Prime Minister of Canada.

After the election of 1963, I was as surprised as I was pleased when Mike told me my job would be National Defence. It was one of the senior portfolios, and I had assumed that he might offer it to someone else. But he didn't, and I was particularly delighted to have Lucien Cardin, who might reasonably have expected a department of his own, as my Associate Minister.

National Defence Headquarters (NDHQ) was located in old, temporary buildings, designated A, B, and C, on the east side of Elgin Street, just a block south of the Lord Elgin Hotel. They had been built to meet the emergency needs of wartime, and the fact they were still in use twenty years later reveals a lot about how governments operate. I moved into the big corner office, which seemed quite grand, although it was little more than a thinly disguised barracks. I had just nicely settled in when Sergeant Major T. "Mac" Macdonald came through a side door with coffee served in elegant fluted china. My instinct as a former enlisted man was to jump to attention, and it took several days to learn to relax when one of the NCOs from the orderly room arrived with the morning brew.

One of the most important jobs for any new minister is to assemble competent and congenial staff. Incompetence can get one into a peck of trouble, and if the staff can't work harmoniously, much effort is wasted on the resolution of internal battles. Marg Bulger had arrived from Toronto a week after the government was sworn in, so I was blessed with a trustworthy and extremely able private secretary. Her team was headed by Miss Edna Kingsbury, an experienced public servant, who monitored six secretaries fully familiar with the internal workings of the department.

I was also assigned two first-class military secretaries, Lt.-Col. R. J. G. (Reg) Weeks and Commander J. M. (Marc) Favreau, who provided the liaison with the services. In the orderly room Mac

MacDonald was assisted by six NCOs, who performed myriad tasks. Driving was the exclusive responsibility of Corporals Yvon (Joe) Gleason and Walter Villemaire. The job of anticipating what might come up in Question Period and providing the necessary briefing material was done by a three-man (one of whom was a woman) parliamentary returns section headed by D. B. Dwyer. Everyone played their part well, for which I was most grateful.

My staff was effectively complete within days, except for the top job of Executive Assistant, essentially the Chief of Staff postition. I was approached by my friend and veteran journalist Jack Macbeth, who made no secret of having his heart set on Defence. Nominees for this post, however, had to be cleared with the PM, and before I had even formally asked for Macbeth, word came that he wouldn't do. He had been a member of the unpopular Truth Squad, which had shadowed Diefenbaker during the early days of the election, and Mike thought that the Defence portfolio was controversial enought without having a principal spokesman who had been a member of the much-publicized trio. The party was in Macbeth's debt, however, so he was assigned to Judy LaMarsh; for me it was back to square one without anyone in the anchor spot.

A few days later inspiration struck. I had been most impressed with the way Wing Commander Bill Lee had performed as Chief Canadian Public Relations Official for that year's NATO meeting, which had just been held in Ottawa for the first time. It suddenly dawned on me that I had one of the best men in the business in my own shop. Lee was an expert. He had topped his class at the United States Air Force Public Relations School, which was renowned as one of the leading institutions in its field.

I arranged a dinner at which Bill and I had a long and animated discussion about the Defence department and the difficulty of keeping the public adequately informed of any steps that might be taken to improve it. Before we parted I offered him the job and gave him twenty-four hours to think about it. After discussing the idea with his wife, Chatty, and Air Marshal Hugh Campbell, Chief of the Air Staff, he agreed – subject to the stipulation that, because he was still in uniform, he be given the title of Special Assistant rather than Executive Assistant. That was immaterial to me, so we had a deal. My staff was now complete and a long, close, and happy relationship was born.

I soon got a taste of the sort of ceremonial occasion that was to form a large part of my job. One of my first assignments occurred on May 31, when I rose at the crack of dawn to head for Kingston, where I was to preside at the graduation ceremony of the Royal Military College. I was greeted by the Commandant, Brigadier George Spencer, who escorted me to the dais from which I took the salute before inspecting the cadets. They were absolutely splendid in their bright scarlet uniforms and pillbox hats, and their drill was as near perfect as one is likely to see. I was proud to be associated with the institution and with the graduands who had mastered a rigorous physical and intellectual course and were about to begin their military careers. The only problem I faced during my performance that morning was that I hadn't worn a hat. That meant I had nothing to remove in acknowledgement of the salute and to honour the colours as they went past. I just bowed my head gently but perceptibly in each case, which seemed to be a suitably appropriate way of expressing my deep respect.

There was something of a repeat performance the next day at Collège Militaire Royal de Saint-Jean, in the village of Saint-Jean, Quebec, a picturesque town on the bank of the Richelieu River. It was our wedding anniversary, so as soon as we could get away gracefully, Ellen and I took off for Montreal to celebrate over dinner at the posh new Bonaventure Hotel. It was a good time to reflect on the trials and achievements of recent weeks and to toast the future.

One of the subjects we discussed at length, which I feared might affect our prospects, was my running battle with Walter Gordon over his proposed Canada Pension Plan. I considered the plan unimaginative, because it addressed only the amount of retirement income, and then only in part, while ignoring the critically important areas of portability from job to job and early vesting rights in private plans, the gross inequities between citizens, and the economic impact of another pay-as-you-go program in which pensions would be paid from current taxes. This is the way Walter was recommending it. To me the proposal smacked more of political gimmickry than fundamental reform.

On the question of equity, vast numbers of people received only the Old Age Pension, while others who worked for the government, General Motors, or IBM, got both the OAP and their company pension. In some cases members of the armed forces had retired on pension at the age forty-five or fifty and had found employment in the private sector. After fifteen or twenty years in the new job, they would then be entitled to three pensions – all supported by deductions from taxable income. This was unfair and unjust and in need of correction. The Canada Pension Plan proposed to perpetuate the inequity by adding another layer.

I objected strongly in cabinet, and finally a mildly exasperated Prime Minister Pearson said, "If you don't like the plan, why don't you produce a better one?", to which I replied, "I would be delighted to." Then came the hooker, I was to be given only ten days to do it.

Nevertheless, I took the PM at his word and busily began to sketch out an alternative plan with some help from Dr. R. W. James, a Defence Department economist. He put flesh on my ideas and together we completed the Herculean task on time. A cabinet document was prepared for distribution.

My alternative plan was universal, funded, totally portable, fully vested from the first day, equitable, and adequate to meet the needs of all retirees. In effect it was something like a Registered Retirement Savings Plan for each individual Canadian. From the day each individual began his or her first job, that person's contributions, together with those of the employer, would go into their personalized fund as a tax-deductible investment trust. Self-employed persons would pay both employer and employee shares.

When cabinet met on June 17, I found that neither the PM nor Walter had taken time to read my alternative proposal, but I was given a good hearing. When I finished, you could have heard a pin drop. Finally Judy LaMarsh broke the silence. She said a decision had to be taken that day to meet the sixty days of decision deadline – a wrong-headed campaign promise we had made to introduce certain items of legislation within sixty days of the beginning of the session. Some ministers said my plan merited further consideration and suggested that the resolution to be put on the Order Paper be drafted in such a way that it would embrace either plan.

As was the case with most cabinet "discussions" of its kind, however, the die had been cast before we met. Pearson had neither the patience to consider genuine alternatives nor the ability to grasp the long-range significance of the issues. He dismissed all further discussion when he said, "the immediate object was to place on the Order Paper a resolution committing the government to do what it had promised to do in order to become a government. A real commitment had been made, which would not be met by the alternative proposal."[6]

Perhaps it was unfortunate that consideration of such an important issue overlapped with the fooferah over Walter Gordon's first budget, though I can't believe that it really made any difference. Too much pressure had resulted from the silly election promise to do so many things of major significance during the first sixty days in office. The result was simply that few decisions, if any, were thought out carefully enough. Certainly that was true of the budget, which shook the Prime Minister's faith in his finance minister, put the fate of the new minority government in jeopardy, and proved a major disaster. The budget proposals dragged on for weeks, until December. The government survived, and so did Walter. But the public's perception of us as a group of competent managers had been shattered. In the Prime Minister's words: "This was the end, however, the quick and almost catastrophic end of the honeymoon."[7]

CHAPTER 2

THE WHITE PAPER
ON DEFENCE

*"If the United Kingdom were today a
recently created State organizing her fighting
forces, it is inconceivable that they would be
separated into three services."*

Field Marshal the Viscount Montgomery of Alamein

L est there be any doubt, my job as Defence Minister involved much more than official luncheons, dinners, military parades, and tattoos. Heaven knows there were plenty of those, and often they were stimulating and good fun. On other occasions they were as tedious and boring as they were time-consuming. Also they provided a ritual temptation to eat too much and drink too much, because it was part of the drill for each unit to attempt to match or exceed all existing records of hospitality. This was the "show" part of the workload, but it was the day-to-day slogging that lay beneath all this that was really important.

The PM had committed the party to establishing a parliamentary committee on defence, which was set up under the chairmanship of Maurice Sauvé. It would study the subject, and although its mandate included consideration of policy matters, its role was advisory and didn't extend to decision-making. That was the prerogative as well as the responsibility of the government. I would undertake an internal review and make recommendations to cabinet.

As my first step as minister, I resolved not to sign anything of substance for the first thirty days. I was well aware that civil servants and the military try to take advantage of the naivety of new ministers by presenting them with a rash of submissions "requiring urgent approval". The odd one might be legitimate, if there has been a hiatus between governments; but far more likely the papers have remained unsigned because the outgoing minister had reservations about them that hadn't been resolved. New ministers, unfamiliar with the background, become fair game for officials flogging pet projects. A natural desire to cooperate can lead to a commitment of money in those early days, and this can limit the minister's freedom to manoeuvre to such an extent that he becomes merely an unwitting passenger, rather than captain of the departmental ship.

To avoid being taken captive I not only held firm but cancelled the general-purpose frigates that Gordon Churchill, my immediate predecessor, had ordered during the election campaign. I suspected that the hastily awarded contracts were more closely related to the ability of the Tory Party to raise campaign funds from the shipyards than they were with defence requirements. Perhaps the frigates were the type of vessel we needed, but what if they weren't? I didn't know, and any delay in deciding just meant that the question would become irrelevant. Besides, there were no detailed plans for the ships and no one knew what the ultimate cost would be. Meanwhile, I received detailed briefings from the three services and the Defence Research Board as to where we were and where we were headed. It wasn't that I was unfamiliar with the subject, but there can be important differences between an outsider's view and an insider's view – and I had to know what they were.

A critical point that disturbed me greatly was the realization that, wittingly or otherwise, each service was preparing for a different kind of war. The air force was thinking in terms of a three- to five-day all-out thermonuclear exchange. The army was thinking in terms of a long war. Only one of its four brigades was up to strength, and even it was ill-equipped. The other three would require months to buy equipment and call up the reserves in a general mobilization, not unlike what was done in the First and Second world wars. The navy had one foot in each camp, with their emphasis on the type of antisubmarine warfare essential to convoy duty, as in World War II.

This was the ultimate confirmation, if any were needed, of inadequate coordination and joint planning at the strategic level. The responsibility lay with the Chiefs of Staff Committee. Instead of spending the time agreeing on the probabilities of different kinds of war and then adjusting their plans and priorities accordingly for different kinds of weapons systems, the committee was little more than a back-scratching club. "You support my bid for new planes, and I'll support your proposal for more ships." However, each chief had direct access to the minister and could present his case without any interference or negative comment from his colleagues. The result was policy by happenstance. The winner in the equipment sweepstakes too often was the service that could get to the minister first, when he was in a good mood, and with his pen handy. That was usually the air force, which was light-years ahead of the other two services in the sophistication of its communications and propaganda networks.

The lack of coordination at the top, and the seemingly haphazard determination of priorities, exercised a profound influence on me as I began to think about the shape of things to come. I decided to work on the White Paper myself, and the first draft was written in longhand. Much of the routine material was cribbed – adapted might be more precise – from the "Report of the Ad Hoc Committee on Defence Policy" of September 30, 1963, an internal document that was to a major extent the product of the committee chairman, Dr. R. J. Sutherland, Chief of Operational Research, Defence Research Board (DRB). This borrowed input was pretty bland stuff, and not really controversial. I also asked Hartley Zimmerman, chairman of the DRB, to write a few paragraphs on the history of his organization.[1] When it came to the sections involving major change, however, I was on my own.

The discussion of the role of the air division in Europe represented one of the most significant departures in the paper. I was convinced that the RCAF was on the wrong track in its preoccupation with nuclear war, and that such a war was near the bottom on the scale of probabilities. It was far more likely that any initial encounter would be conventional, and the problem would be to meet fire with appropriate fire in an effort to prevent escalation. The real need was to enhance the range of options for the Allied Forces, and for our air division that meant acquiring hardware for a dual role – conventional, in addition to nuclear.

This was my strongly held view, and I knew it was also that of the Prime Minister. Somewhat more surprising was the deeply felt concern of our High Commissioner in London, George Drew. In a "Top Secret and Strictly Personal" letter to the PM, dated October 8, he discussed the latest changes in strategic thinking. There would be reduced reliance on early use of nuclear weapons, and consequently an urgent requirement for more conventional capability. Referring to the Allied Forces in Europe he wrote:

> At first it was regarded merely as a "Trip-wire Force", but more and more the impression had developed that it should be regarded as a holding force, and in the event of an outbreak of hostilities there is no doubt that Lemnitzer (SACEUR) and the other senior officers would now expect a reasonably extended period during which there would be what has come to be described as "Conventional War".
>
> Under these circumstances I can only re-emphasize my belief that it would be a major tragedy, even if all the aircraft were fully supplied with the only weapon they can use, if what is generally regarded by everyone including our friends from the United States as the best Air Force in Europe were immobilized as a result of their inability to use the only weapon they possess.[2]

In his "Strictly Personal and Confidential for Personal Use Only" reply of October 14 the PM said Drew's views would "reinforce the position I have taken with the Minister of National Defence" and added "I am assured that this particular matter is being re-examined with a view to changes being made."[3]

Indeed it was. George Drew was dead on. It didn't make any sense to have an air division sitting helplessly on the ground, unable to participate, just waiting for a nuclear war that might never come. Moreover, we knew full well that our air bases were only a few missile-minutes from the Iron Curtain. The chances of the aircraft getting off the ground in a nuclear exchange, without advance warning, were not great. The planes had to be reworked so that they could carry conventional weapons, while still being equipped for the unlikely event of an atomic doomsday.

The biggest proposed change in the White Paper, and one that was far more controversial, was the idea of combining the navy, army, and air force into one unified service. Nearly everyone agreed that we needed more integration of the common elements – at least in principle. It was difficult to argue otherwise when the Glassco Commission had recently done such a splendid job of exposing the waste and extravagance resulting from duplication and triplication. But there was little agreement on the next logical step, which was a single service.

Bob Sutherland had dismissed the concept in a single paragraph.

> One proposal, which seems to appeal to armchair strategists can be dismissed rather rapidly. This is the "purple suit" or single service approach. The rationale of this proposal is that since "integration" is a good thing one cannot have too much of it. The fallacy of this proposal is that it is irrelevant. In terms of the substance of the "integration" issue, it is of almost no consequence whether all military personnel wear the same uniform or whether each man is allowed to design his own.[4]

The pejorative dismissal wasn't surprising, coming from one who was so much in the shadow of Frank Miller, Chairman, Chiefs of Staff (CCOS); but it was a country mile short of being "scientific". Sutherland was right in suggesting that uniforms were almost irrelevant to the integration issue. They were, however, the visual symptoms of a deeply rooted disease – the existence of three independent and competing legal entities in an era when technology and common sense demanded one.

The basic inefficiency of three services was all-encompassing, and affected everything from the trivial detail to the critical issues. "Representation" provided a good example of the former. Officers from the navy, army, and air force would show up at every official function, including innumerable cocktail parties, usually arriving in separate, chauffeur-driven staff cars. The division extended right to the top, as each of the service chiefs felt it necessary to march with the Chairman, COS, and the Commissioner of the RCMP at the opening of every session of Parliament.

Triplication of supply lines, storage, and parts numbers led to some absurd situations. One service would sell surplus material as scrap at the same time that a sister service would be ordering the same item new. In one extreme case, a service sold equipment as scrap to Levy Auto Parts in Toronto and another bought it back at the full new price. There was no cross-referencing and this was especially ridiculous in cases like that of the Mark NC-44 torpedo, which was used by both the RCN and the RCAF. The two services used different parts numbers, so if one service was short of parts for the torpedo, there was no practical way to see if the other could meet the requirement from inventory. Taxpayers' interests were seldom taken into account.

The confusion at the working level was simply a reflection of the rivalry at the top. Cooperation was given lip-service, but in reality the services were three separate fiefdoms, each jealous of its own terrain. This sense of division compromised military judgment, because senior officers in each service were painfully aware that they were team leaders who dare not "let the side down". This could be particularly subversive when senior officers were choosing the right weapons mix for a particular job like antisubmarine warfare from the list of surface ships, submarines, ship-based aircraft and helicopters, land-based aircraft, ocean-floor surveillance systems, and shore-based missiles – especially if some of the systems were the preserve of one service, while others "belonged" to one of its rivals. The RCAF's internal copy of the submission it made to purchase the Argus aircraft, carried the handwritten notation, "This is our chance to screw the navy."

Theoretically, integration of the common services would eliminate many of the day-to-day frustrations, like different inventory numbers for nuts and bolts, cooks' aprons, and torpedo fins. But it wouldn't touch the fundamental aspects of strategic planning, allocation of resources, and choice of weapons systems. Only a unified staff could grapple with these more critical life-and-death decisions. A Glassco Commission researcher told me the commission recognized the magnitude of the dilemma, and preferred the single-service solution, but decided a recommendation of that sort would be politically unrealistic. In its report it opted, instead, for a solution that would remove the common elements such as pay, communications, and supply from each of the three services and put them under the command and control of the Chairman, Chiefs of Staff (CCOS), who would allocate his resources as required. In effect, it was a recommendation for the creation of a fourth service.

The prospect was too horrendous to contemplate. The department was already sinking under the dead weight of its myriad committees. There were committees on land/air warfare, release of military information, accident prevention, clothing allowance, forms control, packaging, magazines, photographic equipment, vehicles, petroleum products, warehousing, awards, pay, records, recruiting, trades, bands, ceremonial, graves and burials – the list seemed endless. Each committee comprised five people: one each from the navy, army, air force, Defence Research Board, and the deputy minister's staff. The Glassco solution would mean adding one extra person, representing the Chairman, COS. The futility would have been compounded as committees met for weeks or months to reach conclusions that were not binding. One or more of the service chiefs would usually thumb his nose at the consensus, and the whole tortuous exercise would be in vain. Even without the addition of another body, one could paraphrase Winston Churchill and say that "never in human history have so many people spent so much time reaching so many conclusions that were going nowhere." In an effort to move one step forward, the Glassco Commission recommended something that could have meant two steps backward.

I don't remember being committed to unification at the outset of my ministry, although Mr. Justice Potts reminds me that I confided my interest in amalgamation on a Muskoka weekend in 1962, citing my own wartime experience in support. Then, the air force had been hogging manpower at a time when the army was desperately short of reinforcements, and I regarded the situation as little short of criminal. In any event, it only required a few weeks as minister to convince me that a single service was the only satisfactory solution. The political practicality of this option was reinforced by the Prime Minister's commitment to substantial change, which dated back to 1960. In the course of a speech on August 5 of that year, he had told the House:

> I suggest to the minister that the time has come to change the organization for one chief of staff whose authority would extend to the three services, army, navy and air force, and perhaps defence research. He would have the chief responsibility for the planning and implementing of defence policy submitted to him by the government.[5]

Mike kept referring to this concept as unification, and it was – in fact, if not in law.

The idea of a single service was not new, and its proponents were not all "armchair strategists" as Sutherland called them. It had been proposed by significant numbers of serving and retired officers of all ranks. Captain J. G. Forth, Royal Canadian Engineers, had published an excellent paper entitled "Unification – Why, How, When" in the *Canadian Army Staff College Journal 1959–1961*. It began: "The existence of three or more separate services in modern national defence forces is an illogical relic of the past perpetuated by inflexible thinking, vested interests and individual service fears of extinction." Captain Forth went on to say, "Historical study would readily show how and why armed forces developed as triplets. But comparative analysis would show just as readily that modern conditions call for a single service." [6]

I knew that the former Chairman of the Chiefs of Staff Committee, General Charles Foulkes, Frank Miller's predecessor, had published a similar paper, "The Case for One Service", so I wrote to ask him for a copy. He forwarded one at once, and in his covering letter of June 13, 1963, he said:

> In reading this it is useful to keep in mind that it was written in 1961 and for a Service Journal, but while some of the detail may be a bit old, the need and principles remain valid. It is a challenging task, but in my view it is the only answer and the Canadian Forces are small enough to try out such a plan. [7]

In his lengthy paper General Foulkes reviewed Canada's first experience with unification – of which I had been unaware – from 1924 to 1927. Major-General Sir James MacBrien was Chief of Staff "with overall authority over the Navy and the military elements of the Air Service." [8] The experiment was aborted in 1927, "amidst rumours of friction in the higher echelons of the services." [9]

More important for serious students of military organization, the paper documented numerous examples of interservice bickering, over postwar establishments, defence research, logistic support for our NATO forces in Europe, the unwillingness of one service to absorb surplus trained manpower from another, and the insistence of each of the three services that it train its own air crew. [10] Reading the record was enough to make me weep. These were the same kind of problems I observed on a day-to-day basis, and the tragedy was that they had persisted for so long. Foulkes's patience, like mine, had run out. He rejected further patchwork solutions and proposed rebuilding from top to bottom. "The plan is based on creation of a single service with one Chief of Staff, a combined administration, and a series of task forces to replace the service field forces."[11]

Major-General W. H. S. Macklin, former Adjutant General of the Canadian Army, had been an even earlier proponent of unification than General Foulkes. An article he published in *Weekend* magazine in 1956 was captioned, "A distinguished soldier takes a long, hard look at the 'archaic' organization of Canada's navy, army, and air force and urges that we Unify Our Three Services."[12] The author's principal points were right on target:

> A unified armed force will give us more defence for less money; World War II proved that there had to be singleness of command; Canada's forces are now governed by a cascade of committees; the Chairman Chief of Staff job is a phony substitute for unity.[13]

General Macklin's radical conclusion was influenced by what he had seen of wartime disasters caused by services operating independently and his experience of successes when they worked in concert.

> The lesson is that the old conception of sea power, land power, or air power as independent entities having little or no connection with each other is completely invalid. None of these forms of military power is of any avail by itself; they are totally interdependent. If we have not learned that lesson by now, if we wait for some future enemy to demonstrate it over again, we shall probably perish in the process.[14]

The principle was clear enough. Historians will recall the earlier unification of infantry, cavalry, and artillery regiments into one army. They had been independent units with their own support services, but in each case the soldiers, gunners, and cavalrymen had to be fed, supplied, and provided with postal, medical, dental, and other services. Eventually it became obvious that it would be cheaper and more efficient to combine the services to meet the needs of all the regiments.

From a military standpoint cost-efficiency was not all that made amalgamation so urgent and significant. With regiments working together in combined operations, it became critically important for the artillery to know the precise whereabouts of the infantry and cavalry. Otherwise, shells might be lobbed into friendly rather than enemy territory. A unified command, while not foolproof, reduced the probability of tragic mistakes.

Several decades of rapid technological change had now brought the navy and air force into the same relationship with the army as the regiments had to each other. The division of roles was no longer clear cut. On the contrary, nearly all operations had become combined operations, involving two or more of the traditional forces. This posed the same problems already faced by the army regiments. Sailors and airmen, too, have to be fed, supplied, and provided with postal, medical, dental, and other services. Therefore substantial savings could be achieved by combining these functions with those of the army.

Again, however, the cost benefits paled in significance compared to military necessity. In combined operations, sea and airborne artillery must know the precise location of land units in order to distinguish friend from foe. Lack of such information and the absence of common communications systems have led to a number of unnecessary tragedies, such as the one related in the following account by Mr. Justice Donald Keith of the Superior Court of Ontario:

> On the 14th August, 1944, when I was a senior Staff Officer in the 2nd Canadian Corps' Headquarters, I was an eye-witness to the devastation that was caused when a major air force attack intended to open the road to Falaise, was unleashed on the Third Canadian Infantry Division, including my own battalion, the Queen's Own Rifles, instead of the German defenders.
>
> Although the aircraft were only a few thousand feet above us, there was no way the land force could communicate with the pilots, except by going through battalion, brigade, division, corps, army, army group to the war office in London, and thence back to the air force commander.
>
> Idiocy prolonged the war by months.[15]

There are many veterans who would say "Amen" to that.

In the Second World War combined operations of two or more services under a single command had been adopted from sheer necessity and to good effect, but that solution still couldn't overcome many of the absurdities resulting from separate services. Words had different meanings from service to service, and this compounded the confusion resulting from incompatible communications systems. Little wonder that most of the great combined-operations commanders, including Lord Louis Mountbatten, Field Marshal "Monty" Montgomery, and General Dwight Eisenhower, ended the war as "unificationists" of one kind or another. Even the controversial Air Chief Marshal Sir Arthur "Bomber" Harris, who tried but failed to bring the Germans to their knees through air power alone, came to favour the single-service concept before he died.

While totally convinced that a single service was the best theoretical solution, I was keenly aware of the limitations imposed by the real world. Bridging the gap from the antiquated organization I had inherited to one in tune with the times would not be easy, and could only be accomplished in stages. I decided that the first step should include abolition of the three "chiefs" positions and the substitution of a single Chief of Defence Staff to whom all three services would report. A consequential change was the elimination of the Naval Board, the General Staff, and the Air Staff in favour of one unified defence staff. Beyond that, in all conscience, the White Paper had to disclose the ultimate aim of the game, so I included the controversial sentence, "This is the first step toward a single unified service for Canada."[16]

Other sections of the paper included a review of policy since World War II, a discussion of the circumstances influencing future policy, a streamlined force structure, with a list of major equipment required to enable the various units to carry out their assigned roles, and a final section on research and its industrial application, which included some of the material provided by the Defence Research Board.

In addition to the changes in organization on the military side, I proposed that the authority of the deputy minister would be increased somewhat and that he would develop, with the cooperation of the military, a ten-year plan encompassing the roles and major equipment required by all three services. This was a first for Canada's Defence Department and provided the organizational framework required for integration of the common services. The object was to establish rational military priorities, which included a substantial increase in air-transport capability, as well as additional sea-lift, as we moved toward more flexible, mobile forces designed to meet the widest range of potential requirements with the fastest possible reaction time. This would only be possible by spending less on "housekeeping" and more on new equipment.

The paper envisaged continued support of NATO, including the brigade group stationed in Germany. The two brigades in Canada that were earmarked for the European theatre in time of emergency were to be re-equipped. At the same time their training was to be broadened to prepare them for a wide range of possible deployment, from NATO back-up to world-wide peace-keeping operations. The fourth brigade in Canada, which had been formed for the Korean War and never disbanded afterward, was to be converted into a compact special-service force and to be provided with air-portable and air-droppable equipment. Air squadrons assigned to NATO would in future be trained to operate in direct support of the ground forces, rather than to remain exclusively in the atomic strike role. To maximize our naval contribution to the alliance, the paper proposed a study to determine the best, most cost-effective mix of antisubmarine equipment available for subsequent acquisition. Finally, increased expenditure on defence research and development was recommended.

With the first rough draft complete, the time had come to circulate copies of the White Paper to my associate minister, Lucien Cardin, and top departmental officials for their comments. The copies were dispatched complete, except for the final section on organization. It is easy to write far-reaching proposals, but getting them accepted is often difficult and certainly not automatic. I had been in politics long enough not to climb out on a long limb only to have the Prime Minister saw it off. Ministers are subject to enough embarrassment and ill-concealed humour without deliberately asking for it. So I decided to seek the PM's blessing and support for unification before presenting the organization proposal to officials.

Reaction to the other sections varied considerably. General Geoffrey Walsh, as reported through Bill Lee, thought it was "well done; no comments other than a suggestion to emphasize the importance to Europeans of a Canadian 'presence' in Europe."[17] Admiral Herbert Rayner was "very impressed", he thought the paper painted "a wide picture with far horizons in bold strokes". He made a few suggestions "designed to strengthen the naval part of the picture".[18] The Chairman, Chiefs of Staff Committee, Frank Miller, recognized the "Sutherlandese", and thought the document might be shortened and simplified for the man on the street. He had a couple of other points, of which the most important was his objection to my statement that the probability of all-out thermonuclear war between the United States and the U.S.S.R. was "close to infinitesimal". He preferred "not great and is decreasing".[19] The same point was raised by Air Marshal Larry Dunlap, who suggested "quite unlikely" as more appropriate.[20] The air force could hardly justify the strike role for a kind of war with such a low probability. Hartley Zimmerman of the Defence Research Board made a number of useful suggestions, and Derry Dwyer, Chief of Parliamentary Returns, wisely pointed out that it might be desirable to include something "to the effect that we may be over extended in the number of commitments undertaken within necessary financial limitations."[21] Deputy Minister Elgin Armstrong's suggestions consisted "mainly of deletions. This seems to me, in a number of areas, material useful for internal thinking but not for publication in sensitive matters affecting our allies."[22] All these comments were useful, and were taken into account in later drafts.

On February 7, with the PM's blessing, I told the Chiefs of Staff about the proposed reorganization and agreed to give them the draft paper in full the next day. My diary records: "The reaction was almost exactly as predicted. John Keyston [sitting in for DRB chairman Hartley Zimmerman] was favorable – thought it was an experiment Canada should undertake which, under the circumstances of their world commitments, Britain and the U.S. could not risk. Walsh was not difficult to convince. Dunlap was apprehensive and Rayner very much so. They were every inch the gentlemen, however, and did not lose control of their emotions. All in all it was not as dreadful as I had feared and I am most thankful to have the experience behind me."[23] Frank Miller, who had a hint in advance, saved his ammunition for the next day.

Saturday morning the two of us had a real "go" from opposite sides of my desk. Frank had no real objection to the headquarters reorganization. No doubt the fact that he, as Chairman, Chiefs of Staff, would become the operating head of the navy, army, and air force had some appeal. His two big bones of contention were the dual atomic and conventional roles proposed for the air division in Europe and the one key sentence that said that the reorganization was the first step toward a single unified force for Canada. On the first point there was no way that either LBP or the government would agree to an exclusive atomic strike role for the air division, which Miller preferred, because it didn't make any military sense; concerning unification, notwithstanding the vehemence of the opposition, I was not about to hide or paper over the fact that this was the ultimate objective of the reorganization. It was one of my most difficult sessions and, no doubt, was the same for Frank. For what seemed like an interminable period, it was a case of an irresistible force and an immovable object. In the end one of us had to prevail, and I wasn't prepared to retreat from the first skirmish.

The balance of the day was spent with Elgin Armstrong, Bill Lee, and Derry Dwyer going over the drafting. My pride was somewhat bruised by the number of proposed changes. I felt these should have been suggested much sooner, since they had all had copies of the original. The real battle, however, was much more important. As I reflected later in my diary, "It is the issue of who is going to set military policy – the military or the government. They had been unfettered so long they just can't get used to the idea of taking direction. The role of the air division is the key."[24] I held out on the fundamentals, the draft was agreed upon, and a copy was forwarded to the Prime Minister. A truce took effect at sundown when the Hellyers dined with the Millers at their gracious home overlooking the Rideau Canal.

Sunday afternoon I took advantage of the opportunity to swim with "Cousin Paul" Martin, as I affectionately dubbed him. It was the principal exercise for each of us, and something we often did together. The Château Laurier pool provided a locker, bathing suit, cap, and unlimited towels for fifty cents, which must have accounted for some of the CN deficit. In any event, we talked about the White Paper and I tried to soften some of Paul's opposition, which originated with Ross Campbell, his assistant under-secretary in External Affairs. I understood External's frustration at not being requested to do the writing, but the department's epithet of "Eternal Affairs" was not entirely a jest. It would take the diplomats forever to agree on a draft, and we wanted to be able to go public so we could get on with the job. Paul softened a little when I explained the urgency, but I knew the war was far from won.

Monday we were both diverted by a visit from Sir Alec Douglas Home, who was Paul's opposite number in the United Kingdom. At a special cabinet meeting Sir Alec told us he thought the Russians had changed tactics and had concluded that all-out war with the United States was impossible. The stakes were too high, and there would be no winner – just two losers. After lunch with Sir Alec, I met with the Chiefs of Staff to discuss means of retiring officers made redundant by integration. The subject was as complicated as it was important. We also resumed our discussion of integration, with Air Marshal Dunlap and Admiral Rayner fighting a rearguard action – "but still controlled".[25]

When I arrived at a Cabinet Defence Committee meeting on Wednesday, I found it had been scrubbed in favour of a ministers-only meeting at 24 Sussex Drive. The reason was soon obvious. "The 'External gang' had swung into action and it was suggested that the whole white paper go to a committee of officials for minute examination."[26] The people at External were still upset that they had had no input in the original draft. Luckily I managed to force an hour's discussion before the aborted meeting broke up. According to my diary: "The PM finally agreed to give the committee a week for discussions after which members would report back to their own ministers. We [Defence] would then present a paper to the whole Cabinet Defence Committee for consideration. I don't know how we will make out. The degree of conflicting views is staggering. Everyone is an expert. If we removed all the offending sections there would be nothing left but the covers!"[27] My apprehension was acute.

On February 21, the Defence Committee, Paul Martin, Walter Gordon, Lucien Cardin and I finally met informally with the PM, the committee chairman, at his home. "I was shocked at the nature of the discussion. The PM was the most sympathetic but he, too, took the attitude that we didn't have to set an example in NATO. He didn't want NATO to break up but was unwilling to support the concept of an 'effective' Canadian contribution. Paul Martin . . . was preoccupied with sovereignty and favoured bringing the Air Division home to augment Air Defence, thereby making it unnecessary to permit dispersal of U.S. interceptors in Canada. WLG [Gordon] suggested cutting defence expenditures an additional 500 million and giving the money to the provinces."[28] Incredibly no one seemed particularly interested in or concerned about integration and unification, which I considered the really "hot" subject on the table. In conclusion the Prime Minister agreed to rewrite some of the sections on foreign policy and let me have them. Based on the discussion, however, I doubted the final version would contain anything definite other than the proposed integration.

For once, I was far too pessimistic. When I got the PM's redraft, the changes were relatively minor – to style rather than to substance. More significant to me was the end run that had been achieved. Now that the PM had been directly involved in the draftsmanship, the likelihood of major changes from External was effectively foreclosed. The boss was "on side" and committed.

The revised version got back to the Cabinet Defence Committee on March 24. There was a large attendance and the atmosphere was a bit intimidating. I made my pitch in favour of the White Paper, but none of the chiefs spoke. The subject was far too important to be rubber-stamped without full discussion, so I pointed out to the Prime Minister, who was chairman, that the views I had expressed on behalf of the department were not those of the Chiefs of Staff, and I thought it was essential that other points of view be fully aired. This opened the floodgate. "Herb Rayner made a spirited plea for further consideration or delay. I admired his action and I was glad that I had insisted he be heard. The others gave varying degrees of support. Walsh was absent, which meant that we had to get along without his positive support except by proxy. External Affairs asked for one little concession which was denied and the paper was approved intact, except for the few changes in wording which had already been agreed upon. I decided to take a chance and let the presses roll. There is no other way to meet the Thursday deadline."[29]

The document was to clear the final hurdle with full cabinet approval the next morning. By then it had been streamlined considerably, but the substance was not significantly changed from the original. It ended with a brief personal statement which reflected my penchant for relating policy to philosophy.

Force, at best, could only deter war and buy time in which men of good will might build a better world.

The White Paper on Defence was tabled Thursday morning, March 16, 1964, shortly after the House opened. To give journalists a chance to absorb its contents in advance, we had used a technique usually reserved for budgets and financial papers. Reporters were locked in the Railway Committee Room, where they could read the paper and write their initial stories. The doors were to be unlocked as soon as I rose to table the paper in the Commons. That way the propriety of not upstaging Parliament could be observed, while still giving newsmen a welcome head start.

The system works well as long as nothing goes wrong, but that morning I had a few anxious moments when Gordon Churchill raised a question of privilege about something Bud Drury had said at the Montreal United Services Institute the night before. This took precedence over the tabling of documents. "We were all worried sick for fear it [the question of privilege] would drag on while we had the reporters locked up. I don't think they would have been too understanding."[30] Mercifully the delay didn't last long, and I was able to table the paper and let the reporters loose while they were still in a good mood.

The initial reaction to the paper was splendid. It even received qualified support from Gordon Churchill and Harold Winch, the Opposition defence critics. One or two newspapers, including the *Toronto Star*, tempered their praise with reservations. Why, they asked, when I rated thermonuclear war as the least probable eventuality, were some of the weapons systems that were proposed "wholly unsuitable" to insurrection and guerrilla conflicts.[31] The observation was valid to a point, but failed to recognize the spectrum of our responsibility, from deterrence to peacekeeping. Experience had shown that meeting diverse UN requirements, for example, was only possible if forces had a wide range of equipment. Our troops in Europe, fulfilling our number-one continuing commitment, needed tanks and heavy artillery. This kind of heavy equipment can easily be left at home when it is not needed, but there is no way it can be obtained in a hurry in the event of a major conflict. As for the continuing nuclear capability, this could not be renegotiated overnight, as some of the dreamers suggested. Whether we liked it or not, I replied to their questions, "We are committed for the present to what was decided in the past."[32]

Most editorial comment was overwhelmingly positive, as the following examples attest. In a two-page spread, *Time* magazine said, "At last, a sense of direction."[33] The Montreal *Star* observed:

Mr. Hellyer could have drifted along, as many of his pre-decessors have done, with an outdated status quo. Instead he has had the courage to uproot the vested interests for which the military establishment has always provided fertile soil. He has also had the imagination to see the form which that establish-ment should take in the context of Canada in this generation.[34]

Canadian Aviation magazine began: "Defence Minister Paul Hellyer's White Paper has been widely heralded as the most forward thinking defence document produced by any govern-ment for the past decade, and probably since World War II."[35] Finally, in a *Telegram* column entitled "Clear Thinking on Our Defense", Lubor J. Zink concluded:

Mr. Hellyer's realistic, non-partisan endeavor to create a lean, integrated force able to meet any exigency deserves the highest praise and full public support. Politicking aside, who can still say that there is hardly any difference between the past and present governments?[36]

CHAPTER 3

HOME ON THE RIDEAU

S oon after the Pearson government was formed, I became convinced that our family would have to move to Ottawa. I had now commuted for fourteen years, and that had been the best arrangement at the time. There was no other way that I could have coped with both parliamentary and business responsibilities. As a minister, however, I found politics was a full-time job, which began at eight o'clock in the morning and ended some time after the eleven-o'clock nightly news six and a half days a week. Sundays were special. We went to church in the morning, and I seldom worked more than two or three hours in the afternoon, with perhaps a little homework after dinner at night. Our children were sixteen, eight, and six, and there was little opportunity to see them except at breakfast – and then only if we lived in the same city.

In July I looked at two or three houses, including the one owned by Rear-Admiral and Mrs. Jeffry Brock. Any one of them would have been adequate to put a roof over our heads, but none was really inspiring. Ellen agreed to visit the capital and spend a couple of days looking around on her own. She checked out three or four places and finally settled on a modest bungalow owned by Robert Bourassa, the future Premier of Quebec. He had been in Ottawa working for a royal commission on finance. It had finished, so he was ready to move back to Montreal. The long, narrow house, which looked much larger from the outside than it was inside, faced the Rideau River about three-quarters of the way downstream, between the Bank Street and Smyth Road bridges. The property was beautifully manicured, which made it very attractive, and was centrally located about ten minutes from everywhere, which was suitable to our needs. The clincher for me was Brighton Beach, a municipally operated swimming hole just a hundred yards away. It looked as though it would be a good place to cool off on a hot summer day.

The move may have seemed inevitable to me, but that didn't mean the family was happy about it. Ellen was a brick about getting everything packed and ready to go, but she shed copious tears en route. It didn't help that, when we arrived, the movers were too tired to finish the unpacking and just went away, leaving the place in a terrible mess, and we were committed – very foolishly in retrospect – to attend one of those innumerable "duty" cocktail parties, which was a tiring part of our work.

The workload at Defence was physically and emotionally exhausting, and was only made tolerable by the incredible diversity. The variety of items crossing my desk had to be seen to be believed. Even then, the decisions in which I was directly involved represented only a small proportion of the department's business. Lucien Cardin, my associate minister, handled the great bulk of personnel and property matters. Millions of other decisions were made by civilian and service officers in the normal course of their duties. If they made good decisions, any publicity reflected favourably on the minister and the department. If the decisions were poor, the minister got the rap. It cut both ways.

Invitations to a wide variety of military, political, and ethnic events poured in at a rate in excess of one a day, and it required considerable time and thought just deciding which ones to accept. Some were considered a "must", like Sunday, September 15, 1963, when I was slated to lay a wreath and take the salute at the twenty-third anniversary of the Battle of Britain, the key date in the RCAF's annual calendar. This turned out to be a lesson in logistic precision.

A day or two before the ceremony, I noted my driver leaving 1982 Rideau River Drive. He explained that he was on a trial run to Green Island at the mouth of the Rideau River, where the ceremony was to be held. He had to know exactly how long it took to get there from my residence, because the senior guests were to arrive at one-minute intervals, with the highest ranks last. I was scheduled to arrive at 1:44 p.m. That meant 1:44, not 1:43, and certainly not 1:45. Heaven help the driver who got out of sequence.

When the day came, watches were synchronized and the precision was awe-inspiring; I don't think we were more than one or two seconds off the arrival target. It didn't take long for the wreath-laying ceremony, the airborne salute of jets thundering overhead, and the traditional march-past to the beat of the "RAF March". You could tell that most of the men in blue were head-quarters desk-pigeons, but they did their best to rise to the occasion.

Two days later I attended a luncheon given by Frank Miller, CCOS, in honor of Admiral of the Fleet Earl Mountbatten of Burma, in the special VIP dining room at the RCAF Officers' Mess, Rockcliffe. In fact it was a double pleasure. Not only did I meet the legendary Mountbatten and establish a working relationship that would continue through my years in the department and beyond, but we ate in one of the best restaurants in the capital region. At that time there were only a handful of top-notch eating-places in Ottawa and Hull – the Château Grill, Café Henry Burger, Le Diplomat, and a few others. None was better than the Rockcliffe Mess. The RCAF spared neither effort nor expense when it came to entertaining top-ranking visitors, and this unique place was the jewel in their gastronomic crown.

I saw Mountbatten three more times within twenty-four hours. That evening I attended a black-tie dinner in his honour at Earnscliffe, residence of the U.K. High Commissioner, Lord Amory. The following morning he came to my office for an official chat before attending a luncheon given by the Government of Canada in honour of the delegates to the Sixteenth Conference of the British Commonwealth Ex-Service League. Roger Teillet, Minister of Veterans' Affairs, proposed the toast to Her Majesty and I did likewise for the veterans of the Commonwealth. In my brief remarks I applauded the success of the North Atlantic Alliance in maintaining peace and stated my deeply held belief that the precious time gained must be used to build a better world. In this regard the Commonwealth was contributing positively by building relationships that were rooted in the hearts of men rather than in law. Lord Mountbatten responded eloquently to both toasts and spoke feelingly of Commonwealth cooperation in war and peace.

Of all the early ceremonies, however, the one that stands out the most vividly was a trooping of the colour by the first battalion of the Canadian Guards at Camp Picton on the north shore of Lake Ontario, on October 19, 1963. The salute was to have been taken by Maj.-Gen. J. D. B. (Des) Smith, who was the Colonel of the Regiment, but unfortunately he had to be absent in Britain. We had met some years earlier, when we were fellow performers in the May Court Show, an annual fund-raising event for an Ottawa senior citizens' home, and I was honoured when he asked me to stand in for him. I arrived at Picton the evening before the parade to attend a mess dinner and be properly briefed concerning the ceremony the following day. I learned that, in the course of a full dress-rehearsal that very afternoon, the commanding officer, Lieutenant-Colonel Willie Mulherin, had demonstrated the stuff of which real professionals are made. Just as the troops were passing the reviewing stand and he ordered the eyes right, a fly lit on his upper lip. He made two surreptitious but unsuccessful attempts to blow it off, but on the third attempt it flew into his mouth. There was nothing to do but to swallow it. There is often a high price to soldiering.

When the Colonel went over the guest list for the following morning, one name stood out, Major-General Arthur Potts. "Good heavens!" I exlaimed! "I will probably get a lecture for going on parade without a hat." I knew that he would disapprove since, during a long chat I had had with his son, Joe, over lunch at the parliamentary restaurant, Joe had insisted that I should buy a hat to wear on parade. I had a little fun in pointing out that his was a very conservative suggestion from one who claimed to be a progressive Liberal. Why was it necessary to buy a hat for the sole purpose of being able to take it off? I reminded him that President John F. Kennedy didn't wear a hat on parade, and I didn't see why any good Liberal should think that I must. It was clear from the conversation that Joe's father shared his view that a hat was required.

In the morning I took my place on the reviewing stand and stood rigidly at attention throughout – only dipping my head gently, as was my custom, to acknowledge the salutes and out of respect to the colours when they passed. Actually I thought I played my part rather well, although I would have been reluctant to say so. At the informal luncheon that followed, General Potts was sitting on the opposite side of the table, two or three places to the left. He was in deep conversation with the lady next to him, but was looking in my direction. "I'll bet I know what you're saying, General," I interjected. "You're suggesting that I should have worn a hat on parade this morning." "Yes," he replied, in his straightforward, no-nonsense way, "But I thought it was damn decent of you to wear a tie." It was a story that was to be repeated many times throughout the years and which I included in a memorial column I wrote after his death in August 1984.

In November the transitory nature of politics and of life itself was indelibly etched on the public consciousness. On November 19, Toronto's mayor, Donald D. Summerville, died suddenly at the age of forty-eight. I was the minister designated to represent the federal government at his funeral on November 22. We were of different political stripes, but he had served his city well, and I was honoured to join civic leaders and colleagues at St. James' Cathedral in paying our last respects. Midway through the service an ashen-faced aide came down the aisle and whispered, "President Kennedy has been shot. They don't know whether he will live or die." I couldn't believe it. Yet I knew it wouldn't be a hoax because no one would play that kind of cruel joke in the middle of a memorial service. It all seemed so incredible. The leader of the free world shot down in his own country? It was the only topic of conversation as we left the church for the committal service. Who could have perpetrated such a heinous crime? My mind flashed back to memories of the Kennedys, of their political rise and struggle, and of the times Ellen and I had been in their presence. A few hours later word came that the president was dead. The most exciting politician to come on stage in decades was gone, snuffed out in the prime of life. The whole civilized world mourned as our hearts went out to Jacqueline, Caroline, and little John.

Although the new U.S. President, Lyndon Johnson, was as different from his predecessor as night from day, the key players of his administration with whom we did business in the areas of foreign affairs and defence didn't change. Secretary of State Dean Rusk and Secretary of Defence Robert McNamara were an impressive team and, from my perspective, very easy to get along with.

Paul Martin and I were soon flying to Paris to join them and our other colleagues at the NATO council. We crossed the ocean non-stop from Ottawa to Paris in one of the RCAF's long-range Yukon aircraft. Paul headed the delegation, which included a troop of his officials from External. I was accompanied by Air Chief Marshal Frank Miller, CCOS, and one of his aides, as well as Bill Lee, Lt.-Col. Reg Weeks, and Marg Bulger from my own office. In conformity with government policy, Nell Martin and Ellen were the only wives allowed, a rule that has been relaxed somewhat since. Finally there were a good number of print and electronic journalists, who accepted free rides without any of the embarrassment that would attach to the practice in later years.

On arrival in Paris we were formally welcomed by a representative of the French government and then taken in tow by George Ignatieff, our ambassador to NATO. We were whisked downtown with a police escort that showed such utter disrespect for the local citizens that it gave me the shivers. Motorists were shooed from the roadway like chickens from a barnyard. I wished that we could skip the escort or, failing that, at least hide the flags flying from our fender staffs, so that the French drivers wouldn't know the identity of the intruders.

Our immediate destination was the Hôtel Plaza-Athenée, avenue Montaigne, a somewhat posh hostelry in the grand European style, although not quite in the same class as the Georges Cinq, where the Americans were billeted. Following a fitful few hours of sleep, our permanent officials to NATO brought us up to date and filled any gaps there might have been in the information we had read on the way over. Canada always played an active part in the deliberations of the NATO council, and it was essential that we be well prepared. That year we were especially well treated as a result of our decision to fulfil Canada's earlier nuclear commitments to NATO and our determination to beef up the capacity of our land forces with some new equipment.

When ministers of the several countries met, the discussion followed predictable lines. The United States was carrying more than its fair share of the defence burden, and other countries, especially the Europeans and Canada, should do more. Another perennial topic was the composition of nuclear forces and the control of nuclear weapons. Was it desirable to have a NATO nuclear force, so that the Americans would not appear to have exclusive responsibility in this field. If so, which nations should contribute? Even more difficult was the thorny question of authorization of the use of nuclear weapons. What were the mechanics by which a decision for a nuclear strike would be taken, and was the process sufficiently realistic to prevent Europe from being overrun while the telegrams were still flying? Then there was the constant necessity for a build-up in conventional strength to raise the threshhold at which nuclear weapons might be required. We also discussed the desirability of greater standardization of weapons and more effective production-sharing between countries to keep costs in line, as well as the ever-present need for further assistance to poorer countries like Greece and Turkey, whose defence budgets were already stretched.

This was largely how the discussion went, with only a few noteworthy deviations, such as an American request that we widen NATO horizons on a global scale to encompass areas of conflict such as Vietnam – a request that fell on very deaf ears. When the agenda, which, in fact, also included the round of official receptions and dinners, was concluded, it was time to go home. We hadn't seen anything of Paris except the fleeting glimpses we got through a car window. It all sounded so wonderfully glamorous, but it was just hard work and extremely tiring as well. It absorbed so much of our pre-Christmas schedule that there was little time available for the myriad chores associated with the season. One bright spot was the trip home. The work was all done, so everyone was relaxed and in a good mood, ready for a game of bridge.

It was the season for giving, and as luck would have it I had something for the Governor General's stocking – with no price tag attached. It was a promotion from Major-General to full General, effective January 1, 1964. To give credit where it is due, the idea originated with Judy LaMarsh, who suggested it to me. She was very sensitive to that kind of nicety, and I agreed wholeheartedly. The gesture was strictly symbolic, because His Excellency was already Commander-in-Chief of the navy, the army, and the air force; but the parchment was a kind of tacit recognition of the sacrificial service the Governor General had rendered his country throughout a long and distinguished career. General

Vanier was as pleased as a child with a new toy and told me it was the best Christmas present he had received that year.

Ellen and I began 1964 with a few days' vacation, and got back to Ottawa just in time for the annual meeting of the Conference of Defence Associations. This is the one opportunity for representatives of the militia, naval, and air-force reserves to get together each year to swap experiences, make representations to the minister, and be brought up to date on departmental plans. In many ways it's a frustrating exercise for everyone involved – at least in a time of tightly controlled defence budgets. The reserves are ready, willing, and able to improve their skills and potential effectiveness, but to do so they require extra money for training and new modern equipment with which to train. This at a time when the regular forces are starved for funds and there just isn't enough to go around. "The forces in being", which are also under-equipped, get first call on available funds. The reserves have to make do with the leftovers, which provide a near-starvation diet.

The next major item on the agenda was an intensive six-day immersion course in the functions of the navy and the RCAF's Maritime Air Command, beginning in Bermuda on Sunday, January 19, and ending at Greenwood Air Force Station, Nova Scotia, on Friday, January 24. It was a trip I was anxious to make, because for some time there had been recurring and disturbing reports of low morale and unacceptable operating efficiency in the navy. A commission of inquiry headed by Rear-Admiral E. R. Mainguy had reported as early as 1949. It made many recommendations, but its main thesis was that elaborate ceremonies should be drastically cut down, that obsolete Royal Navy traditions should be abandoned, and that the Royal Canadian Navy should cooperate more closely with the United States Navy. Little could have changed in the meantime, because, as recently as September 1963, *Maclean's* magazine had carried an article by retired Commodore James Plomer entitled "The Gold-braid Mind Is Destroying Our Navy". In it Plomer paid tribute to the thoroughness of the Mainguy report and said: "On this document, this Magna Carta, an effective navy with high morale and enthusiasm could have been built. But it was not."[1] The article was a slashing attack on "the heart of the problem", which he defined as:

> the self-perpetuating, self-electing group of admirals. Canadian admirals have come to believe in themselves as a social

institution, a marching society, a kind of uniformed Tammany Hall. . . . Arrogantly, they believe that military law, the Naval Discipline Act, and pageantry are all that we need to make a modern navy. . . . In the year 1962, right up to the Cuban crisis, the state of readiness of the fleet was never the subject of formal discussion by the naval board. However, just before the Cuban crisis, the naval board did devote a whole morning to discussing a Tri-Service Handbook on Ceremonial and a new summer uniform for wrens. I know. I was there.[2]

Plomer was merciless.

In my opinion this childish obsession with the pomp of a bygone age is far stronger in the RCN than in any other modern navy. In fact, the highest Canadian officers seem to depend on this, rather than on the job they do, to establish their authority. And it is this attitude of humorless self-importance that causes unrest in the service.[3]

My job was to find out first-hand if the situation was as bad as was alleged.

For administrative convenience the course was divided into two parts. The first half involved the navy at sea in an antisubmarine operation dubbed "Gooey Duck". As the exercise was already under way, I flew to the nearest point of departure, Bermuda. I was accompanied by Vice-Admiral H. Rayner, Chief of Naval Staff; Elgin Armstrong, Deputy Minister of Defence; R. L. Hennessy, Commodore, Personnel, Atlantic Coast; Capt. H. A. Porter, Naval Assistant to Chief of Naval Staff; and Lt.-Col. Reg Weeks, my military secretary.

We were met in Bermuda by the Commanding Officer of Air Anti-Submarine Squadron 880; Commander R. C. MacLean from the aircraft carrier *Bonaventure*; and the local naval liaison officer. The formalities observed, we were soon airborne again for the approximately one-hour flight to join the naval task force on the aircraft carrier *"Bonny"* – three of us in Tracker aircraft, anticipating the thrill of landing on the carrier. Anyone who hasn't shared this experience can imagine that it's like landing on a postage stamp in the middle of the Atlantic. What if the plane isn't lined up perfectly with the deck? What if the tail is too high and the hook misses the arresting cable? What if either the hook or the cable should break? The questions soon became academic after a perfect landing, and the plane came to its wrenching stop.

On board I was greeted by Commodore R. P. Welland, the Senior Canadian Officer Afloat (Atlantic), who was in charge of the operation, Captain R. W. Timbrell, skipper of the *Bonaventure*, and his Executive Officer, Commander W. H. Fearon. Then I was shown to the Commodore's day cabin, where, over tea, I was billeted and briefed on the ship's capability. Soon we were off to the operations room to review developments in the antisubmarine exercise, while Petty Officer Berube, my steward, unpacked my bag and "set-up" the exclusive six-man dinner we would enjoy after meeting the ship's officers and toasting their good health in the wardroom. It was the first, but not the last, time I would be surprised at such extraordinary luxury.

Evening entertainment included night-flying and band music. The circumstances couldn't have been more perfect. The moon was full and the sea like glass. Except for the absence of Mary Martin and the dancing girls, it was just like a scene from *South Pacific* – so soporific that I had difficulty staying awake long enough to absorb the thirty-six pages of briefing material I had been handed. As the night wore on the weather changed, as it so often does after a full moon. The mighty ship began to shake and roll in the raging sea. Fortunately Reg Weeks had had the foresight to bring some Gravol tablets against just such an eventuality, but he had neglected to distribute them. As it turned out, I was a better sailor than my land-based aide, who was the only beneficiary of his own advance planning.

It is said that a surprise a day keeps the blues away, so on day two, I was treated to a jackstay crossing. I was reeled across a thousand feet of ocean on a cable – in very much the same way as pyjamas are hung out to dry on a clothesline. It added nothing to my confidence that the water was still so rough they had difficulty keeping the destroyer-escort *Restigouche* in line with the *Bonaventure*. Eventually all was set, and I was snapped into a harness; but the final instruction, just as my feet left the heaving deck, was far from reassuring. "If anything goes wrong, for Heaven's sake, let go. We will circle around and pick you up." It was just the kind of advice one reflects deeply on when suspended halfway between sea and sky. However, the navy fumbled its chance to drop me in, and I made it. Sometimes a fellow gets lucky.

After a sumptuous lunch with Captain D. L. MacKnight and the officers of *Restigouche*, I was ferried back to the carrier by helicopter to continue observing the exercise against "enemy" subs. The task of the two underwater craft was to evade detection and "destruction" by the surface ships, aircraft, and helicopters, which scoured the three-hundred-mile-square area in search of their prey. I was favourably impressed by the professionalism of the sailors and airmen in locating their quarry with the help of some very sophisticated electronic gadgetry. I was particularly impressed with Commodore Welland, the officer in charge. (Months later, after Welland had been promoted to Rear-Admiral, one of his staff officers was to allege that the exercise had not been as successful as portrayed, and that the Commodore had "cooked" the log of the operation in order to "impress the minister". I must admit I was surprised!)

On Tuesday I was to return to Bermuda, and my "daily treat" was a steam-assisted catapult take-off from the "Bonny". I found it every bit as "exciting" as a deck-landing, as my stomach attempted a fit of rage to assist the plane into the air. Once over the bow, the plane made a small dip in the direction of the ocean, in order to gain momentum, which I thought conveyed a fitting "salute" of appreciation and farewell. Soon I was back in Bermuda and took leave of Commander MacLean, who had been as considerate as he was careful to turn me over safely to Group Captain R. A. Gordon. He was in charge of the giant Argus submarine-hunter, and proposed to give us a "hands-on" seminar in just how these big birds with their bellies full of electronics fitted into the surveillance picture.

For starters, and no doubt the most disconcerting part of the indoctrination, we flew the entire route at three hundred to five hundred feet "off the deck", as they called it. The nearest comparable experience would be driving 1300 kilometers on a washboard road. All of the members of our party, including the Chief of Naval Staff and the Deputy Minister were sick. I was the exception, but it was touch and go. Still, it was a good education, and the only way to understand and appreciate the professionals who had to do it in the line of duty. We landed at the Naval Air Station, Shearwater, across the harbour from Halifax, where we were greeted by the base commander, Captain G. C. Edwards, and Rear-Admiral Jeffry Brock, Flag Officer Atlantic Coast, who took Rayner, Armstrong, and me back to his residence, Admiralty House, for billets.

Brock and his wife were most gracious, and lavished their Old World hospitality on me. This hospitality was made possible, however, by treating ordinary seamen as lackeys. It wasn't too surprising to see them serving drinks and dinner, although civilians were fast replacing military personnel for these purposes. What did shock me was to go to my room and find that some poor sailor had already unpacked my bag, hung up my clothes, and put my underwear in a dresser drawer and my toothbrush in a glass over the sink. My pyjamas were tucked neatly under one of the pillows. I was really appalled. Not that I had any questionable items in the flight-bag pockets to set the rumour-mongers' tongues wagging, but the very idea of being waited on to that extent was foreign to my nature. I was accustomed to packing and unpacking my own bag. "Who do these admirals think they are?" I mused. Such practices seemed an abuse of indentured labour reminiscent of the dark ages.

Dinner was laid to the Queen's taste, with nothing but the most elaborate in china and flatware. It was a congenial and enjoyable feast at which the lieutenant-governor and the premiere were present. They departed after coffee and liqueurs. Admiral Rayner and Elgin Armstrong retired early, leaving me alone with our host and hostess, who chatted amiably about military life, politics, and other matters. There was no hint of the opinions that would be expressed in Brock's book *The Thunder and the Sunshine* twenty years later.[4] Indeed his belated post-facto reconstruction of the evening's conversation is so outrageously false in its implications as to be unworthy of detailed comment. Most of the quotations attributed to me are easily verifiable as views I never, ever, expressed. I didn't say I disliked being Minister of National Defence, because that wasn't my opinion. I wouldn't have said that Defence was the kiss of death for an ambitious politician, because no-one, myself included, thought so at the time. There is equally no possibility that I touted the Finance portfolio as a stepping-stone to the party leadership. The conventional wisdom was just the opposite. Finance, rather than Defence, was considered the kiss of death. What I might have said was that Finance, rather than Defence, was my first choice. There was no secret about that, and it had nothing to do with ambition and everything to do with my reason for entering politics in the first place, which was the hope of introducing some economic innovations.

Our final stop in the six-day marathon was RCAF Station Greenwood, Nova Scotia, where we were greeted by Air Commodore Frederick Carpenter, Air Officer Commanding Maritime Air Command, and Group Captain Ralph Gordon, the base commander who had escorted us from Bermuda. We had another close look at the big birds that patrolled the Atlantic coast and received a full briefing on the interplay between the air and sea elements of our antisubmarine forces. Even more fascinating was the interplay between Carpenter and Brock. Whereas the admiral was prim and proper in the extreme, the airman was informal, a populist in uniform. Carpenter was endowed with a very fertile, creative mind, which is not always an advantage in a big organization like the military. Conformists are more likely to be appreciated than non-conformists, who are often branded as troublemakers. For example, Carpenter thought it was silly to have so many expensive airplanes limited to a single purpose, when it might be possible to give the giant Argus subchaser a dual capability as a troop- or cargo-carrier. So, without benefit of approval from higher authority, he had his men practise stripping the electronic gear from one of the planes to test the feasibility. This kind of initiative was anathema to Brock, who considered his nominal second-in-command both brash and insubordinate. Hints of the tensions between the two men had surfaced briefly during the fomal dinner at Admiralty House and re-emerged regularly in the days to follow. The full fury of Brock's venom was reserved for an attack in *The Thunder and the Sunshine*, after Carpenter had died and was no longer in a position to return the broadside.

By the time I returned to Ottawa, I knew I had my work cut out for me. The navy was going to need a lot of modernization to make it contemporary, and that wasn't going to be easy. However, consideration of such fundamental matters – addressed in a general way in the White Paper – was constantly being interrupted by day-to-day concerns and crises of one sort or another, including the operations of the FLQ. Some of my most embarrassing moments were caused by FLQ break-ins to steal arms and ammunition from defence establishments. A serious break-in at Shawinigan, on February 20, brought both John Diefenbaker and Tommy Douglas to their feet. Three Department of National Defence employees had been tied up while the thieves made off with assorted weapons, and the leader of the Opposition wanted to know what measures were being taken to protect the armed forces and also their supplies from these dastardly acts. The NDP chief wanted to know why round-the-clock protection wasn't available at all defence establishments.

The short answer was that, with so many facilities, the cost would be prohibitive. The following day I reminded the House that, immediately after the first break-in in Montreal, a special commission on security had been established. Its report had just been received and its recommendations were being studied by the chiefs of staff. One recommendation for immediate action had already been put in train. I stated that an "order has gone out to-day that all small arms be withdrawn from reserve establishments where maximum security cannot be provided on an around the clock basis."[5] In addition at least one person would be kept on duty at all times.

This was a temporary measure to give defence officials time to assess the security arrangements in each individual case. The implementation of the order, however, was uneven and not always intelligent. The policy applied to all of Quebec and to adjacent areas of New Brunswick and Ontario but, for unexplained reasons, weapons were rrecovered from many Ontario units long before action was taken in Quebec – even from units in Windsor and Woodstock, which were well beyond the prescribed limits for Ontario. In the Commons I was bombarded with questions that filled many pages of Hansard.

A more embarrassing development in the case was yet to come – one with all the elements of comic opera. An army unit from Kingston arrived at Ottawa's Ashbury College very late at night, and the next morning's newspapers reported that soldiers with fixed bayonets had entered the school and, in what sounded like a nocturnal raid, had picked up the small arms used by the cadet corps. John Diefenbaker was outraged and demanded information from the Prime Minister, who passed the questions to me. The Tory chief wanted to know who had authorized this infamous raid on a prestigious boys' school and later, tongue in cheek, if we had obtained a search warrant.

The explanation was straightforward, if less than satisfactory. The cadet commander had been advised in advance that the detachment expected to arrive at 9:30 p.m. Unfortunately the truck had broken down and the soldiers didn't show up until after midnight, although the college was kept fully informed. The troops were armed, but bayonets were not fixed. In fact the whole operation was carried out with the full cooperation of college officials; but this didn't satisfy the Opposition. Fuel was added to the controversy when Erik Nielsen, MP for Yukon, discovered that some of the rifles picked up at the college were ancient 1917 vintage Cooey .22 calibre; some even had the barrels plugged with wooden stoppers. There were some FN and .308 Lee Enfield rifles and four Bren machine guns at the college, but the public image that emerged was one of soldiers with fixed bayonets raiding a private college in the dead of night to pick up some inoperable rifles that might have been used as props for *The Nutcracker* ballet. It was a cartoonist's dream, and I was skewered mercilessly on the editorial pages. It didn't help when some of the armed service public-relations officers dropped hints to the press that the whole fiasco was due to the imprecision of my original order.

The tempest had just about blown over when the newspapers reported that there had been a mess dinner at Ashbury College the night of "the raid", and a regular force major-general had been present and an eye-witness to the whole incredible scene. When the prime minister read that, he turned purple with fury that the General had been present but had not intervened. I had seldom seen him so angry. At cabinet he demanded to know the general's name. He would be fired forthwith! I refused to disclose the identity of the "culprit", and said that if anyone was going to be fired, it would have to be me. That was the way the system worked. It took considerable time and argument to get the PM calmed down, but I held my ground, and eventually we got on to other business. I never told Maj.-Gen. W. A. B. Anderson that I had saved his career from an early and abrupt end. I would do the same again, even though he was less than kind in his assessment of me at a later stage of my career.

The whole debacle was acutely disquieting. Each service had interpreted the order differently. There was no uniformity. Then, because army weapons had to be sent to army depots, navy to navy, and air force to air force, we witnessed the spectacle of truckloads of small arms moving hundreds of miles in opposite directions from Halifax to Thunder Bay. The exercise was a prime example of tri-service inefficiency, and if there was ever any doubt in my mind about the desirability of unification, that episode removed it.

At the same time, the FLQ crisis was also diverting valuable attention from long-range considerations, like the preparation of the White Paper and the trouble that was brewing in Cyprus. The president, Archbishop Makarios, had refused to observe a provision of the constitution, calling for the establishment of separate Greek and Turkish communities in five major towns on the small Mediterranean island, and this had led to bloodshed between the two factions. Order was restored with the assistance of British, Greek, and Turkish forces, but it was a fragile arrangement, which could have ended, without warning, in open warfare.

The British were desperate for a solution that would reduce the vulnerability of their troops. The Americans were equally concerned about the stability of NATO's soft, southern underbelly, and they thought the alliance should form a force to take over from the Greeks and Turks and reduce the reliance on the British. This idea gained some support, especially in the United Kingdom, but it was subsequently vetoed by Makarios, who preferred a UN force under the supervision of the security council. Problems of financing, jurisdiction, and control appeared almost insurmountable as the situation on the island continued to deteriorate. On February 3, 1964, still plagued by other problems, I noted in my diary: "The Cyprus thing, too, is boiling. It is almost certain that we will be asked for troops. Someone said that it would not be politic to send the Van Doos. The GOC [General Officer Commanding] Quebec command disagrees and so do I."[6] The situation rumbled on as everyone looked for an acceptable formula, and on February 19 the PM made a brief statement, setting out the conditions that were essential to Canada's participation in a peace force. He also assured the House that the matter would be referred to Parliament before any final decision was taken respecting Canadian participation.

Five days later, Marcel Lambert asked the PM for an update on the UN Secretary General's plans for Cyprus, "and in particular, has there been a further request from the United Nations for the use of Canadian troops in Cyprus?"[7] In reply the Prime Minister said the matter was still under consideration, and as far as troops were concerned, "there has been no additional request made of Canada for participation in any such force but, as the House knows, we have laid down certain conditions which we feel should be observed before Canada participates in a force of that kind."[8] Privately he was less diplomatic. When I asked him for his latest views the next morning – because we couldn't make plans in a vacuum – he replied: "We probably won't participate at all. Let them cut each other up. We certainly won't go in just to help the British."[9]

For almost three weeks the question was front and centre in the Commons, as the diplomatic dithering continued. In the end it was Paul Martin who pulled the chestnuts from the fire. At the Prime Minister's suggestion, he had gone to New York to tell U Thant that if Sweden would participate, he would announce Canada's decision to join a UN force. He found, to his dismay, that the possibility of Swedish cooperation was still in limbo, and the UN Secretary General was pessimistic about success. It was at this stage that Paul decided to phone some of his fellow foreign ministers directly, in an effort to break the deadlock. He succeeded. As he recalls in *A Very Public Life*, Vol. II, "The result of my phone calls was the establishment of the UN force in Cyprus. After everything had been arranged, I telephoned a rather surprised U Thant in New York to tell him the good news."[10] It was one of Paul Martin's finest hours.

I was called back to Ottawa from a speaking tour in Winnipeg. I was having dinner with Richard Malone, publisher of the *Winnipeg Free Press*, when the summons came, and a number of important departmental decisions had to be made on the spot. Dick was sufficiently impressed with my "crisp and decisive" manner that he later reported favourably to the PM. In the capital the defence department was ready. I hadn't taken the PM's earlier reservations too seriously, and a contingency plan for sending troops to Cyprus had been prepared. In this case the department deserved full marks for doing its job well, and we were in a position to act on a minute's notice.

Everything came together on March 13 when the PM asked for parliamentary approval. An emergency debate was held that evening with only a little procedural kicking and screaming from the Quebec Créditistes, who alleged that their parliamentary privileges were being abused. Meanwhile, we had our first contingent in the air and on its way before the debate began. It could easily have been recalled if Parliament had denied its approval, but at least we would gain a few critical hours if, as expected, Parliament concurred in the government's decision.

Everyone was impressed with Canada's quick response. In *Mike*, Vol. III, the PM recorded the U.S. reaction.

President Johnson was amazed and filled with admiration at our ability to act so quickly, and I think this may have changed his attitude toward Canada. He phoned me again the night we began our airlift to say: "You'll never know what this has meant, having those Canadians off to Cyprus and being there tomorrow: you'll never know what this may have prevented." Having praised us for our action, he concluded: "Now what can I do for you?" I replied: "Nothing at the moment, Mr. President." But I had some credit in the bank.[11]

I have talked to one American-born economist who thinks it may have been this "credit" which influenced the United States to sign the Autopact in 1965.

CHAPTER 4

REPRIEVE

The early months of 1964 were not easy for me. In addition to the FLQ crisis and the pressure of trying to get the White Paper approved and published, there was the ever-present threat posed by the Canada Pension Plan. I had considered the question thoughtfully and arrived at the conclusion that I couldn't support another unfunded plan in addition to the Old Age Pension. It was too much at odds with the long-term interests of the baby-boom generation who would have to pay the taxes for both. I would oppose the idea to the extent of my ability, and when I lost the battle, as seemed inevitable, resign.

The plan had not enjoyed the swift and easy passage its sponsors had hoped for. Its complexity had resulted in numerous redrafts, and provincial acquiescence was far from automatic. In fact, since Quebec had decided that it would prefer a funded plan of its own, the CPP could no longer be touted as a national plan.

On February 24 the PM indicated that the Canada Pension Plan would be ready within a couple of weeks. "It looks as if we plan to plow ahead; oh well!" I recorded wistfully and somewhat fatalistically in my diary. "It looks as if I have a few days' 'reprieve.' "[1] Meanwhile Walter Gordon got the bright idea that the pension issue would provide a good excuse for seeking a fresh mandate from the people, and I got wind of the scheme for a new election. On March 7 "I had lunch with Jack Pickersgill and put him 'in the picture'. Obviously he didn't have a clue that a crisis was approaching and an election probably imminent. He didn't say much, but he was obviously shaken."[2]

It seemed a bit strange to be pushing ahead with the defence White Paper, knowing that I probably wouldn't be around to implement it. Still, I was never one to let what might happen tomorrow interfere with what has to be done today, so the show went on. The March 26 publication of the White Paper was something of a triumph in its own right – especially when the reaction was so overwhelmingly positive. Nevertheless, reality had to be faced, and I wanted the PM to know exactly where I stood on the CPP before the final decision was taken.

On April 9 I was granted my "long awaited interview with the Prime Minister. After a couple of awkward moments we had a good chat about the Canada Pension Plan. I outlined my objections on social and economic grounds. He admitted that he had been advised to hold an election on this issue and also that a poll had been taken to get the public 'temperature'. I suggested that part of the election plan was a 'dump Hellyer' campaign. He said he didn't think this was so, but suggested it was difficult to know motivation. He undertook to check again the question of portability between the CPP and the Quebec Plan and let me know his findings on Tuesday. Re. the White Paper, he agreed that the reaction was excellent. He said that some had thought it was a risky proposal and some thought it would be suicidal. I wonder who?"[3] Mike's mild reaction to my allegation that Walter wanted to get rid of me was tacit confirmation of the degree of tension the CPP debate had produced.

That meeting was the prelude to a gruelling weekend trip to the West Coast, scheduled to begin the following morning. I had little doubt it would be my last as Minister of National Defence. Saturday morning I addressed army, navy, and air force officers and NCOs at HMCS *Naden* – 1,000 all ranks in the morning and 875 in the afternoon. Rear-Admiral William Landymore, Flag Officer Pacific Coast, provided lunch in between. It was quite worth while from a public-relations standpoint.

At Harrison Hot Springs I worked some of the kinks out of my aching back in the hot pool before joining my host, W. S. (Stan) Haggett, chairman of the board of the Air Industries Association, for dinner. My address came on Monday. "The group was so starved for information that my mediocre presentation was received with great acclaim."[4] We returned to Vancouver's Sea Island Airport by RCAF helicopter. Ellen and Marg Bulger found this most interesting though, as I recall, it was also a bit bone-jarring. The flight back to Ottawa was uneventful but "my back and shoulders are really bothersome. The terrible fatigue accumulated over these weeks has caught up with a vengeance."[5]

That same day, while I was away, Bill C-90, to amend the National Defence Act, was introduced and given its routine first reading. Its purpose was to implement one of the major recommendations in the White Paper on Defence. Specifically, the bill provided for the replacement of the positions of Chairman of the Chiefs of Staff Committee, Chief of the Naval Staff, Chief of the General Staff, and Chief of the Air Staff by a single new position designated as Chief of the Defence Staff. Although the proposed change represented the first and probably most important move in the integration of the armed forces under a single defence staff, it all seemed rather academic if my career was about to founder on the shoals of the Canada Pension Plan.

Tuesday noon, I went to the cabinet table in the northwest alcove of the parliamentary restaurant for lunch. When Mitchell Sharp arrived, he said, "There have been some dramatic developments over the weekend."[6] He explained that these included new demands for tax-sharing with the provinces and a plan to adopt a pension plan along the Quebec lines, which would permit the same benefits for all Canadians and portability from coast to coast. When the House met at two o'clock that afternoon, the PM made a brief explanation in reply to a question from John Diefenbaker, and I could hardly wait to get the story. Later, when I saw him privately, he said that the government had moved far enough in my direction that I should agree to stay. That seemed to be the case. The CPP was still a half-baked plan, but at least it would be funded in the short-term, and an important element of universality had been restored. The immediate gains were enough to justify a stay of execution – a reprieve that would permit me to soldier on.

What had happened in the interim is difficult to piece together, but this much is known: Tom Kent and Maurice Sauvé went to Quebec City for a weekend meeting with the Québec people in a last-ditch attempt to try to reach a compromise. The meeting was arranged in great haste and maximum secrecy – so much secrecy, in fact, that no one bothered to advise Judy LaMarsh, who, as Minister of Health and Welfare, was nominally in charge of the issue. That Sunday they received Premier Jean Lesage's assent and, according to Judy, "on their return, Kent met with the Prime Minister, Walter Gordon, Guy Favreau, and perhaps others. He made his report and the Prime Minister urged him on."[7]

When Judy learned that we were to make an accommodation with Quebec, she was livid. She didn't like the funding provision at all, not because she was opposed in principle, but because she felt she had been made a fool of. She had bought Walter's line holus-bolus and "had spent a solid year making speeches about our pay-as-you-go scheme."[8] In the end there were compromises on both sides, and cabinet accepted them. Judy capitulated on the grounds of universality. "There was no other way if there were to be a system of universal pensions across the whole of Canada. One for nine provinces was unthinkable and probably unworkable."[9] No one ever admitted that I had influenced the outcome. My only clue was that Walter Gordon didn't speak to me for three weeks following the reversal in policy. That was to be the clearest indication that I had been a factor in the decision.

Walter had warmed perceptibly by the time I saw him on May 6, just after he got back from a trip to Vancouver. He said the Prime Minister was given great credit for his diplomacy and skill in working out the settlement with Quebec. Then he added: "That isn't exactly the way it happened. It was more like a game of poker when you have only one move left and it is an all-or-nothing decision. It doesn't always work out so well."[10]

Before actually walking the plank on this issue I had decided it would be prudent to get an independent opinion from someone whose judgment I trusted. So on April 2 I had sent a copy of the proposed CPP, together with a copy of my alternative plan, to Graham Towers, former Governor of the Bank of Canada. I thought he had the best financial mind the country had yet produced. His reply wasn't received until after the government changed course, but his comments are well worth noting:

I share your apprehension in regard to the Canada Pension Plan, even as amended. The inequities could be formidable. . . .

I am aware that objecting to an apparently desirable public programme because of its costs tends to be regarded as highly reactionary. My objection is based on the assumption that if a country overloads itself with fixed payments, it will in due course be forced to reduce the value of the payments by depreciating its currency, an enticing but dangerous form of fraud. Up to a point a government can get away with it, without destroying confidence, as few people understand what is being done to them. As a continuing and repeated solution it is fatal to progress. Forgive this homily. Put it down to my sensitivity as an ex-central banker.[11]

Mr. Towers showed unusual prescience. He continued: "Turning to your alternative plan, I think it is workable and much better for the country than the Canada Pension Plan.[12]

While the pension plan was never far from my mind during this tense and difficult period, it was just one of the many hot potatoes that I seemed to be juggling most of the time. In addition to the FLQ crisis and the White Paper, there was the Cyprus Force, the Special Committee on Defence, plans to reorganize National Defence Headquarters, and myriad other concerns too numerous to mention. Little wonder that the strain spilled over on the homefront. On February 23 I noted, "The whole family is unhappy about being in Ottawa and naturally blame the whole thing on my political career. It is quite a sacrifice, and the going seems to get tougher all the time."[13]

Wherever I went, people assumed that, since I was Minister of National Defence, my mind was a depository of official secrets. While it is true that I had a good grasp of current numbers and of future plans, there were few cases when I was privy to something I considered a genuine "military secret". There were many subjects that I couldn't discuss, even though you could read a reasonably accurate account of them in the *New York Times*. Official silence was based on the theory that, although a potential enemy might have assembled the facts and figures, you never provided the luxury of confirmation.

One of the few cases during which I really felt it was important to keep my mouth shut began when Air Marshal Roy Slemon, NORAD's Deputy Commander-in-Chief, phoned from the Prime Minister's office to ask for an appointment. When we met, he had to admit that the secret was so hot that he had only planned to tell the PM, but my boss had made it clear that it was his duty to inform his minister. Slemon said the USAF had developed an experimental fighter, the A-11, capable of flying at three times the speed of sound. It was being subjected to test runs along the coast of British Columbia and across the Arctic to Thule, Greenland. The USAF was quite confident that it wouldn't be detected by radar, but just in case it was, we should know it was friend rather than foe. He couldn't overemphasize the necessity of keeping the whole operation hush-hush.

My lips were sealed and I didn't discuss it with anyone, not even Frank Miller, though I assumed he would be *au courant*. Only a few days passed before Slemon phoned again, but this time to say "President Johnson has announced the successful development of the A-11 and flight testing to Mach III. The military are to say nothing. We [Canadians] will say 'a very interesting development; we will follow its application with great interest.' "[14] I phoned the Prime Minister, but he had already heard directly from the President, who said, "I don't want you to read it in the newspapers."[15]

On another occasion Bob McNamara told me about the development of the cluster bomb, its variations, and the havoc it could wreak. This information, too, was "top secret", and I was honour-bound not to say a word to anyone. Only a few months elapsed before I read in the newspapers that U.S. troops had been using top-secret cluster bombs in Vietnam. That made me wonder if anything is ever secret for long. I don't want to create the impression that I treat the subject lightly, because I don't; but in my experience it is just as likely to be the taxpayers who are really in the dark as it is any potential enemy.

The secrets that were most frustrating, from my vantage point, were those the military refused to reveal to their "political masters", as they called us – with a trace of tongue in cheek. The transport capability of the RCAF was a classic case. For many years the workhorse of the fleet had been the old C-119, known as the "Flying Boxcar" because of its unusual shape. Then an order came through for four "copies" of the more modern Lockheed C-130 Hercules, which I approved. About that time I read in the press that hairline cracks had been detected in the C-119s and that the entire fleet had been grounded while repairs were being made. I asked Frank Miller about this and was assured there was nothing to be concerned about. The Boxcars would soon be as good as new, and serviceable for years to come.

I was sceptical on two counts. The C-119s were old and seemed to belong to an era long since past. Then there was the undeniable fact that the RCAF didn't want to spend money on air transport. They abhorred the thought of being seen as "truck drivers for the army". Any airman worth his salt had to be a "Captain of the Clouds", an air-superiority, one-on-one type, just like you see in the movies. If the department had any money for airplanes, the RCAF wanted it to be reserved for fighters.

I understood the importance of air superiority in wartime, but it was one task of many. Men and materials have to be moved quickly, and the kind of flexible mobile force I envisioned needed airlift. There might be times when ox-carts or trucks would be fast enough, but there would be others when time was of the essence. I decided to find out where the C-119s were being repaired and check our capability first-hand.

I learned that the work was being done at Downsview and decided to drop in without notice to prevent the kind of snow job to which visitors are often subjected. Consequently, on my next trip to Toronto we landed at de Havilland Airport, where the RCAF Station was located, and instead of loading into the waiting cars, walked over to the office. The commanding officer was absent, and a flight-lieutenant was manning the phone. He called the Acting CO, who was elsewhere on the station, to advise that the minister had just arrived and would like to look in the hangar where the C-119s were being repaired. I could hear only one end of the conversation but realized instantly that it was one of those hilarious Laurel-and-Hardy exchanges. The Wing Commander obviously didn't believe a word of what he was hearing, and must have insinuated that his subordinate was smoking pot or otherwise in breach of regulations. Perhaps he asked if Snow White and Cinderella were visiting as well. After several exchanges the flight-lieutenant sensed that I was getting anxious and ended the conversation by advising his superior that we were going to the hangar and he could meet us there if he wished – which is how that part of the story ended.

When we walked through the hangar door, I was flabbergasted. Mechanics were rebuilding whole sides of the airplanes – ribs, skin, everything. Instead of having some innocuous hairline cracks of no account, the airplanes were, as I had suspected, worn out. They were suffering from the fatigue of a long life in the air. The next time the subject was on the agenda for a staff meeting, I had the advantage of being better informed than anyone else present. We decided, despite the protests that were somewhat muted in the face of the evidence, that we would purchase sixteen additional C-130s and dispose of the Boxcars. The wisdom of that decision has been confirmed by the fact that the Hercules have been used extensively by the Canadian Armed Forces in almost every major exercise and operation in which they have been engaged for more than two decades.

The explosive power of the atomic bombs assigned to the RCAF's No. 1 Air Division was an even more closely guarded secret the military was reluctant to reveal to anyone – especially a politician. I was told the weapons could be adjusted to give them more than one level of explosive power, but no details were provided. It was only when I demanded, point blank, to see the figures, that I was told the bombs were capable of yields ranging from a few kilotons to something in excess of two megatons. I could now understand the air force's desire to avoid the kind of public relations "explosion" that would have been inevitable had this information become public.

May 1964 was another busy month for military ceremonial and official functions. For sheer drama the episode that topped them all was triggered by the death of the great Indian statesman (Pandit) Jawaharlal Nehru on May 27. The PM and Paul Martin put their heads together, but let the night pass without deciding who should represent Canada at the cremation ceremony. Neither of them was free to go, so Thursday morning the Prime Minister phoned to say they had decided on me. At that stage, however, I was told I had only minutes to get ready. The RCAF didn't have a jet aircraft which could make the journey in time; but the U.S. representative, Secretary of State Dean Rusk, had generously agreed to give me a lift in the President's plane – if I could get to Washington fast enough to meet his deadline for takeoff to Delhi.

Moving quickly was one of my well-honed skills, but this was ridiculous. I had to get various inoculations, obtain traveller's cheques, pack, and get to the airport in no time flat; and that's just about how long it took. An army driver picked up the traveller's cheques at the main branch of the Bank of Montreal. They were to be signed later. This wasn't according to Hoyle, but was part of a special arrangement Edna Kingsbury of my office had for just such emergencies. A military doctor administered shots "on the run", and Ellen put some of my clothes on the bed so I could pack in three minutes instead of the usual five to ten. Twenty-seven minutes after hanging up from the PM's call, I was at the airport and ready to go. Bill Lee, who came independently from his home in west Ottawa, arrived a couple of minutes later, with his car steaming and the police in hot pursuit.

It was all to no avail. We sat in the RCAF's 412 Squadron terminal for what seemed like an eternity, while Washington decided if there was any point in us trying to make it. Finally we were told that there wasn't. Rusk had taken off without us. Nevertheless, in addition to setting an all-time record for attempting the impossible, I used the incident in evidence when Canada eventually acquired long-range jet-transport aircraft for the Canadian Armed Forces.

On June 4, I attended the first National Prayer Breakfast held at the Château Laurier. It was sponsored by a group of parliamentarians, including Robert Thompson, Walter Dinsdale, Ross Macdonald, and others. Dozens of Senators, MPs, and heads of diplomatic missions turned out, including Prime Minister Pearson, Opposition leader John Diefenbaker, and NDP leader Tommy Douglas. The idea was to get public leaders to acknowledge the spiritual dimension of their work and to take just a few minutes off to reflect on it.

Although most of the work for the breakfast was done by the parliamentarians, the concept had originated south of the border with Abraham Vereide, a Norwegian immigrant who had been a social-worker in Seattle in the 1930s. He found that ameliorating problems like poverty and inadequate housing was extremely difficult in the face of a city administration that was uncaring and allegedly corrupt. So he got a few businessmen together for breakfast to discuss the impasse, and this developed into a weekly time of prayer and Bible study. Together they turned the city around, cleaned up the corruption, and began to get things done. With this success Vereide extended his influence to members of State legislatures and later to senators and congressmen in Washington. Thus the Prayer Breakfast movement was born.

Vereide and his young cohort and understudy, Doug Coe, had invited me to address the movement's Seventh World Conference to be held in Bad Godesberg, near Bonn, Germany, on June 12. At first I demurred because there seemed no way that I could work it in, but shortly after, an opportunity came up for me to make a visit to our troops in Cyprus. I had wanted to go at the outset, but had been advised by External to give the soldiers time to settle in. The time was now ripe, so it appeared that I could combine the speaking assignment with official visits to Bonn, London, and Cyprus. I agreed to go.

That was the easy part. Tying the loose ends together and getting ready was something else. I was particularly busy reviewing the dossiers of senior military personnel before deciding who to appoint to the new integrated staff envisaged by Bill C-90, which had been given second reading and then referred to the special committee on defence. The plan was to pass the bill before the House recessed for the summer, and then proclaim the new law on August 1. That would be the historic day the individual service chiefs and staffs would be replaced by an integrated staff reporting to a single chief of defence staff – assuming, of course, that Parliament gave the necessary approval. In any event, I had to be ready.

At least one of the four or five top officers in the new organization had to be a French-speaking Canadian, and I had difficulty deciding who it would be. Major-General J. P. E. Bernatchez, Vice-Chief of the General Staff, was the senior man. He had an excellent war record, was a first-class officer, and on paper his qualifications were perfect. Yet he had a slightly diffident personality, and I couldn't envisage him as one destined to go right to the top. This was an important consideration because we were involved in a serious game like chess, where it was necessary to consider more than one move in advance. It seemed to me that the ebullient Jean Victor Allard was a more likely candidate to be the first Francophone Chief of Staff. This became the plan, though I sensed there would be repercussions from setting seniority aside. My intuition was correct.

Early the next morning, Saturday, June 6, I received a call from Esmond Butler, Secretary to Governor General Vanier, saying that His Excellency would like to see me. I guessed that it was about Maj.-Gen. Bernatchez, so I agreed to drop past Government House on my way to an air show. His Excellency began in his kindly way by reviewing the constitutional niceties. He fully realized that, although he was the Commander-in-Chief of the Forces, he was bound to accept my advice without question; but could we just talk as friends, which is what we did. Later, I recorded, "The interview was much easier than I anticipated. H.E. did not dispute our judgment but was concerned by the fact that Bernatchez had been planning the 50th birthday celebrations for the Van Doos and that now, after 20 years as the senior officer of the regiment, he was to be superceded. It is without a doubt a personal tragedy of some magnitude. No solutions were offered – except a look at the Col. of the Regiment post [an honorary position that would have allowed him to complete his plans for the celebration] – and the problem was left with me. My regard for H.E. rises each time I see him. A few of his type and we could have a peaceful world."[16]

Monday morning "General Bernatchez came to see me first thing. I offered him the Paris Posting [NATO] to replace Air Vice-Marshal Bob Cameron if he chose to stay in the service. He had his mind made up, however, and we agreed on a press release reflecting the fact that he had declined a senior posting. His attitude was much calmer and more relaxed than it was Friday. A copy of the press release was sent to His Ex. the Gov. Gen'l."[17] I really felt sorry about the whole affair, but I couldn't see any other way. Bernatchez's release was the key move, and the coast was now clear to complete the slate of senior staff changes that would have to be announced soon after my return.

Tuesday was the final day of preparation before leaving for Bonn. It was also a most controversial day in the hearings of the House of Commons Special Committee on Defence as it reviewed the ramifications of the bill based on the White Paper. Air Marshal Wilf Curtis and Maj.-Gen. W. H. S. Macklin were witnesses. Curtis said the individual service chiefs should remain, and Macklin said he was diametrically opposed to the idea. "I wound up the evidence at the evening session and, 'surprise', the Bill [establishing a single staff reporting to a single chief] was referred back to the House of Commons. There is always something to be grateful for."[18]

Early Wednesday morning we took off for Bonn. Our group included MPs Walter Dinsdale, Paul Martineau, W. H. A. Thomas, Sig Enns, Bob Thompson, Andrew Brewin, and James R. Tucker, who wanted to attend the Prayer Breakfast Conference.

Staff assistants included Bill Lee, Marg Bulger, Reg Weeks, Mac Macdonald, Robbie Robinson, and Squadron Leader Roy Sturgess, who went along to help with RCAF liaison. We arrived at 11:30 p.m. local time and drove about thirty minutes to Bad Godesberg. It was the first time I had seen the Rhine up close, and it was beautiful in the light of a summer night. The river-barge traffic was very heavy, carrying millions of tons of coal and other products from the industrial heartland to the sea.

The landscape was even more lovely by day, with the seven hills of *Snow White* fame dominating the skyline on the other side of the river. Bad Godesberg had also been the site of one of the meetings between Neville "Peace in Our Time" Chamberlain and Adolf Hitler. Reg Weeks and I had lunch as guests of the West German government, and soon after this, I was advised by Conference organizers that the speaker for Thursday night had not arrived. I agreed to fill in with my speech, which had been scheduled for the next day. By then the content had been worked over to my satisfaction, and it stands up well enough that I would still use it today. It wasn't the kind of speech that rated much attention in the secular press, and extensive coverage was limited to the *Catholic Register*, which dubbed me "The Minister of Peace".

I spent Saturday and Sunday with the troops. A helicopter took me first to the Sennelager training area, where the Brigade Group was exercising. Morale was high, and the soldiers were looking forward to receiving their new armoured personnel-carriers the next year. We had a mess dinner in the forest, after which arrangements were made for me to sleep in a van. It proved to be too short, so when lights were out I switched with Bill Lee. He enjoyed the privacy of the van, and I enjoyed the leg-room in his tent.

Much of Sunday was spent at the RCAF's 3 Wing in Baden and later at 4 Wing in Zweibrücken. There I saw the first quick-reaction alert (QRA) in operation. "Three and Four Wings went operational at 1:00 p.m. local time today. They are very proud and morale should zoom back now."[19] After witnessing the QRA we headed back to Bonn to pick up the balance of the party en route to Marville, France, where we were to remain overnight.

Monday morning Ellen and Marg peeled off for London, the MPs returned to Canada on a regularly scheduled RCAF flight, and the rest of us left for Nicosia, Cyprus. We had been in the air for only a few minutes when one of the Yukon's four engines conked out. The captain explained that we would be flying down the Italian boot and would never be more than seventy-five kilometers or so from an airport. He wasn't really alarmed about safety, so the decision to press on or turn back was mine. Since returning for repairs would have thrown the whole schedule into a tizzy, I opted to fly on.

Our touchdown in Nicosia was about an hour late because of the decreased speed. Brigadier A. James Tedlie, Colonel Edward A. C. Amy, and the UN Commander, Indian Lt.-Gen. P. S. Gyani, were there to greet us. A Guard of Honour from the Royal 22nd Regiment had been standing in the beastly heat for hours, and if it had been within my power, I would have awarded each man a medal on the spot. I have often wondered if that kind of torture would be considered cruel and inhumane punishment under the new Charter of Rights. The formalities completed, I was whisked off to the High Commissioner's residence for a reception. No sooner was a cool drink placed in my hand than I was asked if I had ever been swimming in the Mediterranean. No, as a matter of fact, I hadn't. "Pity," came the response, "because there's nothing in the world like it. Unfortunately there is no time on your schedule to work one in." Later I was checked into the Ledra Palace Hotel where, for the first and only time in my life, armed guards stood watch round the clock. Col. Amy wasn't taking any chances.

Tuesday morning I was briefed on the Nicosia Zone, which seemed to be the heart of the trouble, visited the UN base camp, and drove along the Green Line, which separated the warring Greek and Turkish factions. Cyprus was so beautiful that it was heartbreaking to see it torn apart. The depth of the division became even more apparent following separate visits to the President, His Beatitude Archbishop Makarios, and the Vice-President, Dr. Kutchuk. The former appeared to be a strong and cunning leader, while the latter seemed little more than a figurehead.

When the President greeted me, the first thing he did was put on an enormous mitre, which allowed him to tower over the tallest visitor. In combination with his long, flowing beard, the Bishop's headdress made him a most imposing figure. I was escorted to the palace garden, which was a showplace in itself – a classic mix of ancient artifacts and exotic flowers. We discussed the apparently intractable problems of Cyprus at length, and there was no hint of give and take in Makarios's position. He said he would not tolerate another "imposed solution", though for the life of me I couldn't see any other way out of the impasse. My conclusion was shared by Lt.-Gen. Gyani as well.

The only ray of hope was a hint of pragmatism in the Archbishop, which I gleaned from a story he told of his earlier years. He had been raised in abject poverty, but by dint of hard work and good luck he gained admittance to a theological seminary. He applied himself and progressed well. His studies were a real challenge, and he especially enjoyed the plain but abundant food. When he completed the course he was invited to dine with the Bishop, where he tasted the excellent food and fine wine that graced that office. His superior took advantage of the occasion to point out that the time had come for Makarios to grow a beard, which was a required badge of the order. The young man refused.

"But members of our order have worn beards for a thousand years," the Bishop explained.

Makarios shook his head.

"In that case you will have to return to the farm from whence you came," said the Bishop. "I will call a car."

When it arrived the two men shook hands and Makarios thanked his mentor and said good-bye.

"Don't throw your whole life away, my son," the Bishop counselled as a parting shot.

The car drove off. It got only as far as the gate when Makarios ordered the driver to stop and back up. He had already decided that if the Bishop didn't relent and call him back by then, he would capitulate. The lure of the Bishop's table – and his own future prospects – appeared far more appealing than the subsistence level he was returning to. As he stepped from the car, the two men embraced and Makarios agreed to grow a beard, the badge of his future authority.

Early Wednesday morning I was off to see the 1st Battalion (Van Doos) in action. Our party, which included Major Pat Tremblay, C Company, took a helicopter to one of the forward positions and watched the troops supervising the harvest; in several other cases a section of a company would be split between the Greek and Turkish enclaves in a village, with young corporals nineteen to twenty-one years of age acting as ambassadors between the groups. I wrote, "They are really splendid – I don't

know when I have been so favourably impressed."[20] Our next
stop was a hilltop outpost midway between Greek and Turkish
machine-gun positions – not the most comfortable "bird's nest"
imaginable. I chatted with our chaps in both official languages
and headed back to the helicopter. Reg Weeks followed, hopped
aboard, and banged heavily against me as he hit the seat. "Move
over," he ordered, in his most authoritative tone. "Sir," he added
somewhat sheepishly a moment later, as he turned his head and
realized it wasn't necessary to "make room" for the minister,
who was already on board.

Our whirly-bird flew northward to the magnificent ruins of St.
Hilarion castle from which we got our first glimpse of the
Kyrenia shoreline. It was magnificent. Later, in Kyrenia, one of
the officers went through the same old bit about the wonders of
swimming in the Mediterranean. That was the third time – same
question, same answer. We lunched with the Van Doos. Then I
thanked them for their hospitality and left by helicopter for
Nicosia airport and our farewell to the troubled island, which, in
peaceful circumstances, could have been paradise on earth. Our
next destination was El Arish, on the Gaza Strip, where Canadians had been serving with a United Nations Emergency Force;
but our plane was too big and too heavy to land at the desert
airstrip, so we had to put down at Beirut and switch to a smaller
Twin Otter.

We flew south parallel to the Israeli coast, and I will never
forget the scene from my window as our plane turned east toward
the shoreline. Both sides of the border between Israel and the
Gaza Strip were clearly visible. On one side a huge combine was
harvesting the grain. On the other, scarcely a thousand yards
distant, women were beating out the kernels on a threshing floor,
exactly as they had in the time of Christ. I had the feeling of being
caught up in a time machine encompassing two millennia. When
we touched down on the makeshift strip, I was greeted by the
United Arab Republic Liaison Officer and taken to Camp Rafa
for a mess dinner. One of the first topics of conversation was the
Mediterranean Sea, and swimming. Had I ever experienced this
unforgettable sensation.

"Not yet," I replied.

"It's really too bad that there is no provision on your
schedule."

Colonel Donald Rochester, the Canadian Commander, must
have noted my ill-disguised exasperation, because he quickly

added: "The only possible time would be at six o'clock in the morning."

"We'll go," I said, which seemed the only way to end the irritation. It wasn't yet dawn when Col. Rochester and the Canadian physical-training instructor arrived in a jeep, and the three of us headed down the narrow sandy road for the twenty-minute ride to the sea. The noise of the engine brought the Bedouins from their tents, and although it was difficult to interpret their reaction, I suspect they thought we were somewhat demented, but I was beyond caring. The splashdown was absolutely exhilarating. The hour may have affected my senses, but I decided that the reality did justice to the extensive advance billing.

After breakfast I addressed all ranks, who were standing in the hot sun – not an ideal posture from which to absorb a serious speech. Jackets were removed and the troops were told to "stand easy", but the heat was still oppressive. Fortunately for everyone, my remarks had to be cut short as a result of an unexpected and humbling refrain. Every time I opened my mouth to share a few wise words, a donkey tied to a nearby fence went "hee-haw". When I stopped, it stopped, and when I began again, it took its cue from me. The comic relief probably averted thirty cases of sunstroke, and whether the straight man was some kind of a mascot or a hired saboteur, I never knew. However, I got the point, declared a truce, and spared my audience further exposure to sun and flow charts. My time with the men did convince me, though, that morale was not high, and this was due largely to the length of the tour of duty, a point that had also been a concern of the men on Cyprus. I undertook to see what could be done about it.

I had lunch at the Headquarters mess. Music was provided by a kilted Indian band, which was as professional as it was splendidly outfitted. A painting of a Bedouin woman carrying a huge jug of water on her head was taken from the wall and presented to me. In response I not only thanked the officers for their kindness but mentioned my profound impression that the desert areas could be made to yield unbelievable wealth if, for example, atomic energy was used to desalinate water from the sea. I considered it an exciting challenge to use the tools available to modern man to create the "miracle". I was later dismayed to learn that, even before I got home, Paul Martin had received an official note of protest from the Egyptian government, claiming that I had taken sides in the dispute. That was nonsense, as I had gone out of my way to be even-handed. My enthusiastic vision of the desert blooming like a rose had been taken out of context.

We left the Middle East that afternoon, June 18, for London. The following morning I saw Julian Amery, British Minister for Air, about the possibility of a deal on the manufacture of the McDonnell F-4C aircraft; Lord Jellicoe, First Lord of the Admiralty, to review naval ship-building; and Peter Thorneycroft, my opposite number in defence, on all aspects of defence, including NATO strategy. Lionel Chevrier, by then our High Commissioner, gave a luncheon at which all the ministers were present. Admiral Mountbatten was also there as a result of his keen interest in the White Paper and what we were doing. "They are so interested that Strong (UK Chief of Military Intelligence) has just done a paper for Mountbatten about our internal organization,"[21] I noted in my diary. After lunch I visited the Canadian Joint Staff and spoke to all ranks. "We can make some savings here," I recorded after the event, having seen duplication and triplication of positions.[22]

When we got back to Ottawa I was able to report that our troops were doing well, but would be happier if their tour of duty was shortened, which it subsequently was. I wasn't naive enough to believe that there could be any quick solution to the Cyprus question, but little did I dream that our troops would still be there more than two decades later.

PTH in RCAF summer uniform, waiting to be
posted to Initial Flying Training School, 1944.

With wife Ellen and daughter Mary Elizabeth,
rehearsing Christmas carols.

Singing the role of Escamillo with Patricia Rideout as Carmen at the Banff School of Fine Arts, August 1954. (George Noble, Banff)

Checking the voters' list in Trinity with Jenny and Helen Michniewicz, December 1958.

Inspecting the Maginot Line in France while visiting Canadian troops with fellow MPs, including John Diefenbaker and a number of his future cabinet ministers, fall 1955. (National Defence Photo)

Celebrating the by-election victory with Trinity campaign-workers
December 15, 1958. (FEDNEWS)

Getting a warm reception from leader Mike
Pearson on arrival in Ottawa after unexpected
victory, January 1959. (Toronto Star Syndicate)

Listening to private secretary Margaret Bulger
in parliamentary Centre Block office, 1963.
(National Defence Photo)

At a mess dinner with H.E. Governor General Georges Vanier (seated,
centre), Associate Minister Lucien Cardin (seated, right), and senior
staff. (Standing left to right): Vice-Admiral H. Rayner, Hartley
Zimmerman, Air Marshal C.R. Dunlap, Air Chief Marshal F. Miller,
Elgin Armstrong, and Maj.-Gen. J.P.E. Bernatchez. (National Defence
Photo)

Crossing from the aircraft carrier
Bonaventure to the destroyer *Restigouche*
by jackstay, January 1964. (National
Defence Photo)

With Vice-Admiral H. Rayner, Deputy Minister Elgin Armstrong, and
Rear-Admiral Jeffrey Brock after dinner at the admiral's residence,
Halifax, January 1964. (National Defence Photo)

The minister with "Spitfire", the mascot of the Royal Canadian Dragoons Reconnaisance Squadron on the Green Line in Nicosia, Cyprus, June 1964. (National Defence Photo)

Conferring the degree of Doctor of Laws, *honoris causa*, on the Right Honourable Louis S. St. Laurent at the Fall Convocation of the Royal Military College of Canada, Kingston, Ontario, October 3, 1964. (National Defence Photo)

Enjoying a private joke with new Associate Defence Minister
Léo Cadieux, Spring 1965. (National Defence Photo)

Relaxing with senior headquarters officers and their wives after dinner
at the mess, 1965. (National Defence Photo)

With Group Captain Gil Gilespie (left),
Commanding Officer RCAF Station Uplands,
greeting General Lyman L. Lemnitzer (centre),
Supreme Commander, Allied Forces in Europe.
(National Defence Photo)

Ellen Hellyer reviewing the Guard of Honour at the launch of the
Canadian submarine *Onondaga* at Chatham, England, September 25,
1965. (Royal Navy Photo)

CHAPTER 5

TROUBLED WATERS

T he amendments to the National Defence Act, consequent on the White Paper, were given Royal Assent on July 16,
1964. The bill provided the green light to get on with the reorganization of defence headquarters. Its most critically important
object was a fully integrated headquarters with a single chain of
command. The heads of the three services were lopped off, and
their authority vested in one officer, to be known as the Chief of
Defence Staff (CDS). Also the Naval Board, the General Staff, and
the Air Staff were eliminated and replaced with a single Defence
Staff, organized along functional lines.

   The process of picking personnel for the top jobs in the new
integrated headquarters required much thought and balanced
judgment. I had already decided that Frank Miller, Chairman,
Chiefs of Staff, would be the first CDS. I knew him well and
admired him greatly. He had all the right qualities, except one: he
was adamantly opposed to unification. General Charles Foulkes,
a former Chairman, Chiefs of Staff Committee, wanted the job,

and had been lobbying the PM and me on his own behalf. His offer was gratefully declined, however, because bringing him out of retirement would have been a terrible blow to the morale of serving officers. It would have said, in effect, that none of them was qualified. The only other contender was Lt.-Gen. G. Walsh, Chief of the General Staff. I thought that he was favourable to unification, although I have since been advised that this may not have been the case. More important, he lacked the confidence of the other services and was close to retirement age. So Frank got the nod, and Walsh was slotted in as Vice-Chief (VCDS).

Of the other two chiefs of services, Vice-Admiral Rayner preferred to retire and Air Marshal Dunlap accepted a posting to Colorado Springs as Deputy Commander-in-Chief of NORAD, succeeding Roy Slemon, who had held the position for quite a while. Dunlap toyed with the idea of a headquarters post, but Miller advised him not to have any part of it, probably anticipating rough waters ahead. So Dunlap opted to move sideways while the coast was clear, and his departure, along with Rayner, opened the way for some upward movement in each service.

To be effective the senior team had to include a judicious mix of skills, professional training, and personalities. The integrated staff had to be able to work harmoniously in order to get the job done. Advice came from all sides, including from Bill Lee, whose tiny, concise memos became well-known to insiders as "Leegrams".

The reorganization job was ongoing, time-consuming, and emotionally draining, so it was fortunate that there were interludes to break the monotony and ease the tension. One was a trip to Alberta to open the Calgary Air Show on July 4. It was also Stampede time, and that was part of the attraction, because this was one great Canadian tradition that I had not yet witnessed. Part of the ritual, if you had the right contacts, was an invitation to Harry Hays's legendary Sunday-morning breakfast. Harry was a former Mayor of Calgary, who had won as a Liberal in the 1963 election to become federal Minister of Agriculture. As a cabinet colleague, I was welcome on his list.

The morning began with preparation of the mysterious "sillabub" eye-opener. I was intrigued to see paint and varnish cans of liquid being emptied into a giant milk can, and being topped by a few squirts of milk direct from the cow's teats. Ice was added before copious quantities were issued to the assembled throng. Harry never revealed the prescription for his secret potion, but a taste-bud analysis indicated roughly equal parts of grapefruit juice, pineapple juice, and gin. It seemed a marvellous prelude to the mountains of bacon, sausages, and scrambled eggs that followed. I must confess, however, that it was the only time in my entire life when I arrived at church exhaling an admixture of carbon dioxide and alcohol.

The Calgary Stampede had been such good fun that I was happy to return to Alberta on July 14, though this time on an entirely different kind of mission. My guides were Hartley Zimmerman and Archie Penny of the Defence Research Board, which had undertaken to set off a big blast of five hundred tons of TNT at the Board's Suffield Research Station in cooperation with the U.K. and U.S. governments. Suffield comprised a huge expanse of prairie grassland that was ideal for experiments with materials and devices that might improve our defensive capabilities against atomic, biological, and chemical warfare.

When we arrived in Ralston, via Medicine Hat, the weather was not propitious, so we had to cool our heels for a couple of days, and this allowed us to take in the local stampede and rodeo. When zero hour finally came, the explosion was indescribable! A million pounds of TNT is a lot of explosive, and it created a fireball not unlike the small atomic bombs it was intended to simulate – just what was needed for purposes of measuring the shock waves and other effects. Having witnessed the event and seen the damage it created, I was infinitely grateful that it was just a simulated atomic blast and not the real thing.

On July 30 the House paid tribute to Sir Winston Churchill on the occasion of his retirement from the House of Commons at a ripe old age. The Prime Minister and other party leaders spoke glowingly of the great man's accomplishments. What a remarkable impact he made on the western world by being the right man in the right place at the right time. He rallied British and Allied spirits by holding Hitler at bay across the English Channel and then by preparing to liberate continental Europe from the Nazi yoke. His success was all the more remarkable, considering that, as far back as 1926, it was said that his parliamentary career was finished. One of my favourite Churchillian anecdotes dates from his eighty-fifth birthday. A Tory back-bencher, assuming that

Churchill was out of earshot, told the MP beside him, "They say the old man's getting gaga." Without turning, Churchill said: "Yes, and they say he's getting deaf, too."[1]

August 1, 1964, was the red-letter day when the RCN, the Canadian Army, and the RCAF came under integrated management – integrated, not yet unified. The transition was so smooth that it didn't create a ripple. Two or three of the senior positions were filled only on an interim basis, but when the moves were complete, headquarters organization was as follows:

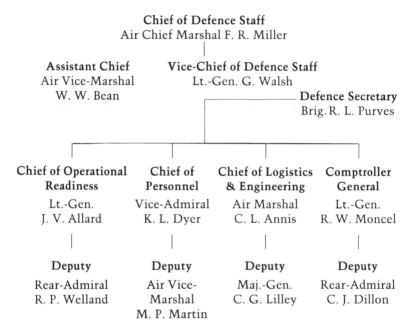

Chief of Defence Staff
Air Chief Marshal F. R. Miller

Assistant Chief
Air Vice-Marshal
W. W. Bean

Vice-Chief of Defence Staff
Lt.-Gen. G. Walsh

Defence Secretary
Brig. R. L. Purves

Chief of Operational Readiness	Chief of Personnel	Chief of Logistics & Engineering	Comptroller General
Lt.-Gen. J. V. Allard	Vice-Admiral K. L. Dyer	Air Marshal C. L. Annis	Lt.-Gen. R. W. Moncel
Deputy	**Deputy**	**Deputy**	**Deputy**
Rear-Admiral R. P. Welland	Air Vice-Marshal M. P. Martin	Maj.-Gen. C. G. Lilley	Rear-Admiral C. J. Dillon

There were a couple of jobs that I considered of doubtful necessity. One was Operational Readiness, headed by Lt.-Gen. Jean V. Allard and his Vice-Chief Rear-Admiral Welland. I thought the function could have been filled by the Vice-Chief of Defence Staff (VCDS), and there is little doubt it would have been if it hadn't been for Allard. The natural position for him was VCDS, but he and Frank were so totally incompatible that that solution wouldn't wash. I suspect the Operational Readiness slot was invented to sidetrack Allard from the direct chain of command. I was also suspicious of the position of Assistant Chief of Defence Staff. It appeared to be redundant, but it was a convenient means whereby airman Wilf Bean, who thought very much as Frank thought, could keep a watchful eye over General Walsh's shoulder. I capitulated because the time comes when one gets tired of arguing. I had achieved the substance of what I wanted and could afford to bend a little in putting up with anomalies. Having eleven men do the work previously done by sixteen was a step in the right direction. The position of Defence Secretary, the liaison between the military establishment and the minister's office, which had been abolished by General Pearkes when he was minister, was re-established.

The scaledown was consistent with my decree calling for a thirty percent reduction in headquarters personnel. It was an arbitrary figure, but experience had convinced me that the establishment was bloated beyond belief. I was certain that an integrated staff that was thirty percent smaller could manage all the forces efficiently. Nothing that has happened since has changed my view on that point.

Another change of considerable significance complemented the change in organization. I reactivated the Defence Council, which hadn't met since January 1963. The first four meetings in July followed the traditional format, but beginning in August, with the advent of a single defence staff, it became the nerve centre of the system.

I acted as chairman, with Lucien Cardin as vice-chairman. Other members included CDS Frank Miller, VCDS Geoff Walsh, Deputy Minister Elgin Armstrong, and the Chairman of the Defence Research Board, Hartley Zimmerman. Our secretary was Ron Sutherland, with Group Captain W. M. Garton acting as secretary for the military. Other officers who were invited included the chiefs of Personnel, Logistics, and Operational Readiness, and the Comptroller General. This ensured a good balance of tri-service experience. A representative of External Affairs, usually Arthur Menzies, sat in, and someone from Defence Production was invited when equipment purchases were being discussed. Bill Lee, my personal right arm, and Colonel, later Brigadier, Lou Bourgeois, the new departmental Director of Public Relations, were always included, so that when they were talking to the media or public they would know exactly what was going on rather than relying on second- or third-hand information.

Defence Council operated very much like cabinet. The chairman was the final arbiter, but all of them had a chance to state their views before decisions were taken. Also, because all matters of importance were considered by the council, it was no longer possible for representatives of the three environments to do "end-runs", privately, to the minister. Everything was on the table and everyone was in the picture.

This was a far cry from the way Defence Council had operated previously. An item from the January 21, 1963, meeting provides a glimpse of the old system. Council was considering the consolidation, not amalgamation, of the historical sections:

> The three Directors met with the Co-ordinator Joint Staff on 30 November 1962 to proceed with the integration of the Sections, but the Navy and Air Force refused to admit that the Minister had given any direction for integration but was mainly concerned with reductions in staff, and consequently no progress was made.[2]

That is the way the system used (not) to work.

In order to integrate and streamline the defence establishment, many officers would be made redundant, but if we relied only on attrition to reduce the numbers, it would be light years before anything like a normal rate of promotions could be restored. With constipation at the top, morale would suffer all down the line. It was essential that we get authority for a "golden handshake", prepare redundancy lists, retire some officers prematurely, and establish a promotion rate that would at least offer some hope to the up-and-comers – both officers and NCOs. A policy of "up or out" would have to take effect.

The magnitude of the problem at the top was unequal among the services. The air force was easiest to deal with because there was a steady stream of senior officers approaching retirement age. The army wasn't too bad, but the navy was a corker. Once Rayner left, there were no admirals even close to retirement age; they all had a number of years remaining to serve. Breaking a logjam, both to accelerate promotions and to provide openings for younger officers who were more amenable to the single-service concept, was going to require some major cuts.

The first casualty was Rear-Admiral Jeffry Brock, Flag Officer Atlantic Coast. I had phoned him in Halifax on August 3 and asked him to come to see me, which he did on the fifth. I explained the problem, and pointed out that we had to create some movement. He was told that he would go on retirement leave in November. My diary notes: "He took it like a real man. I was proud of him."[3]

In his memoir *The Thunder and the Sunshine*, Brock reveals a very different picture from the one I recorded at the time. He says:

> I glanced across to Frank Miller. His face had turned the colour of old parchment, and he had bitten his lower lip so that blood trickled onto his chin.
>
>   . . .
>
> I got up to leave. Frank Miller, still speechless, put his arm on my shoulder as we approached the corridor exit from the Minister's office. I opened the door and turned to nod in Hellyer's direction but he had followed me across the room. And suddenly, halting before us, he said in a simpering sort of voice: "Admiral, I really hate doing this to you because I just love your family."
>
> I almost vomited on his feet but Frank Miller, grabbing me firmly around the shoulder, led me gagging and gasping down the corridor, muttering as we went: "That bastard. That lousy, dirty, rotten, cheating bastard. He's broken every promise he ever made."[4]

That quotation attributed directly to Frank Miller sounded as much unlike him as the words Brock put in my mouth sounded unlike me, so I decided to write Frank, which I did on July 18, 1985, for confirmation or otherwise. My query read, in part, as follows:

> Dear Frank:
>
> I presume you have seen the enclosed reference from Admiral Brock's book. I wonder if you would be kind enough to confirm whether or not the quotation is accurate.
>
> If it is, would you also be good enough to list the broken promises. I am having some difficulty recalling them.[5]

On July 27 he replied:

> Dear Paul:
>
> It was good to hear from you despite the unfortunate subject that led you to write.
>
> To answer your specific questions, I have not read Brock's book.
>
> After 20 years I cannot remember what I said to him afterwards, but I do remember trying to calm him down from his

very distraught condition. In doing so I very much doubt that I made the statement attributed to me. It does not reflect my opinion of you and the wording is not such as I usually use.

I know of no promise you have ever broken.

On one point I am sure. I never bit my lip until it bled in your office.[6]

These are two very different versions of history and I will have to leave it to readers to decide which is the more authentic.

When the second volume of Brock's autobiography, *The Thunder and the Sunshine*, was published in 1983, it was generally assumed that he was fired because of his opposition to unification. This is not correct. He was prematurely retired because he was an anachronism – a traditionalist holding up his hands to stem the tide of the future. His devotion to the outmoded class distinctions inherited from the Royal Navy was inappropriate to the modern Canadian navy after World War II. Myriad sources cited his name when discussing the problems set out in such depressing detail in the Plomer article and the Mainguy Report, and his unpopularity with subordinates had been noted on a senior-officer assessment list that had been prepared for me.

In addition, I had read a classified document Brock had prepared for the Chief of the Naval Staff, outlining the navy's equipment and personnel needs for the decades to come. In his book, Brock recites some of the high compliments he received for his efforts, but to my mind the report was totally void of realism. Considering the limits of probable defence budgets, if his recommendations had been followed, the fleet would have required every available nickel, with nary a cent left for the army or air force. It was typical of the conventional thinking of the senior officers of the day, in which the other services didn't seem to exist – with the exception of a token nod in their direction. Brock's plan was for a World War II type navy, which would leave the other services to row their own boats. In addition, his firmly entrenched model of officer-seaman relations dated him beyond argument. Clearly, in my opinion, he wasn't someone to be promoted "up" and consequently a prime candidate to go "out".

From my perspective there was never any thought of promoting Brock to Vice-Admiral, and if anyone gained a different opinion from his memoir, it probably had to do with a game I suspect the senior headquarters officers were playing with me. After themselves accepting all the three-star positions I had allotted for the integrated services, the headquarters officers suggested that the field commanders at Halifax (navy) and St. Hubert (army) should also be three-star. This would have raised Brock to a three-star position. The fact that the air force already had a three-star position as Deputy Commander-in-Chief NORAD was used in evidence. I felt betrayed by the back-door method and object of the proposal, and I was determined to resist.

If I had it to do over again I'm not sure that I would have fired Brock. His book recalls in living colour his incredible love of pomp and circumstance and of being in the company of important people. It would have been simpler to post him to one of the NATO positions in Rome or Paris, where he would have been in his element and too far removed to impede progress at home.

A happier note involved the preservation of HMCS *Haida*, one of Canada's most famous World War II fighting ships. She was "paid off" and would have been scrapped had it not been for a group of former naval officers who decided *Haida* should be preserved as a visible reminder of Canada's proud and outstanding contribution to the Battle of the Atlantic. I was approached for encouragement and assistance with the project, which I was happy to provide. We rounded up equipment to replace what had been stripped from the aging hull and towed the powerless vessel through the St. Lawrence Seaway. Thousands of hours of volunteer labour by her sponsors and naval reservists retored much of *Haida*'s earlier lustre, and she now rides proudly at berth at Ontario Place, opposite Toronto's Canadian National Exhibition park.

At the end of August I headed north to spend the final weekend of the summer season at Arundel Lodge, our "non-profit" tourist resort in Muskoka, which I had acquired from Curran Hall when I left the company. Early Saturday morning Ellen took the car and headed for Ottawa to get the children ready for school. I was left all alone to close up on Sunday when the staff was gone. I put on an old suit with badly frayed sleeves and loaded up our battered pick-up truck. By the time I cleaned out the refrigerator, there was nothing left but two slices of dry bread and one very small bottle of Muskoka Dry ginger ale, which I took along.

Halfway to Ottawa I stopped for gas. As I pulled into the gas station I noticed a hitchhiker and decided to offer him a lift when

I left. He was still there as I pulled out, and he cheerfully climbed aboard. I asked him if he had had lunch and he said no, so I offered him one of my two slices of dry bread and apologized for not sharing the ginger ale, which I had already started.

After we finished eating I asked him where he was headed, and he said Petawawa. He was a soldier, he advised, though he was wearing civies at the time. Then he asked me what I did, and I said I, too, worked for the Department of National Defence. He asked where. "In Ottawa," I replied. "In the minister's office," I added, after further prodding. But what, specifically, did I do in the minister's office, he demanded, at which point I admitted that I was the minister. This caused a silence that lasted until we reached the fork in the road where I turned south and he went north to Petawawa. He thanked me for the ride, then, as an afterthought, he added a very hesitant "Sir".

A few weeks later, in early November, Ellen and I visited Petawawa, where we were guests at the 8th Canadian Hussars (Princess Louise's) Military Ball. I recounted the incident to the commandant, Maj.-Gen. R. Rowley. "Oh yes," he replied. "The story is all over camp about the nut who thought he was the minister of defence."

One of the many battles being fought in cabinet at that time concerned constitutional reform, including an amending formula which would permit patriation of the British North America Act. On August 27, 1964, the PM had brought to cabinet his recommendation, which would entrench the principle of provincial unanimity in respect to constitutional change. This was to take effect before the antiquated division of powers between governments could be altered. The question was so important that a special cabinet meeting was scheduled for the next day. Walter Gordon cautioned the PM not to give the impression that the federal government, under pressure from Quebec, was prepared to contemplate a weakening of federal powers. Yet that was implicit in the discussion. I was more concerned with the amending formula than with the politics of the situation. "I played the part of devil's advocate, as usual, and pleaded that the enactment of a law to enshrine the 'unanimous consent of the premiers' might produce a constitution too rigid to be workable, even worse than at present."[7] The PM argued that the existing situation, which required that we go to London for amendments, was the least satisfactory of all. The formula that he was proposing at least had the merit of not requiring unanimity for all classes of amendments. "Just the important ones," I thought as he went on to explain that the government had been committed at the federal–provincial conference in Quebec. That's how we got into many difficult situations – commit first; think later.

Negotiations continued, and it seemed for a while that agreement would be reached. Then at a cabinet meeting on Septembr 29, Guy Favreau reported a "friendly if disturbing" three-hour meeting with Paul Gérin-Lajoie [one of Lesage's ministers].[8] Favreau thought Premier Lesage was prepared to proceed on the basis of the 1961 formula, but Lajoie thought it failed to reflect changes that had taken place in the political climate since. It was apparent that Quebec would ask for new conditions, including a revision of section 91(1), setting out the federal powers, prior to patriation. The mood of cabinet was changing, and I sensed that most ministers wouldn't be too upset if the talks failed – apart from the embarrassment of another rebuff from the provinces. "It is a far cry from the day I stood virtually alone in opposition to the proposal to accept the rigid formula merely for the sake of change."[9]

The debate was repeated almost verbatim at caucus the following day. "Although almost everything had been said I put in my 2 cents' worth. I made a strong pitch for flexibility. A changing environment and changing technology demand constant reconsideration. States, provinces, and constitutions are made for the service of man. They should not be strait-jackets to prevent action when action is required. My outburst was well received except, perhaps, by Jean-Luc Pepin and one or two of the more rabid Quebec nationalists. LBP, instead of being angry as he might have been, referred to it as a 'moving speech'. He characterized it as 'damn the constitutional torpedoes, full speed ahead.' Not quite accurate, but not bad."[10]

When, many months later, the Prime Minister advised cabinet that the negotiated deal was off, I said, "Hallelujah" – to his mild astonishment. He shouldn't have been surprised after listening so patiently, so often. In reality, I felt more strongly about the issue than many of my colleagues. I abhorred the thought of giving any single province, no matter how big and important, an absolute veto over all significant constitutional amendments for all time. It defied common sense. There was no way of knowing then that after two decades of additional infighting my cherished hope would be realized: a patriated constitution, embodying an element of flexibility. It was well worth waiting for. Once having achieved the "impossible", it would be an unspeakable tragedy to wantonly give it up.

Saturday, October 3, 1964, the fall convocation at the Royal Military College, was one of the great days of my career. I recorded in my diary, "I have the honour of admitting the Rt. Hon. Louis S. St. Laurent to the degree Doctor of Laws – RMC. A strange twist of history that the last of his ministers, half his age [forty-one as against eight-two] would be in this position. He is a truly great man – he spoke out for Canadian unity. A pox on our newspapers who gave him only half the space they would give a rebel separatist."[11] I was also deeply honoured to have my parents present. It was their first military function of note, and they enjoyed it immensely. "They are wonderful people and I am very proud of them."[12] Ralph Campney was another guest and rode with me to Ottawa for dinner following the near-perfect ceremony, most of the credit for which belonged to Air Commodore L. J. "Birch" Birchall, the legendary "Saviour of Ceylon", who had taken over as College commandant.

On Tuesday, October 6, I boarded the lumbering old C-5 for another trip west, my third in a matter of weeks. I was met in Calgary by Maj.-Gen. J. M. Rockingham, the General Officer Commanding Western Command, Brigadier Bruce MacDonald, and Col. Frederick Clifford, who took me on a tour of Currie Barracks and other defence installations in the area. "I addressed the troops but unfortunately they were standing in a cold hangar and it was no place to speak. Results were not good."[13]

Wednesday morning we took off for Moose Jaw and a quick tour of the station, followed by a chance to address the officers and airmen in the theatre. "The problem here seems to be the same as it was in the Air Division – leadership. A/V/M Greenway is not favourable! He started telling me that the surplus 500 aircrew were due to reductions in commitments. Three minutes later he told the truth – that Hugh Campbell had ordered the buildup at the time of the Berlin crisis even though there was not a requirement!"[14] My visit confirmed again that, at bases where the leadership was favourable, integration was smoothly effected. Where leadership was not favourable, it was not.

Thursday, after breakfast at the mess, I was flown to Rivers in one of the two-place Tudor training aircraft. En route we decided to do some acrobatics. For me it was the first time in more than twenty years, and the first ever in a jet. I "followed through" on all the manoeuvres, and the pilot managed to create the impression that I was doing some of the flying, which I occasionally did, without taking undue risk. The sensation was marvellous and I was convinced the young pilots would have great fun flying the Tudors. The flying lesson was so engaging that we lost track of time and arrived at our destination twenty-five minutes late – an unforgivable "no-no" with the military. The Rivers base was interesting and almost integrated.

On my return to Ottawa I found considerable tension surrounding the upcoming visit by the Queen. From the outset there had been fear for her safety, considering the situation in Quebec, with Lord Mountbatten and others urging that the trip be cancelled. The Prime Minister took the view that, if anyone cancelled the trip to Quebec, it had to be Premier Lesage, because he had requested she visit Quebec City as part of the centenary celebration of the Charlottetown and Quebec conferences that gave birth to the Canadian federation. Her Majesty indicated no concern, but she did request that the Quebec visit be followed by two days in Ottawa over the Thanksgiving weekend, and cabinet concurred.

The Royal couple landed at Summerside RCAF base safely on Monday, and the Charlottetown part of the schedule went off without a hitch. The real test for jittery security men was about to begin as the royal yacht *Britannia* steamed up the St. Lawrence toward Quebec City. Late Friday afternoon, after sorting through the most urgent items that had accumulated on my desk while I was out west, I took off with Ellen for Quebec with the Lamontagnes, the Dupuis, and René Tremblay. The two of us dined at Le Vendôme, a small restaurant near the hotel, and then went dancing at the Château. "It was one of those rare pleasurable evenings when no official duties encroach."[15]

The Lieutenant-Governor of Quebec, the Hon. Paul Comtois, and Madame Comtois, Premier Jean Lesage and Madame Lesage, and Quebec Mayor Wilfrid Hamel and Madame Hamel, met the Royal Party at dockside, Wolfe's Cove. We were involved only as interested and concerned visitors as the royal motorcade moved through Lower Town to the Parliament buildings and hundreds of students deliberately turned their backs on Her Majesty, as though they were afraid of being blinded by the exposure. Our turn to participate came after lunch, with the inauguration of the memorial of Le Royal 22ième Régiment (the Van Doos), of which Her Majesty was Colonel-in-Chief, and a military display in her honour.

Just getting to the Citadel where the ceremony was to be held was not easy. We had to take an alternate route in order to get past the demonstrators. "The R22R performed magnificently as always and fortunately the rain held off, but it was cold. Admiral Brock and Mrs. Brock were present and it was not just the weather which was cold! We had a lovely chat with Her Majesty before the reception [for officers of the regiment, following the ceremony]. We spoke of Cyprus, separatism, etc. Her Majesty was quite down on the irresponsible press who gave the impression that they could hardly wait 'for the shooting to start.' "[16] She also mentioned that, although the young separatists had turned their backs, they couldn't resist taking a quick peek after she was past. I noted that "Prince Philip was not too favourable toward integration. Brock must have briefed him."[17] The State reception that evening was a perfect glittering spectacle, marred only by the conspicuous absence of one minister, René Lévesque.

Thanksgiving morning I greeted Her Majesty at the Cenotaph in Ottawa and escorted her to the dais. The television coverage was quite good and the friendly reception by the crowd was a welcome change from the icy greeting at Quebec. Tuesday morning I was among those who went to the airport to say farewell. Group Captain W. L. "Gil" Gillespie, the base commander, had assembled a large coterie of schoolchildren, who gave Her Majesty a rousing send-off. "A few of those at Quebec City would have helped. We all heaved a sigh of gratitude when the Air Canada DC-8 took off safely. It will be interesting to see what the long-term effect of the trip will be. Certainly the immediate reaction is not good."[18]

John Diefenbaker was outraged by the whole affair and raised Cain in the Commons. Paul Martin, who was Acting PM, handled him deftly and promised that a resolution of loyalty would be presented. It was delayed by one day because the Prime Minister was in Toronto to address the Empire Club. "He spoke well – with passion – of the Queen's visit and on national unity. I was proud of him."[19] He was back in the House Friday morning when we finally got the address of loyalty to Her Majesty. "Dief stood and started singing [God Save] the Queen. We all joined quickly except one Créditiste. He will get the headlines."[20]

With over three-quarters of 1964 gone, I appreciated that the months, to date, had been good for my public image. The tone had been set early in the New Year in articles like "The 'Wonder Boy' Carves His Niche" by Charles Lynch of Southam Newspapers. Under dateline Ottawa, the lead paragraph in the Hamilton *Spectator*'s version read: "At the age of 40, Paul Hellyer is writing his name into Canada's military records alongside those of our big defence ministers of the past – Sir Sam Hughes, James Layton Ralston, and Brooke Claxton."[21]

As already mentioned, the reaction to the White Paper in March was almost universally positive, and any criticism was pretty well dismissed in terms like those of a Calgary *Albertan* article, reprinted in the Kingston *Whig-Standard*. The mini-editorial, entitled "Military Toes" began:

> Mr. Hellyer's chief crime, it seems to us, is that he is looking farther ahead than his critics: and that he has tramped on the toes of one of Canada's most sacred cows, the entrenched military establishment, in order to do the things he feels are necessary.[22]

An article "Pearson's Star System Blinks Out, but . . . Martin and Hellyer Show New Sparkle" by Ron Collister in the Toronto *Telegram*, was comforting to me, but didn't help my popularity with other members of cabinet. After reviewing the performances of the principal and best-known players, the report card ended with the sentence, "After Mr. Pearson, Martin and Hellyer are now the men to watch."[23]

Most prestigious of all was a cover story "Special Report: Canada's Paul Hellyer – Why a Single Service Is Best", which appeared in the Washington, D.C., magazine *Armed Forces Management*, published for the military executives of the free world.[24] No one could recall when any Canadian had been given similar prominence in the U.S. journal.

It was a time when I was getting the breaks. Several colleagues had been plagued by bad luck, and it is possible that their misery was diverting press attention from my would-be critics. Also I was fortunate in the timing of one or two events like the move from Toronto's University Avenue Armouries and the construction of new quarters for the militia.

On October 18 I turned the sod for Moss Park Armoury, on the east side of Jarvis Street between Queen and Shuter in Toronto. This was the beginning of the end of a long and controversial story, which had begun years earlier when I was parliamentary assistant to Defence Minister Ralph Campney. The Province of Ontario wanted to take over the site of the historic old University Avenue Armoury, just north of Osgoode Hall on the boundary of Chinatown, for a new Court House. The request was a political hot potato from the outset because the stately, block-long building was sacrosanct to tens of thousands of Torontonians who had enlisted there in two world wars, and it had been a headquarters for many militia units and veterans' organizations in between. The pressure for the province to change its plans became insistent, and I dreaded facing the decision.

One really has to dig to find advantages in being defeated, but escaping responsibility for the destruction of the Armoury was a blessing. When the Tories won the 1957 election, the whole matter was dumped in the lap of the incoming Diefenbaker administration, and the Minister of Defence, George Pearkes, in particular. Not only was he a distinguished and decorated veteran, he had the additional advantages of representing a B.C. riding and being on the same side of the political fence as John Bassett, publisher of the Toronto *Telegram*, but it still wasn't easy for him to let the University Avenue Armoury go. Nevertheless, the decision was made. One new facility, Denison Armoury, was built in North York, and I arrived back on the scene just in time for the windup – construction of another, the Moss Park Armoury. It would share with Denison the honour of replacing the old facility. Consequently, I escaped from a traumatic episode pretty well unscathed.

Still, as the leaves turned, and then fell, I realized I would have to make decisions concerning the units that would be housed in the new armouries. These decisions would be equally difficult, would land me in a barrel of hot water, and would test my resolve.

CHAPTER 6

RESERVES, RUMBLES, AND REORGANIZATION

O f all the aspects of the defence reorganization, one of the most difficult was streamlining and reducing the size of the reserves. I set out the parameters when introducing the defence estimates on December 5, 1963. The militia would be cut from 51,000 to approximately 30,000; the RCN reserve strength would be reduced from 4,000 to 2,700; and the RCAF part-time flyers would be pruned even more drastically, from 2,200 to 800, which allowed the retention of only six squadrons and their associated wing headquarters, all of which were to be located at bases used for other purposes in order to keep overhead at a minimum. This did not reflect my "devastating stewardship",[1] as Peter Newman calls it in his book *True North* Not *Strong and Free*; the reductions were simply part of a long list of cost-saving measures proposed by the Chiefs of Staff in the face of a drastic curtailment of defence expenditures, ordered by Finance Minister Walter Gordon with the full backing of the Prime Minister.

Many of the cuts, which included paying off a number of the navy's auxiliary vessels, closing and consolidating supply depots,

and transferring responsibility for the Northwest Highway system and the administration of Fort Churchill in Labrador to other
departments, were painful. None was more so than the reduction
in the reserves: but we had to save a few million here and a
million or two there. None of us downgraded the reserves, as
Field Marshal Montgomery had when he equated their military
capability to that of the Salvation Army; but we did have doubts
about their cost-effectiveness. Many units were far below
strength, and too many of the reservists were overfed World War
II veterans whose age and physical condition would have made it
difficult for them to shape up in an emergency. Faced with the
task of setting priorities, the Chiefs of Staff decided to conserve
as much money as possible for the "forces in being". It was a
judgment call with which I fully concurred.

At the outset I announced which naval divisions and RCAF
reserve squadrons would be affected, but the militia was much
more complicated and difficult. My colleague Lucien Cardin set
up a commission headed by Brigadier E. R. Suttie to study all
relevant aspects of the situation and make recommendations. At
the same time he asked Commodore Robert I. Hendy and Group
Captain J. W. P. Draper to consider and offer advice on the
continuing roles of the navy and air force reserves. When their
reports were received, they were reviewed at the highest level,
first with the Chiefs of Staff, and then, in the case of the Suttie
Report, with the General Officers Commanding the various
regions.

I became directly involved due to the political sensitivity of the
issue. Unlike the full-time forces, where changes are primarily
important to the limited areas directly affected, there were hundreds of reserve units with strong emotional ties in every major
town and city. Any tampering would be potentially perilous, and
eliminating units could be political dynamite. For this reason the
reorganization of the militia was given one of the most careful
examinations undertaken during my term as minister. There
were twenty-two separate meetings of two to three hours' dura-
tion. Every factor was weighed and evaluated from all points of
view before we decided which units would be transferred to the
Supplementary Order of Battle (SOB).

We followed the Suttie recommendations carefully but not
slavishly, and when we had finished, it was clear that well-known
named units with battle honours and proud traditions would be

eliminated in Montreal, Halifax, Winnipeg, Edmonton, and Vancouver – in almost every major city in Canada. It would have
been untenable if Toronto were the only exception. There were
too many infantry regiments in the city, and one of them had to
go. When the criteria was applied objectively, it was the Irish
Regiment of Canada that had the lowest point score.

I don't think it really would have mattered which unit was
bottom of the list, because all hell would have broken out in any
event. Toronto has a long history as a garrison town, and military
roots run deep. Consequently, each unit had its coterie of enthu-
siasts and a powerful association to support its activities. Although I drew warm applause when I told a Toronto audience
that we had to streamline the reserves, recruit younger men, and
get better value for the taxpayers' dollars, I knew darn well that if
in the next sentence I had added, "and that means unit 'x' will be
transferred to the suplementary order of battle", some of the
same people would have booed. There is a giant gulf between
principle and practice when one's own ox is being gored.

Once the list was made public, the reaction was predictable.
With few exceptions, every unit that was deactivated made extended representations to have the decision reversed. John
Turner brought a delegation from the Victoria Rifles; Grant
Deachman made a pitch on behalf of the Irish Fusiliers of Vancouver. We heard from every city, but none of the representations compared in volume and intensity with those on behalf of
the Irish Regiment of Canada. Letters poured in from Paul Martin, Ross Macdonald, Arthur Laing, Marvin Gelber, Gordon
Keyes, John Connolly – even from the Prime Minister's office.

Mr. A. Callow, President of the Irish Regiment of Canada
Veterans' Association, even wired the Queen asking her to rein-
state the regiment to the active list. In accordance with constitutional protocol, Her Majesty referred the telegram to His Excellency the Governor General, who in turn had his secretary
Esmond Butler refer it to me. When it landed on my desk my
secretary, Marg Bulger, herself of Irish descent, had affixed the
notation "The Irish believe in going to the top."[2]

On November 26 I received a delegation from the regiment in
my House of Commons office. It comprised Gerned S. Horgan,
Q.C.; Major, The Reverend D. F. Rowland, M.C., D.D.; and L. H.
Nerlick, Esq. We went over all the same old ground. Why the
Irish? Because their effective strength was almost ten percent

below that of the Toronto Scottish, which was second-lowest in the point score. Once it had been determined that Toronto would have to give up one infantry regiment, the decision was strictly objective; no favouritism was shown. The explanation was not accepted.

That was just one round in a battle that continued for months. An editorial entitled "Shillelaghs for the Minister" in the *Star Weekly* began:

> The shillelaghs are whistling around the head of Defence Minister Paul Hellyer these days. Members of the Toronto Irish Regiment and their friends are protesting vigorously against the defence department's decision to de-activate the regiment. This is only a foretaste of the storms Mr. Hellyer can expect from all parts of Canada as his plans for streamlining the militia go into effect.[3]

Having said that, the *Star* supported the policy.

> We can sympathize with the feelings of militiamen who see a familiar unit, with a proud tradition formed in two world wars, disappearing. But the changes now being introduced are necessary and inevitable.[4]

Those were my sentiments, exactly, and I was deeply disturbed by Padre Rowland's public declaration that the reason the Irish Regiment died was because it lacked political support in high places. That simply wasn't true! The Montreal, Winnipeg, Edmonton, and Vancouver regiments all had high-powered political support, but that didn't save them; and of all the units none had anything like the extent of political backing enjoyed by the Irish. It had ten times the support of the others, but that couldn't be allowed to interfere with what had been a fair decision. If I had capitulated on one decision, the whole package would have been undone, with renewed demands for reversals from coast to coast.

There were many compromise solutions put forward in respect of the Irish. It was suggested that the name be assigned to an armoured regiment. Another was to rename a Sudbury unit. This idea, popular with the CO, was not endorsed by the junior officers; later it was resurrected, because nearly everyone wanted to keep the Irish on the active list. I was enthusiastic as long as the total number of units and their geographical distribution remained intact. In the end, the 58 Field Regiment (RCA) located at

Sudbury, Ontario, was converted to infantry and redesignated the Second Battalion, Irish Regiment of Canada (Sudbury). The Toronto Irish generously provided some dress uniforms for the new outfit. The Irish Association wasn't too happy with the solution, but at least one battalion of the kilted Irish remained on the active list and the overall reduction, which had been so difficult to achieve, was not affected.

One of the interesting aspects of politics is what requires cabinet approval and what doesn't. As far as I can recall, the entire reserve forces reorganization was never considered by cabinet. There had been concurrence with the principle, which was dictated by budget allocations. We also advised ministers and MPs which units in their ridings would be affected before the list was made public. But the details were never discussed by cabinet, despite the potential for far-reaching political repercussions.

In the context of such extensive delegation, I was both astonished and amused when I read the agenda for cabinet of November 13. An item under my name requested authority for the expenditure of an additional $7,000 to hire civilian ski-instructors to help train the biathlon team preparing for the 1968 Winter Olympics. The former minister had received a request from the Canadian Amateur Ski Association to train and enter an Armed Forces team in the Olympic event; and Defence Council, at its July 6, 1964, meeting, had reconfirmed the commitment. We had already authorized expenditures of $30,450 from departmental estimates, but it became apparent that some top civilian instructors would be required if the team was to reach an acceptable level of expertise. Treasury Board had no particular objection to spending the extra $7,000, but decided the item should be considered by cabinet as a whole.

When cabinet met, my sixth sense told me that treating the subject seriously would lead to a half-hour discussion on the origin, purpose, and desirability of the project, when dozens of really important items were waiting for attention. It was definitely a case for the light touch if we didn't want to get off on a tangent.

"What's this all about, Paul?" the Prime Minister asked, after reading the item aloud.

"I really don't know, sir," I replied, "but I think its some kind of a contest where soldiers ski until they are too exhausted to go further, so they fall in the snow and shoot for a while; then they get up and ski some more until they're all worn out, and drop again; the exercise is repeated until they cross the finish line."

He gave me one of his broad grins, indicating that he, too, recognized the ridiculous aspect of wasting cabinet's time on such minor matters. "Agreed?" he said, and the item was carried after less than two minutes.

The list of more important matters requiring cabinet attention included constitutional amendments, "contracting out" legislation, the Canada–U.S. Autopact, the flag debate, and the perennial issue of the Canada Pension Plan, which had not yet cleared all the hurdles. Another, the Rivard Affair, which the Prime Minister was to describe in his memoirs as "one of the most sordid and vindictive episodes in the history of the House of Commons", was waiting in the wings.[5]

The first hint of this issue had come a year earlier when the five maritime transport unions were placed in trusteeship following an inquiry by Mr. Justice T. G. Norris into the operation of the union. The president of the Seafarers' International Union, Hal Banks, who had originally been brought to Canada by the Liberals, fled the country while free on bail pending appeal of a conspiracy conviction. The Liberals were accused of collusion in his escape and of making no effort to get him back. This was not true, because we had decided to prosecute, but we were hamstrung by the fact that conspiracy was not an extradictable offence. The Opposition, however, was unmoved, and did its best to create a climate of suspicion and innuendo.

It was against this background that we faced the first of the so-called scandals that rocked the government. Lucien Rivard was a notorious gambler and criminal wanted in the United States on narcotics charges. While in a Montreal jail awaiting the outcome of extradition proceedings, he escaped and disappeared. The government was immediately accused of complicity, because it was alleged that Raymond Denis, executive assistant to Immigration Minister René Tremblay, had attempted to bribe Pierre Lamontagne, the Montreal lawyer who was counsel for the United States government in the extradition proceedings against Rivard, not to oppose bail for him. The RCMP investigated and prepared a report for Justice Minister Guy Favreau. On November 22, 1964, the day before the Justice estimates were to be debated in the Commons, Favreau informed the Prime Minister that the police investigation had been completed, but that in his opinion as a lawyer, "no successful prosecution was possible since it would be simply Denis' word against that of the man who had accused him of offering the bribe."[6]

Although Favreau expected tough opposition in the Commons, he was ill-prepared for the barrage led by Erik Nielsen, John Diefenbaker's chief hatchet man. The debate went badly, and the government agreed to a judicial inquiry by Chief Justice Frédéric Dorion of the Quebec Superior Court. This might have sidetracked the issue – which is often the purpose of judicial inquiries – if Doug Harkness hadn't asked the PM when he had first been informed of the affair. The PM replied: "Mr. Speaker, I think I was informed on the day before his [Favreau's] estimates were brought before the house."[7]

In his memoirs Pearson said this reply referred only to his lack of knowledge of the details. It is just as likely that he was stricken with the kind of panic that overtakes nearly all politicians at some stage in a time of crisis. In any event the answer was incomplete at best, and totally misleading at worst. As early as the summer of 1964, Gordon Robertson, Clerk of the Privy Council, had told him there was trouble in the Immigration Department "over an indiscreet Executive Assistant [Raymond Denis]."[8] Then on September 2, on the flight back to Ottawa from the Centenary Federal–Provincial Conference at Charlottetown, Guy Favreau had taken advantage of Mrs. Pearson's temporary absence to sit beside the PM long enough to advise him of allegations of bribery against Raymond Denis. He added that the whole matter had been turned over to the RCMP for investigation.

In view of this, Favreau was shaken to the core by the PM's denial of any previous knowledge of the affair. He assumed that it had been just a lapse of memory, and he fully expected his boss to set the record straight at the earliest possible opportunity. To his credit, that was Pearson's initial instinct. He recognized the terrible damage to Favreau's image and was inclined to make amends. The majority in cabinet agreed and urged him to act immediately, but there were two or three powerful dissenters, led by Walter Gordon. They recommended continued silence, presumably based on the somewhat callous theory that ministers are expendable, whereas prime ministers are not.

The matter dragged on for days, and the publicity surrounding the affair was terrible. The subject was on cabinet agenda at almost every meeting, because it was uppermost in our minds. Almost every day one or more of us urged the Prime Minister to set the record straight, but to no avail. He gave no reason for the hesitation. In his book *The Shape of Scandal*, Richard Gwyn quotes an aide as saying:

> I think it was simply disgust. He was appalled at the thought that an accusation of lying – and this was bound to be made as soon as he corrected the record – could be made against him through a chain of such incompetence. I think he was disgusted at the thought that after a lifetime in the public service his word could be doubted.[9]

Finally, on December 16, all hell broke loose again when the press learned from the Dorion Commission that the Prime Minister had, in fact, known about the affair long before November 22. In explaining the situation to cabinet on the morning of December 17,

> Mr. Pearson said that when he had first met with Chief Justice Dorion following the establishment of the Commission of Inquiry, he had told the Commissioner that a statement would be made on this matter as soon as possible in the House of Commons. When, earlier that week, the opposition had turned down a proposal for a question period, he had decided to submit his clarifying statement to Chief Justice Dorion and it was this statement that had been put on the record of inquiry the preceding day.[10]

It was a lame excuse, because he could have risen in the House of Commons on a question of personal privilege to put the record straight at any time. Instead, he followed a procedure that gave him the worst of all possible worlds. Not only did it appear that the truth was dragged out of him, but the correction was made outside the Commons, which is considered unpardonable parliamentary conduct. In the process Pearson not only tarnished his own image, he nearly broke Favreau's heart, because the ever-loyal Justice Minister had kept mum to protect his boss, even though his own reputation was being tattered.

When *The Shape of Scandal* was published the following year, the Brantford *Expositor* carried a banner headline "Pearson Fiddled While Favreau Burned".[11] The story was based on Richard Gwyn's assessment of the affair, suggesting that:

Two ministers, Pickersgill and Defence Minister Paul Hellyer, came close to resigning. To them, and to others in the administration, the issue was a moral not a political one: Guy Favreau's reputation was being torn to shreds and nothing was being done to shield him.[12]

This report was not correct, as Jack Pickersgill points out in a recent letter to me that puts the conflict in perspective.

I was exceedingly unhappy about Mike's long delay in correcting his recollection and about the manner in which he chose to do it, but I never contemplated resigning. I still cannot see what kind of ground one could have given as a third party for resigning. I am sure you would have felt the same way, however indignant you might have been. It was a sorry time in our affairs as a government.[13]

Jack is correct and our recollections are identical.

If my concentration on the so-called scandals was less than total, it was only because I had major and minor problems of my own. The reorganization of headquarters was proceeding at a reasonable pace, while senior staff were turning their attention to the field command structure. Superimposed on these two major undertakings was the first integrated defence budget and a five-year equipment program for the Armed Forces.

Shrinking a military headquarters by thirty percent is a complicated procedure. It created surplus personnel, who had to be posted elsewhere or retired. As the overall strength was being reduced at the same time, there were limited opportunities for alternative employment. Our two-sided policy offered a pragmatic solution. On one hand we gave generous financial treatment – the "Golden Handshake" – to personnel slated for early retirement, and on the other hand we guaranteed a minimum number of promotions at each rank level to offer hope and encouragement to those who remained in the service.

Frank Miller volunteered to prepare a redundancy list of officers, and when I got my first look at it on October 21, my heart sank. "Top man on the Air Force list is A/C Fred Carpenter – the only senior RCAF officer wildly enthusiastic about integration. Also on the list, W/C Harvey, who will get out and continue to throw knives. This will never do![14] As I stated earlier, my opinion was that Carpenter's principal handicap was possession of a creative mind, coupled with his penchant for intellectual honesty. When, some time earlier, the Chief of the Air Staff had asked him to write a paper on the future of the RCAF, instead of recommending a bigger and better air force, he had suggested it be amalgamated with the other services. The brass were livid with rage, locked up all copies of the report, and labelled it so "top secret" that not even the minister at the time was allowed to see it. Freddie's fate was sealed. There would be no more promotions for him.

Before making up my mind about Wing Commander Harvey, I decided to talk to him, and invited him for lunch on October 27. Harvey had succeeded Bill Lee as head of the RCAF Public Relations Department and was a vehement opponent of integration. When we met, "He was very nervous and quite bitter. I was nervous too. We had a good chat on what we are trying to do. I asked him if he would like to stay in the RCAF or get out. He preferred to go and I think it would be best to accede."[15] I was fully aware that if I let him go he would cause lots of trouble, but he was already doing that in speaking "off the record" to the press. The difference was that as a civilian he would be doing it openly and honestly, aboveboard. That was more compatible with my basic philosophy, which was "If you can't be loyal, get out, and speak your mind freely." I sent the redundancy list back to Miller with Carpenter's name scratched out and an okay for Harvey, who went on to fulfil my expectations precisely. He got a job as a public-relations officer with Massey-Ferguson and used his position to oppose me with all his considerable talent.

Having set the target of thirty percent reduction for the entire headquarters, I couldn't very well exempt my own military staff. Certainly it wouldn't have been politic. I looked at my orderly room and concluded that it was top heavy and that reductions could be made. The first casualty was Sgt.-Maj. T. "Mac" Macdonald, who had become as much an integral part of the minister's establishment as eggs are to an omelette. Mac had wanted a promotion to Warrant Officer I, but I didn't think the job deserved the rating, although he, as an individual, certainly did. When I said I couldn't persuade myself to fatten the establishment at the very moment I was asking everyone to think lean, he opted to go. Concurring may have been a mistake, because his next job was at the Prime Minister's residence, 24 Sussex Drive, doing many of the same things. He claims that he always spoke well of me, but it would have required superhuman effort never to let his disappointment register.

The next NCO to exit was Staff-Sgt. T. P. Collins, another longtime orderly-room stalwart. We had a farewell party for him, as we had for Mac, and it was in his response to our presentation of a small gift that the secret of the overstaffing came out. The Department of National Defence used to have its own private railway car, which I recalled as I listened to his story, and two crews of "cook-stewards" had been established to man it. The crews alternated, as did the members of each team, who were equally qualified as both cook and steward. With the onset of the jet age, however, the railway car was used less and less, until Defence Minister George Pearkes finally decided to dispose of it. The car was sold, but the crews were kept on staff, even though their original *raison-d'être* had disappeared. I had always wondered why there were six NCOs in the orderly room, in addition to my drivers, and at last I knew. Many similar stories had come to my attention during my years in Ottawa, but most of them were apocryphal. Ironically, the first *bona fide* example emerged right under my nose.

We were able to make savings in personnel in the support services as well. Where there were three recruiting offices in each city, we closed two. The intelligence branches of the three services were combined, and the number of authorized jobs reduced by about one-third. The overblown RCN, RCAF, and Army public relations divisions, as well as the leaner departmental one under Bill Dumsday, were amalgamated. Dumsday, who had reached retirement age, stepped down and left the new four-in-one organization in the capable hands of Colonel Lou Bourgeois, who reported to the deputy minister. The number of personnel was cut dramatically. Equally important, the department now spoke with one voice instead of with the often contradictory "party-line" views expressed by the individual services. It is worthy of note that the elimination of triplication and quadruplication in these areas saved taxpayers many millions of dollars.

One of the most difficult aspects of this evolutionary process was the attempt to develop an integrated budget and equipment program for a five-year period, so everyone would know what they were doing – or could do. Individual branches still competed for funds, which was only natural, but all the conflicting demands had to be rolled into one, with the active involvement of the military staff and without end runs to the minister.

This was a change of monumental proportions in the way things were done, and one not easily accepted. On October 21, I had a direct confrontation with Frank Miller, whose views were about 180 degrees apart from mine. "He doesn't really believe in the No. 1 priority – re-equipping the Canadian Army. We have a chance to save $1½ to $2 million by buying an extra 500 M113s [armoured personnel-carriers] now. He argues that there is no point in having equipment without shipping. Correct – but there is equally no point in having an army without equipment. We are going to order 500 M113s."[16]

Frank may have been afraid that, if we spent money on the army, there wouldn't be enough left for a tactical airplane for the air force – especially the F-4. If so, he was right; but the F-4 wasn't the number-one priority. Under the old system the air force, because of its superior public relations and pressure, would probably have got its plane, and everyone else would have got nothing. Under the new system the airmen had to stand in line like everyone else, until their needs topped the priority list. That wasn't easy for Frank to accept, because he was, after all, an airman of the old school – tough as nails in support of the belief that airpower is the only force of substance. Curiously, many air-force officers considered he had "sold out" because of his involvement in the integrated staff, and they looked to W. "Iron Bill" McBride as their advocate and leader. How wrong they were in their appreciation of Frank. He was about as dedicated an airman as I have ever met.

On Sunday, October 25, I bumped into Commodore J. Deane and had a chat about the navy equipment program that he had been working on. It was beginning to take shape. The formal briefing, on Monday, was quite well done. "It is a big improvement on much of the staff work we have been getting. The presentation on the Provider [supply ship] is something I have been waiting for. It clearly demonstrates that an extra Provider on each coast will increase our 'on station' capability more for the cost involved than anything else we could do. The DDH [Tribal Class destroyers with helicopters] seem to make sense. Also an updating of the balance of the DDEs [destroyer escorts] with better sonar, asroc, etc. All in all not a bad program."[17]

An interesting sidelight to the organizational changes taking place, and the new sense of movement, was a subtle but significant shift toward innovation. Two major examples related to the Tribal Class destroyers. The first was bridge control, which would allow captains to "drive" their ships without resort to the traditional telegraph to the engine room. This development had long been resisted by the old Naval Board, and it had been left to the Defence Research Board to sponsor an experiment to determine the worth of the idea. A destroyer escort had been equipped with makeshift bridge control, so the principle could be tested by fifteen of the younger skippers. If my memory serves me correctly, twelve of the fifteen found a definite improvement in their ability to manoeuvre the ship with ease and accuracy, especially in docking. So the DDHs were the first Canadian naval ships to incorporate a system that had long been in use commercially.

The other departure from precedent was the engines. The DDHs were the first navy ships to be equipped with gas turbines. A principal advantage lay in the time required for refit. Ships powered by conventional steam-boilers could be laid up for months when the engines required major overhaul. The turbines could be replaced in forty-eight hours by simply opening hatch doors on deck and having a crane lift the old turbine out and lower a new or rebuilt engine into place. Connect a few nuts and bolts, and the ship is ready to put back to sea. It is highly unlikely that either of these major departures from conventional practice would have been possible had the old Naval Board still been in existence.

On November 9, Defence Council met for the purpose of consolidating the three service programs within a single budget of $1,550 millions for 1965-66 and an assumed annual increase of two percent to 1969-70 to offset inflation. Some of the specific items approved were as follows:

In addition to the three "O" class submarines already on order, the navy got a third replenishment ship and four additional helicopters; the army was given more money for armoured personnel-carriers in addition to the mechanized howitzers already approved; the air force got money for fifteen Buffalo aircraft and four more C-130E Hercules, but the maritime replacement program was deferred by two years and the express provision of a new tactical aircraft was deleted in favour of a balancing item which included tactical aircraft.[18]

It was not a package designed to please the air force, which saw the things it didn't want, the Hercules and Buffalo transport aircraft, moved forward, and the thing it did want, the acquisition of a new tactical airplane, deferred. The RCAF's number-one priority, and heart's desire, was removed from the definite column and put effectively on hold. This sowed the seed of a continuing controversy, discussed at greater length in the next chapter.

The four additional Hercules were advanced to take advantage of an existing production run, with prices that wouldn't be available again. The Buffalo "buy" was one of those double-barrelled decisions, designed to give the army greater mobility while lending support to a struggling and oft-battered aircraft industry. I never shared the view of some of my colleagues that military purchases should be decided primarily in the interest of Canadian industry. Whenever there was opportunity to meet both military and industrial objectives, however, I was most sympathetic and did everything reasonably possible to give Canadian businessmen the break. But military priorities took precedence.

That was the crux of the argument that raged over a British proposal for a joint program to build the McDonnell F-4 aircraft, equipped with Rolls-Royce Spey engines, in Canada. Defence Council, at my insistence, had decided that the tactical aircraft would have to take a back seat to more urgent equipment needs; but other departments and other ministers thought differently. I spoke to Walter Gordon about the airplane deal at lunch on December 1, just after he had met secretly with several government officials. He assured me that the group did not include "interested parties", but that wasn't the whole truth. I had seen the party leave his office, and one of the officials was Simon Reisman, Deputy Minister of Industry, who was very much an interested party.

The following afternoon, Walter, Bud Drury, who was responsible for defence production, and I met in the PM's office to discuss Bud's proposal to join forces with the British. Walter read a memo he had written to the PM, which seemed to support me, but concluded by supporting Bud. The inconsistency became the object of some instant mirth. Still, he told me, "Frankly, I am more interested in the industrial considerations than I am in carrying out your program."[19] He remained behind to bend the PM's ear after Bud and I left, having agreed to a small Cabinet Defence Committee meeting at the PM's residence the next day at which tactical aircraft as well as urgent parliamentary business could be discussed.

When the Cabinet Defence Committee, chaired by the Prime Minister, subsequently reconvened in formal session, it endorsed the position I had recommended, and on December 8 the entire five-year Defence Department program went to cabinet for approval. My memorandum was considered in tandem with Bud's. We also had the cabinet committee report that not only recommended that my submission be adopted for planning purposes, but also recommended that the British authorities be informed that the Canadian government was not in a position to reach a conclusion on future aircraft needs of the RCAF, but did not consider that the F-4 would meet Canadian Forces requirements.[20]

The discussion was long and far-reaching. Walter Gordon said that expenditures for all departments might exceed his $7.45 billion limit, in which case there might have to be a further scaling down across the board. He argued that traditionally Treasury Board had become too much involved in details of expenditures and that departments should have more authority within the overall sums allotted to them. Before this could be done, however, they had to be equipped to exercise more effective financial control.[21]

I said there was no real disagreement on the procedure to be followed, but some months before cabinet had adopted overall limits to avoid ad hoc decisions. The Department of National Defence program was an overview within the prescribed limits. We were willing to meet with Treasury Board and justify elements of the program, but some overall direction was needed. Defence was the only department with a declining budget, both in absolute terms and as a proportion of government expenditures relative to Gross National Product. We could live within the $1.55 billion ceiling for the next year and still meet increases in pay and allowances, but only if cabinet was prepared to agree immediately that there should be no action to acquire tactical aircraft during the fiscal year 1965-66. I also said that the course being followed by Defence should be extended to other government departments, to provide a basis for evaluation of priorities among government programs.[22]

The Prime Minister said it was not unreasonable to have Treasury Board review the program at this stage. In his view the most important decision reached by the cabinet committee on defence related to the F-4 Spey aircraft. At the end of the meeting, cabinet agreed to refer my five-year plan to Treasury Board, and noted with approval the decision to inform the British both that the F-4 did not fit our requirements and that it was Mr. Pearson's intention to discuss the matter with Prime Minister Harold Wilson when he visited Ottawa.[23]

The Prime Minister did remember to mention the F-4 deal when Wilson arrived the next day. He was pleased to note that the British leader was far less concerned than might have been expected, although he did want us to consider the Buccaneer as an alternative choice for the tactical role.

One day later, in what must have been an all-time speed record, Walter Gordon reported that Treasury Board had agreed to the defence budget. Our five-year program was pretty well determined, with the exception of the tactical aircraft that was to be the *cause célèbre*.

Walter also made a deal with me on the disposal of DND equipment. He said we could keep the money realized from the sale of surplus land or equipment to spend on new capital requirements. Until then I couldn't persuade the department to part with anything, because the proceeds went into the consolidated revenue fund. This lack of incentive led to ridiculous situations. In Victoria, for example, we had a stack of guns that were purchased for installation on the bows of merchant ships in wartime. Not only had they been taking up valuable storage space for almost twenty years, but the department hired commissionaires to guard them. Once the deal with Walter was struck, the guns were sold. So was a lot of other obsolete junk and surplus property. As a result we realized quite a few million dollars, which were spent on new equipment.

We were moving forward on several fronts. On November 19 and 20, Frank Miller had convened a Senior Commanders' Conference. In his new capacity as Chief of Defence Staff, he brought senior navy, army, and air force officers together to discuss a wide variety of subjects, including headquarters organization, a proposed Canadian Forces communications system, manpower policies, integrated defence programming, development of a common pay system, and many others. It was an opportunity to exchange views with one of the most impressive assemblies of military brass in Canadian military history.

It was a cold, snowy morning, and after Frank explained the purpose of the conference, I gave the multicoloured assembly a thirty-minute welcome. The atmosphere inside was as cool as it was outside, and I suggested that officers should get enthusiastic about integration and the change in policy or else turn in their badges and take the special benefits available to them. At the end of the day, Frank held a reception at the RCAF Rockcliffe Officers' Mess, and by then the ice was beginning to melt, as officers of the different branches began to get used to each other.

At noon on Friday I hosted a luncheon and the thaw continued. "They were beginning to appreciate the sense of history, i.e. this is the *first* time the senior commanders of Canada's three armed forces have sat around a table and talked to each other. I think they found it quite interesting! People are people! The atmosphere had improved so much that one of my pessimistic 'spies' reported favourably. 'Army-enthusiastic! Air Force mostly neutral give it a try. Navy skeptical to anti – particularly Landymore. But overall, most encouraging.' "[24]

Generally speaking, I was in a positive mood as we prepared for the NATO Council meeting that would take us to Paris on December 12 for five days. The warning bell concerning Admiral Landymore's attitude at the Commanders' Conference hadn't really registered, and I was elated by cabinet's concurrence in my five-year program. Everything seemed pretty well under control when Ellen, Bill Lee, Marg Bulger, Frank Miller, Marc Favreau, and I boarded the lumbering old RCAF Yukon to join Paul and Nell Martin and our respective officials from External and Defence.

Paris and the NATO meeting were virtually photocopies of the previous year, so there is no need to elaborate on either. One incident stands out in my memory, however, and that was a late-night verbal shootout withFrank Miller over the role of the RCAF Air Division in Europe. We were discussing the relative merit of a single atomic strike role, as agreed to by the Diefenbaker administration, and the dual atomic or conventional warfare capability that had become the Pearson government's policy. Frank was strongly in favour of the former, while I was equally adamant in support of the latter. I pointed out that I knew from Bob McNamara that all the targets assigned to the RCAF were also targeted by the U.S. Strategic Air Command. Some targets were covered as many as three, four, or five times by different missiles or bombers. His argument was that blasting something from the face of the earth three or four times was more conclusive than doing it just once. We debated whether it was possible to be deader than dead, as we pointed fingers at each other in mock simulation of point-blank mutual annihilation.

It was one of those futile circular arguments that goes nowhere and was totally irrelevant anyway. We weren't stripping the F-104s of their ability to be first, second, third, or fourth to get through to their assigned targets in the event of all-out nuclear war; we were simply adding a capability for conventional operations that was ten times more likely to be used because McNamara had forbidden General Lyman Lemnitzer, Supreme Allied Commander, Europe (SACEUR), to use NATO's strike aircraft independently from the U.S. Strategic Air Command. In other words, Lemnitzer's strike force would sit helplessly on the ground until Washington decided on a course of mutual annihilation for the United States and the U.S.S.R. That could be quite a long wait, and as George Drew and others had pointed out more than a year earlier, it didn't make sense to have planes sitting helplessly like so many stationary ducks. Eventually Frank and I were too weary to argue and packed it in to rest up for the trip home and for Christmas, which was just around the corner.

Tuesday, after Christmas, Defence Council took its first look at the proposed command structure for the future, which I had asked them to prepare for my consideration. "It is very interesting but gives me the impression that, if implemented without amendment, we will wind up with more brass and more bodies than we have now. Clearly this is not acceptable and we will have to take a very close look at the whole proposal. The principles may be all right, but this looks like another example of adding a strata on the top."[25]

The military were fighting a rearguard action. As in any large, hierarchical organization, there was a propensity to maintain or expand career and promotion opportunities, rather than to contract them. Convenience often took precedence over common sense, and this was seldom more obvious than when the Assistant Chief of the Defence Staff, Air Vice-Marshal Wilf Bean, gave us a look at his terms of reference and setup. He said the staff couldn't possibly be reduced by thirty percent and still do the work. Bean had solicited the support of Arthur Menzies of External Affairs to shore up his contention that the intelligence group would suffer if cut substantially. "Somehow they were *not* convincing. We are spending far too much money in this area and something should be done about it. A firm hand must be exercised if we are not to get in serious trouble – good old Parkinson's law!"[26]

Despite the resistance, which was inevitable, my diary entry for December 31, 1964, contained a positive summation. "The end of the most tense, difficult, frustrating, and yet productive year of my life. It is incredible, but yet the time cycle from last year's preparation of the White Paper seems like an eternity. We have been most fortunate in many respects, such as the timing of our announcements. On the credit side has been the painstaking work and preparation in respect of:

1. The White Paper and reorganization of defence headquarters.
2. The militia reorganization – a real tiger.
3. Preparation of the first controlled five-year defence program in the history of Canada. Integration is proceeding well, but must go even better in the year ahead."[27]

CHAPTER 7

THE MAPLE LEAF FOREVER

E arly in 1965 Ellen and I took a few days off to relax in the sun. We headed for Guadeloupe, a tropical paradise of volcanic origin. We had been there only a couple of days when the telephone rang one morning about dawn and the operator said there was a Lieutenant Smith in the lobby to see me. Consternation! I wasn't yet fully awake, and the last thing in the world that I wanted to do was see Lt. Smith, whoever he was. I asked that he be put on the line, and learned that he was an RCN pilot from HMCS *Bonaventure*, who had obtained special permission from the French government to land at Guadeloupe in order to hand-deliver an urgent, top-secret message from my associate minister, Lucien Cardin.

I was nonplussed. Should I take time to dress? Was the message of a nature that could be prudently discussed in a hotel lobby? My mind wasn't yet quite in gear when I invited Lt. Smith to our room, where I could read and reply to the message in some privacy. Had I been wider awake, I would have been more considerate of Ellen, who pulled the sheet over her head in self-defence. The message, when I read it, said simply that the French Ambassador to Canada urgently wished to meet with me about the possibility of the RCAF choosing the Mirage as a tactical aircraft. I can't recall the exact wording of my reply, but I suspect it was a bit terse. I couldn't conceive of any subject less welcome as an interruption to a badly needed rest.

We returned home in time for me to dash off for Paris on February 9 for a two-day special meeting of NATO defence ministers. While there, the ministers considered the 1970 NATO Force Goals that were to be provided by member nations, nuclear planning and procedures, and selective release of SACEUR's nuclear capability. This reflected the restrictions that had been imposed by Washington concerning the use of strike aircraft without prior approval from the Pentagon – probably the most important development in years.

On the way back across the Atlantic on February 12, the captain of our airplane picked up a news broadcast from Ottawa saying that Lucien Cardin was being named Minister of Public Works, and Léo Cadieux would be the new Associate Minister of Defence. In a way I was happy that Lucien was getting a department of his own. He deserved it, although he would be sorely missed, because he had been most conscientious in dealing with the thousands of pieces of paper that had been directed to him. Also, his lot had not always been easy. I tried to keep him informed of my plans, but the changes were so monumental and fast-moving that I sometimes slipped and made his task more difficult. His replacement, Cadieux, was unknown to me, and I wasn't sure I would recognize him if he walked into my office. He was sworn in on February 15, the day Canada's new flag was proclaimed after one of the most protracted and bitter debates on record.

The subject of a flag for Canada had been discussed for years, but the final push really began on May 19, 1964, after the Prime Minister's now-famous speech to the Canadian Legion, when he had been booed by the veterans after suggesting that Canada should have a flag of its own. He informed cabinet that, following his rough reception, he had received sixty-three telegrams, of which fifty percent were in support. He told us he would have preferred to defer consideration, but because of the campaign of the Canadian Legion, he had come to the conclusion that the matter would have to be dealt with quickly or it might be lost by default. Advice on heraldic implications would be sought from John Matheson, MP, Col. A.F. Duguid, and Lt.-Cmdr. Alan B. Beddoe, RCN (retired).[1]

When cabinet met on May 12 there was a long discussion on the history of flags. A proposed design was presented that had three maple leaves conjoined and blue bars at each side. Mr. Beddoe said that the maple leaves conjoined were historically correct, but that blue bars were not really appropriate. He agreed that the Red Ensign was a fifth-rank flag, in the sense that it was superceded by all the others. In reply, the Prime Minister said he liked the blue bars.[2]

On May 25, Mr. Beddoe, who was recognized as a leading heraldic artist, produced designs based on the previous discussion, and cabinet approved resolutions to introduce a new flag, to make "O Canada" the national anthem, and to make "God Save the Queen" the Royal Anthem.[3] The following day cabinet approved a design incorporating the three maple leaves and blue bars that was agreed upon the previous day, but with leaves slightly enlarged.[4] This was the flag that became known as "The Pearson Pennant".

While the flag debate raged on in Parliament and country – with raged being the most appropriate word – the defence department was having its own internal debate on what the proposed change meant for us. On July 20, 1964, Defence Council was briefed on the implications. We asked the Personnel Members Committee to re-examine the flag question, considering two alternative propositions: that if the proposed new flag were approved, it should be the only one used by the Armed Forces; alternatively, that the new Canadian flag be used by the armed forces in addition to a new standardized ensign.[5] On July 27, Rear-Admiral M. G. Stirling, chairman of the Personnel Members Committee, showed members some preliminary sketches of military ensigns, but noted that both the RCAF and RCN had a preference for maintaining their distinctive ensigns.

Meanwhile Lord Mountbatten came to see me to implore that the RCN continue to fly the White Ensign, so that all Commonwealth navies would wear the same flag. He said that he was a messenger for the Queen and that it was her wish. Whether that was literally true, I never knew. Mountbatten was considered "royalty", and he may have been her agent, but it is just possible that he was putting words in Her Majesty's mouth. In any event, I was appalled. In a constitutional monarchy, I had been taught, that sort of thing simply isn't done. Still, out of friendship for Mountbatten, I promised to raise the matter with the Prime Minister. When I did, Pearson dismissed the suggestion summarily, though he subsequently raised the question in cabinet after Mountbatten approached him directly.

When the sixth report of the special parliamentary committee on a Canadian flag was presented to the House of Commons on Tuesday, October 29, 1964, it did not recommend the so-called Pearson Pennant. After forty-five meetings, and *in camera* testimony from twelve expert witnesses, the committee eliminated all but two of the approximately two thousand designs that had been presented to it. At that stage the Tories decided to play a little trick. Confident that the Liberals would remain stubbornly faithful to the three-leaf design, the PCs decided to vote for the single-leaf version that subsequently became the Canadian flag. Imagine their surprise when the Liberals switched horses and backed the Tory choice. For the Prime Minister it was a typical – but in this case a very sensible – compromise.

Badly outmanoeuvred, the Tories vowed to continue the fight in the House. They were determined not to adopt a flag that did not include the Union Jack. Their opposition was a fair reflection of the division in the country. Like other MPs, I received scores of letters both for and against a new flag. Those in favour usually included a copy of their own favourite design. Those who were opposed were much more vitriolic, and often quite abusive in their language. For them I prepared a form letter that was intended to be both conciliatory and informative. The debate on the motion for the House to concur in the committee report continued for weeks. Finally on December 14, after 270 speeches, the government imposed closure, and the report was adopted, with the Tories still opposed.

On January 20, 1965, cabinet agreed that February 15 would be Flag Inauguration day. Several ministers, however, took serious objection to a proposal that there be no ceremony and that the Red Ensign be lowered the night of February 14 and the new flag raised the morning of February 15. I was particularly adamant and pointed out that "Canadian veterans and service people would be disturbed if the Red Ensign were not to be properly retired in the same way that regimental colours were from time to time." On a related matter, I added that while the newspapers were conveying the impression that the navy was not prepared to accept the new flag, I had received very little correspondence about the discontinuance of the White Ensign. I was confident that the use of the new flag by the navy would not create any serious difficulty.[6]

When the big day came there were few hitches. I drove to Parliament Hill with the Red Ensign flying for the last time from the staff on my car fender. At the ceremony, purely by chance, I stood near the former Prime Minister, John Diefenbaker, who had declined the opportunity to speak and who shed a few tears. For the majority the mood was movingly reported by Ottawa *Citizen* staff writer Jim Rae in his full-page article headed "Ten Thousand Cheer Raising of a New Flag".

At first, as the ceremony transferred itself from the rotunda of the Parliament Buildings to a platform outside, the proceedings seemed stiff and drawn-out.

The vast and swelling crown was numbed both by the damp cold and the monotony of waiting. The sun was glimpsed only once in a while.

The music was sombre; the day was gray; the people were solemn.

Prayers were given as the Red Ensign was lowered for the last time, bundled up and marched off.

The sea of faces surrounding the Peace Tower registered a single, sad expression as though for a state funeral.

Gloom was in the very step of the three NCOs representing each of the armed forces, as they returned across the wooden platform.

But now, suddenly the presence of the bare mast stirred the curiosity of the crowd – a curiosity that grew into suspense as the three NCOs unfolded the new flag and held it outstretched.

There were more prayers – but uplifting prayers this time. And eyes that should have been closed were glued instead to that bare, white 25-foot flagpole on the platform.

The suspense became almost intolerable before the magic moment arrived – before the new flag moved its first jerky foot up the staff to the accompaniment of guns booming in the distance.

Emotions that had been pent up for more than an hour erupted into a mighty cheer just as the Maple Leaf flag reached the top of the mast for the first time.

The sun was out now; and a light breeze was tickling the newborn flag, much as a mother might fondle the feet of her baby.

Faces that had been sombre only moments before, now were all smiles. Cameras of every description were thrust high in expectancy as gradually, the wind rose and filled the new flag like a blossoming sail.

What a picture! . . .[7]

At cabinet on February 16, Jack Pickersgill said that "the inauguration of the national flag, including the Ottawa ceremony, had been a great triumph for the Prime Minister. The flag would do steadily more good for the country as the years passed."[8] And so it has. It took me a while to get used to it at first because, like the Prime Minister, I had really preferred a design that included blue. But somewhat later, when I saw it raised by Canadian troops on exercise, glistening in the sun against a backdrop of snow-covered Norwegian hills, the love affair began.

My responsibilities didn't end with the inauguration. I was instructed to cancel permits for merchant ships to fly the Blue Ensign and the departments of Defence and Public Works were put in charge of disposing of all the old flags in an appropriate way. Surplus White Ensigns from the navy were sold to New Zealand at cost, and Red Ensigns were made available to schools and Legion branches for their use. In addition, I received letters from quite a few individual veterans asking how they could obtain one of the old flags as a memento, and in each case one was mailed without charge.

A major handicap during my term as minister was the lack of analytical staff to review military submissions. The deputy minister's office was first class in its areas of operation, but these did not include the one function of most immediate interest to me. There was some capability in the Defence Research Board, but again, short of secondment, the expertise was not available on a day-to-day basis. I kept thinking of an early RCAF submission to purchase additional CF-104 Starfighter aircraft. I had had to do all my own staff work to decide that they weren't needed. A later proposal to discharge five hundred surplus aircrew didn't turn out as well because I didn't take time to think through what the consequences might be. In fact they were disastrous, and might have been avoided if someone had systematically questioned the assumptions inherent in the RCAF submission.

Consequently, in early January 1965, I had sent the deputy minister a memorandum reminding him of my interest in the establishment "of a number of positions for staff to assist in the analysis and cost-effectiveness analysis of military briefs."[9] I was opposed to the idea of a large systems-analysis group like the one in Washington headed by Dr. Alain C. Enthoven. For many reasons Canada's requirements were much more modest, and I thought six analysts would be ample. Their responsibility would be to examine the premises on which submissions were based, consider the cost-effectiveness, and report possible alternatives. In short, to supply the minister with the right questions to ask in order to be assured of the validity of a proposal before he signed on the dotted line.

The assistant deputy minister (Finance), J. S. Hodgson, elaborated on my memo and outlined the functions performed by Bob McNamara's staff in a paper for my deputy minister, Elgin Armstrong, dated February 5, 1965, but after that the project was "lost" and never really got off the ground.[10] Many reasons were given for the delay, but none of them were definitive. I could only surmise that the opposition came from the men in uniform. The Canadian military didn't want a clatch of civilian whiz-kids second-guessing their decisions. That is natural enough, but from the minister's side of the desk, I can only say that their decisions often needed a thorough review, and there is no way that anyone can adequately perform this function single-handed.

In March my principal concern was working on a new command structure for the forces. As with the White Paper, I did the first rough cut myself, drawing an organizational chart on a piece of paper and listing the functions in the boxes. These charts were turned over to the defence staff as a guide of what I had in mind. Prior to integration, each service had had its own type of organization. The air force was organized along functional lines, with commands related to specific tasks in Air Defence, Transport, Training, and so on. The army, on the other hand, observed geographic lines of demarcation, with separate Eastern, Quebec, Central, and Western commands. The Navy enjoyed a happy combination of the two concepts because, except for its reserve units, its functions were concentrated in the Atlantic and Pacific oceans.

In an era of joint operations and military task-forces, it seemed to me that the job to be performed was of greater relevance than where it was to be performed. Consequently, I preferred the functional-command concept, because it provided the greatest flexibility. At the same time, thanks to integration, the number of commands could be reduced from eleven to six, with considerable saving of overhead. For once the majority of my senior advisers concurred, and at an historic meeting on March 29, Defence Council approved the new structure – with the exception of Maritime and Materiel commands, which were subject to further study. There was some question as to whether we should have one or two maritime commands, and this was subsequently resolved in favour of one.

March 31 was a horrendous day. "It started off with Jean Allard telling me he is going to resign as a result of his failure in respect of bilingualism in the Armed Forces. I tried to convince him of 'the truth' that the proposed command structure had no real connection to the problem of making French-speaking Canadians feel 'at home' in the Armed Forces. It is a separate problem and I am willing to give it some real attention. I dislike his 'using' politics and threatening to resign from time to time. On the other hand, there is some foundation for his complaint."[11]

When I wasn't putting out fires in the department, I took advantage of every possible occasion to explain the reasons for the reorganization, because I knew that once they were understood, people were much more sympathetic and often supportive. For that reason I welcomed an invitation from Air Commodore Frank Ball to address the students at the RCAF Staff College, Armour Heights, in North Toronto, on May 10. They were the future leaders of the air force, and it was both an opportunity and a challenge to speak to them and answer their questions. When I got back to my office, I was handed a memo which read: "Mr. Lee phoned to give you the following message: 'Have heard that Group Captain Gordon (here) received a call this afternoon from his brother Group Captain Gordon (Toronto) that your RCAF Staff College speech was a smash success and very much impressed the students.' "[12] A letter of appreciation from Air Commodore Ball, saying how helpful the exchange had been was more moderate in tone, but nevertheless reassuring. He suggested that it be made an annual event.[13] For the record, I did return a year later, with equally positive results.

On May 18, my colleague Jack Nicholson hosted a dinner for Earl Mountbatten at the Country Club. "The Admiral is all for us – thinks we are doing a great job. He does not support the idea of a single uniform, however. It was fascinating to hear him on this. His wonderful objectivity ended when he came to this subject, where he substituted 'Sailors have always worn dark blue with brass buttons.' He described my December letter to Denis Healey as brilliant, which I think is too generous, and would like another report to take back with him. He is a fascinating character."[14] (My letter to Denis had been just a brief résumé of our reorganization and the rationale for it.)

We were back on the subject when we met again on May 21. "A really, truly, genuinely hectic day. From the crack of dawn the pressure was unbelievable. Bill [Lee] gave me replies to Air Force Association Resolutions to approve. Lord Louis Mountbatten arrived at 9:30 and stayed for 1 hour instead of $\frac{1}{2}$. We had a most interesting discussion on NATO strategy and on integration. Again he urged me to give Denis Healey a real sales-talk at the Paris meeting next week. He believes that Healey must make decisions by July or the whole reorganization will be set back years."[15]

The following week, when I spoke to Denis Healey in Paris, as requested by Mountbatten, the U.K. minister was favourable to the principle of integration/unification, as was every other NATO defence minister with whom the subject was discussed. "You're absolutely right," he told me. "But if you think I'm going to go through that kind of political hassle, you're crazy." It wasn't lack of understanding of the advantages of a contemporary military organization that kept the British from leaping into the present; it was the minister's fear of the slings and arrows of outrageous politics.

One more difficult decision was whether to continue development of the hydrofoil or not. The hydrofoil was our segment of a three-country project in cooperation with the United States and the United Kingdom. Each country agreed to test a craft of different size and design, on the understanding that its findings would be shared with the other two partners. The cost of our hydrofoil had escalated from $26.3 to $36.2 million, and there was pressure to drop the whole project. I finally ruled otherwise because it was a Canadian commitment. Had Canada defaulted, there would have been a big gap in the range of knowledge.

Unfortunately Canadians are ultraconservative when it comes to pure research. We like to know the end use in advance, although that isn't always possible. When we put the first Canadian satellite in orbit, for example, there was no known commercial use for the contraption. Today there are dozens of uses. Similarly, with the hydrofoil, we wanted to know more about the problems of delivering power to a propeller through a long shaft and to gain information about the seaworthiness of such a craft. There was never any firm plan to adopt it for naval purposes – as the press kept insisting there should be – although it might have been a welcome addition had money been available for further development. It was research for research's sake, and a small Canadian contribution to a pool of knowledge from which we always got more than we gave.

On June 7 all the senior commanders were brought to Ottawa to be briefed on the new command structure, which was now complete. It was my second chance to give them a little pep talk about getting on with the job. Later, I recorded: "The command structure has been *very* well received both internally and externally. I think it makes a lot of sense and the reduction from eleven to six will save us a lot of overhead and money.

"All of the new commanders are delighted with one exception – Maj.-Gen. Anderson. He is quite disappointed and doesn't really think the new structure will keep the militia alive. I don't think the problem is insoluble if we work at it. However, he shouldn't take the job [Mobile Command] unless he is going to be enthusiastic."[16] The following day: "Reaction still very good! Our solution seems to have general support."[17]

Of all the decisions facing a Minister of Defence few are as fraught with potential danger as the choice of a new tactical aircraft. C. D. Howe's decision to suspend work on the Avro jetliner in favour of an all-out effort to design and build the CF-100 was highly controversial. The same was true of the successor Avro Arrow, which helped scuttle the Diefenbaker regime after the early test aircraft had been put to the torch. Certainly the subsequent decision to acquire the American F-101 Voodoo, an airplane inferior to the Arrow, did nothing to restore public confidence. Then the Diefenbaker purchase of the F-104 Starfighter, soon dubbed "The Widow-maker", for the air division in

Europe remains controversial even after a quarter of a century. Every minister involved in the selection process succeeded in getting his fingers burned, and I was no exception.

In my case the story had really begun with the White Paper, which stated a need for a new tactical aircraft to replace CF-104 Starfighters in Europe and then the CF-101 Voodoos in North American defence. The need was there, although it certainly wasn't urgent at the time. The White Paper was looking ahead.

Nevertheless, its presence on the list was sufficient invitation for the aircraft companies to line up in the hope that their planes would be chosen. The stakes were high; so it was no surprise when the first pitch in favour of the Douglas A-4E Skyhawk had come in the summer of 1964. The A-4E was designed for use on U.S. aircraft carriers, and the RCN really hoped that it would be suitable for the *Bonaventure*. Next, in September, Lockheed had come along with a modified version of the F-104. Giving them the time of day was really just a courtesy, because there was no way that I was going to buy more high-altitude aircraft for low-altitude flying. Grumman paraded their A-6A and General Dynamics their famous TFX – the result of Bob McNamara's attempt to force the USAF and USN jointly to develop an aircraft for use by them both. Not unexpectedly, the U.S. military scuttled the experiment. Other presentations included the McDonnell F-4, in current use by the USAF, and the Northrop F-5, which was a beefed-up and armed version of the T-33 trainer used by air forces around the world.

Of all the planes the F-4 was undoubtedly the most suitable. That was the RCAF conclusion and my own. Had I been able to buy it, I would have been a hero with the airmen. But by November I was caught in a vice. When, for the first time ever, we had consolidated the programs and budgets of the three services, the total sums didn't fit. Walter Gordon's stringent limit of $1,550 million for our budget wasn't enough to meet the essential requirements of the army and navy and leave enough for a tactical aircraft. So finally, at the November 9 meeting of Defence Council, I removed the purchase of a new aircraft from the essential list as the fight raged on.[18]

The airmen pulled every conceivable trick. Old Man McDonnell, the aging dynamo who was both CEO and founder of the giant company, came to see me personally to apply pressure. A production-sharing deal with the British was "sweetened" to the point at which it became an offer difficult to resist. Then, in a somewhat transparent attempt to force the RCAF's size-twelve budgetary foot into Cinderella's size-six appropriation shoe, Frank Miller proposed that the airmen would settle for sixty-four aircraft – far too small a number to meet the operational requirements. At the same time, behind my back, he told Fred Kearns, the president of Canadair, where the F-4 would have been manufactured, not to pay any attention to the figure of sixty-four in his plans and cost-estimating. Once the initial approval was obtained, the RCAF would "find" the money to keep the production line going.

The attraction of the production-sharing proposal was very great, and I understood the view of colleagues who supported it. But the principle at stake was whether we were going to spend limited capital funds on the items of military equipment of highest priority or on one of the lowest. That was the issue. The battleground had narrowed on December 8, 1964, when cabinet decided not to accept the British deal.[19] In effect the F-4 was eliminated, and the contest narrowed to the A-7, A-6, and the F-5. The lobbying for each of these took on a new intensity. I didn't like the A-7 because it was single-engine, and after our accident rate with the Starfighter, I was more than a little nervous about a single-engine aircraft. The A-6 was rated the best of the lot, but it still wasn't really good enough for the intended roles. The F-5 was little more than a trainer with guns hung on it, although the USAF was supplying them to their Vietnamese allies.

I was so angered by the extent of the air-force machinations that I didn't know which way to turn. From a strictly military standpoint the obvious course was to drop the tactical aircraft from the five-year equipment program altogether. This extreme solution was moderated by cries from the aircraft industry, which didn't see how it could survive for five years in the absence of any military orders. By the time we could afford a tactical airplane, there might not be any industry left to build it. Also, I really wanted a plane that would allow the airmen to practice the ground-support roles that they had abandoned at the end of the Second World War.

Luckily, the air force had inadvertently provided me a way out. The same list of their equipment needs that mentioned the tactical fighters also included a replacement for the T-33 "T-Bird" trainer. I decided that I could kill three birds with one stone: I could keep the aircraft industry alive, if only barely, give the flyers a plane that would be quite adequate for practising ground-support techniques, and provide a T-Bird replacement, all at a very modest cost for retro-fit to trainers when a new tactical aircraft finally became available.

It was a good compromise, and on July 4, 1965, the same day that Larry Pennell, the new Solicitor General, and Jean-Luc Pepin, Minister of Mines and Technical Surveys, attended their first meeting, cabinet approved the purchase of up to 125 North-rop F-5A Freedom Fighter aircraft for $215 million, subject to satisfactory arrangements for production-sharing with Canadian manufacturers.

The decision was announced in a press release the following day, but that didn't end the war of nerves. Airmen used the press to try to establish in the public mind that the CF-5 was an irresponsible choice. They also began to undermine the project by recommending an assortment of expensive extras that would increase the cost out of all proportion to the effectiveness of the aircraft. The solution was to make them live within the $215-million ceiling approved for the project. They were given the choice of more airplanes with fewer extras or more extras with fewer airplanes. It was an excellent discipline – perhaps the only one that public servants understand. It worked miracles, and many of the unnecessary changes, which I recognized from my own experience in the aircraft industry, were dropped.

Twenty years later, when the new CF-18s went into squadron service, the CF-5 conversion to trainers began exactly as planned, except, regrettably, at least a decade later than the most pessimistic assumption.

CHAPTER 8

ANOTHER MINORITY

At cabinet on January 26, 1965, the day Sir Winston Churchill died, the Prime Minister advised us that he was not entertaining the possibility of a spring election.[1] It seemed odd that he felt obliged to say anything, and if his purpose was to be reassuring, the statement had just the opposite effect, at least for me. It reinforced the suspicion that he was under intense pressure from Walter Gordon, who was hell-bent for an early vote.

My concern had nothing to do with my own re-election prospects in Trinity. In the January issue of *Maclean's* I was named "one of the outstanding Canadians of 1964".[2] This kind of publicity had given me a high and positive profile with electors and I felt that my riding was reasonably safe. I opposed Walter's plan for an early election simply because I felt an election was unnecessary and unwise. The people were very much against it, and Walter vastly underestimated Diefenbaker's ability to ridicule the government's handling of the so-called scandal and the effect this would have on the hustings.

Walter had developed too great a reliance on political polls. He was a pioneer of this technique in Canada, and had been instrumental in persuading Lou Harris, the renowned chief pollster for the U.S. Democratic Party, to establish a branch office in Canada.[3] Harris, and later his alter ego, Oliver Quayle, became principal advisers to Walter, Keith Davey, and Tom Kent on questions relating to the political pulse of the nation. For a long time this fact was not well publicized, because it wouldn't have looked good to have had Americans meddling in our political affairs, and it certainly wouldn't have enhanced Walter's image as a Canadian nationalist. Consequently, even most members of cabinet were unaware of Harris's activities.

In December 1964, Walter had sent the Prime Minister a memorandum urging an early spring election, and this was probably why Mike felt he had to deny the possibility to cabinet. But Walter didn't give up, especially when Oliver Quayle's early 1965 polls showed that the Liberal edge over the Tories had widened. He also feared that, if the election were not held that year, we would be stuck until a new redistribution bill, changing riding boundaries, came into effect late in 1966. I suspect that he had other reasons as well. His cosy relationship with Pearson had been eroded by the public reaction to his first budget, and his standing in the party was ambiguous, with strong factions both for and against him. As promoter and chief architect of an election that yielded a majority, he could re-establish his position as unquestioned number-two man in the party.

In addition to holding contrary views about the need for an early election, Walter and I continued to differ on the best approach to the development of social policy – this time on the subject of health insurance. I thought that we should ask for an in-depth study, beginning with the nature of the problem and progressing to alternative solutions, stating the advantages and disadvantages of each. It didn't seem either logical or sensible to assume that we would simply opt for some imitation of the British system, with all its imperfections, without so much as wondering if there was a better way.

The need for health insurance was basic and well understood. The level of medical services available to rich and poor people was not comparable. Equally distressing, was the fact that there were countless tragic cases in which serious and extended illness had resulted in medical and hospital bills far beyond anything a family could pay. Savings were lost, insurance was cashed in, and houses or farms were mortgaged to satisfy claims that had resulted from circumstances beyond anyone's control. It was the luck of the draw, and not even the middle-income well-to-do were immune from the spectre of financial disaster.

In the search for a solution it seemed obvious that the criteria should include: equal access to the best medical care for rich and poor alike; minimum red-tape; and the least incentive for people who can well afford their own routine "throat checks" to take advantage of the system and demand services just because they are "free". My colleagues were deeply concerned about the need for universal access, but most simply heaved a sigh of resignation when it came to questions of bureaucratic excess and possible abuse. I decided to think through the maze and consider what I would recommend if it were my responsibility.

When the subject was discussed in cabinet on July 16, 1965, in the context of determining a government position on health insurance for a federal-provincial conference, I put forward an alternative to medicare. After my experience with the Canada Pension Plan, I didn't prepare a cabinet document but simply made an oral presentation to see if I could elicit any interest. My formula was designed to satisfy all three of the criteria I had set out. All would go to the doctor and/or hospital of their choice, and all would be responsible for their own medical bills up to a limit of two percent of their income. They would be one hundred percent insured for expenditures in excess of that amount. Those with $100,000 annual income would pay their own bills up to $2,000. Those earning $30,000 would pay up to $600, while people with no income would pay nothing. No one would be subjected to financial hardship as a result of medical expenses, because the burden would be proportionate to their ability to pay. At the same time, the fact that the majority would pay most of their medical expenses in a normal year would relieve governments of the responsibility of collecting and then disbursing billions in routine transactions and would eliminate much of the abuse experienced by the British and the Swedes.

To ensure that a temporary lack of cash would not deter anyone from seeking needed medical attention, and also to guarantee that doctors and hospitals would be reimbursed for services provided, patients could send their bills to the Government Insurance Agency for immediate payment and subsequent adjustment in Income Tax calculations. Expenses might be averaged over two or three years to discourage people from "storing" medical problems for the specific purpose of incurring major expenses in one taxation period, but apart from a few minor technical details, there was no fine print to detract from the simplicity and efficacy of the plan.

When I finished my presentation every cabinet minister who spoke – and most of them did – said it was a better, more efficient, proposal than the one before them. There were no exceptions. Walter Gordon was the last to speak. He, too, said it was a better plan. "But," he added, "it wouldn't be politic." With those five words, rational debate ended; the discussion of alternatives was over.

None of this discussion was recorded in the cabinet minutes, which simply stated: "Mr. Hellyer said he objected in principle to the whole approach government was taking to the question of social security. To his mind, the object of social security was to insure those risks which were beyond the financial capacity of an individual to meet; it was not for the state to provide complete services to individuals regardless of their means."[4] That is someone's loose interpretation of what my plan was all about.

I still think it was worth pursuing. It would have allowed rich and poor equal access to the best medical services available, while avoiding the acrimonious debates to which we have been subjected. There would have been less abuse, lower overall costs, faster service, and shorter queues. Governments would not have been burdened with raising such vast sums. We could have avoided the necessity of governments setting fees for services, under which the worst of doctors are overpaid and the best and most skilled specialists are vastly undercompensated. As I have often argued, you can get away with averaging for MP's salaries, where the numbers are small and everyone is working in the same place. If you want to be an MP there is no choice. The principle doesn't work as well with doctors and other professionals, who are free to move to other jurisdictions where they enjoy greater freedom.

Meanwhile, the pressure for an early election never let up. Pearson equivocated, however, and when it was too late for a spring election, Walter started plumping for the early fall, even though the cabinet was almost universally opposed. The uncertainty continued all summer, which was enough to keep everyone on tenterhooks and make advance planning difficult if not impossible. On the one hand it was business as usual, while on the other hand no opportunity to influence voters favourably could be ignored. This was reason enough for Jack Pickersgill to suggest that I represent him at the opening of the Swift Rapids Lock on the Severn River, thirty-six miles from the western end of the Trent-Severn canal system. The lock replaced an original, antiquated marine railway, dear to the memories of many boaters. Jack's rationale was that, as a senior Ontario minister, my participation would be politically more beneficial than his. While this explanation made some sense, I was also aware that he would be relieved of the necessity of forsaking his idyllic New-foundland hideaway and travelling almost halfway across the continent just for a strenuous one-day function. I was happy to accept what seemed to be a mutually advantageous proposition.

Ellen and I flew from Ottawa to Muskoka Airport, where we transferred to an army helicopter from 1 Transport Helicopter Platoon for the short hop to our point of embarkation. There we were to join a convoy of small boats for a six-mile cruise to the lock. When we landed and got out of the helicopter, Ellen headed directly into the path of the tail propeller, which was invisible to the naked eye. Shouting was useless against the roar of the en-gine, so I resorted to what our daughter Mary Elizabeth, who was on hand to greet us, described as "very strong non-verbal com-munication". Fortunately Ellen caught a glimpse of my "steely blue eyes" and the horror on my face and froze in her tracks un-til someone could lead her out of the path of danger. Tragedy averted, the balance of the day was very pleasant. Sunny skies, etched by fleecy clouds, were a flattering backdrop for the flotilla of vacationing boat-lovers.

When cabinet met on September 1, the results of highly suc-cessful lobbying by Walter Gordon and Keith Davey were clearly evident. When the election talk had begun months earlier, nearly the entire cabinet was opposed, but one by one the majority, including Jack Pickersgill, succumbed to the sales pitch. At one point, in an effort to soften my opposition, I had been shown Oliver Quale's polling results. They were becoming increasingly ambiguous, although they still registered a substantial Liberal lead. I was underimpressed because a poll is like a small snapshot of political opinion over a specific time-frame. It doesn't tell you what people will think a month or two later, any more than a photo taken on a sunny day will indicate cloud and rain in the days to come. The Prime Minister followed the unusual procedure of asking each minister for an opinion, and all but four had taken the bait. Maurice Sauvé was negative, as was Watson MacNaught, presumably because he knew he couldn't win his own seat – which is the way it turned out.

When he finally came to me the Prime Minister said, "I already know what you think." We had met privately in his office, where I told him it was very unwise to call an election mid-term without a clearly identifiable issue. Walter intended to campaign on the necessity for a majority – presumably to obtain a mandate to implement new social programs like medicare. But this reason didn't make sense in the public mind because we had just succeeded in introducing a new flag and the Canada Pension Plan, and in making major amendments to the National Defence Act without benefit of a majority. Some of these, the flag in particular, had been controversial, and subject to stiff opposition, but there was no clear case of insurmountable obstruction. It was far more likely that the so-called scandals would become the issue. Paul Martin was the last to be called on, at his own request, but when the time came he said nothing. In the second volume of his memoirs, *A Very Public Life*, Paul states that he had misgivings, and shared them with the PM the day before cabinet met.[5]

Still the PM didn't act, so I was off to Vancouver to attend a regimental dinner at the invitation of Colonel T. Inglewood and then came right back to Toronto for the Canadian National Air Show at the waterfront of the CNE on September 3. On September 4 I left for Quebec City for a weekend with the Canadian War Correspondents' Association. We bussed to Lake Le Gîte, north of Quebec City, where fishing was the advertised weekend attraction. The fishing, however, was no match for the yarns told by veteran newsmen like Frank Swanson, Charles Lynch, and Gil Purcell, Canadian Press's legendary general manager. I don't recall seeing many trout, but I do remember that this was the second and most recent occasion when I had observed copious quantities of alcohol being consumed before breakfast. It was an association ritual to fill every available pail with tomato juice and gin to help open eyes heavy from late-night partying.

I was just nicely back from the annual replay of myriad famous wartime battles, when an election was called for November 8, and another verbal battle in the seven-year Pearson–Diefenbaker war began. The tactics, for some of us, were compromised by lack of prior notice. My calendar was partially filled with official engagements, which would be embarrassing to cancel. Serious campaigning had to be wedged into the available gaps. I couldn't possibly skip the official opening of Toronto's magnificent new city hall on September 13, for example, nor the RCAF's Battle of Britain ceremony on Sunday, September 19 – not that there were any votes to be gained, but because people really expect you to show up when you say you will.

On September 24 we left for England, where Ellen was scheduled to christen the second of our new "0" class submarines, HMCS *Onondaga*. Normally this would have been a seven-day affair. We were guests of the British government, which had purchased tickets for concerts at London's Royal Festival Hall and had planned an extensive and interesting program. In the circumstances, however, the visit had to be what the military call a "fast turnaround". Ellen refers to it as "the time I flew to England for lunch", which is a slight exaggeration, but only slight.

We arrived at London's Savoy Hotel in the evening, after a daylight flight across the Atlantic. We were all preregistered by Her Britannic Majesty's public service and were handed keys by an assistant manager who escorted us to our rooms. When it was Lou Bourgeois's turn our host said, "You're on the fourth floor, Mr. Burgess," which underlined the centuries-old problem of communications between French and English. Lou was born in Saskatchewan and so used to mispronunciation that he didn't raise an eyebrow.

Saturday was Ellen's day. We departed from London early for Chatham, where HMS *Victory*, Admiral Nelson's flagship, had been launched in 1765. On arrival the guest of honour was afforded the full treatment, which included meeting the dignitaries, naming the ship, inspecting the guard, and taking the salute for a march-past of units of the Royal Navy and Royal Canadian Navy. She performed with great dignity and aplomb, though there was one small hitch. The champagne bottle didn't break on the first try. As a precaution the shipyard had sawn the glass more than halfway through and suspended the bottle in a vice-like contraption designed to smash it against the prow when a cord was pulled. But it didn't break, either the first time or the second. The dockyard's chief constructor, who may have designed the failsafe device, was pressed into service, and the third try brought champagne cascading over the bow. Ellen then took a gavel and struck the control panel that sent the *Onondaga* gracefully through the line of British and Canadian flags into the Medway, as the eight thousand guests, including 1,200 Canadian sailors from four ships, gave three cheers for Mrs. Hellyer and then, at her lead, three cheers for the men and women who built the ship. It was an awe-inspiring combination of sound and sight.

I had played no official part, being present only as the spouse of the sponsor, but I did keep a close watch to see if the British had learned anything from their experience in launching *Onondaga*'s sister ship, the *Ojibwa*, just days earlier. On that occasion, I was told, one would have been hard pressed to believe that the submarine was not destined for the Royal Navy. No high Canadian officials had been invited, our flag was not flown, and the band played "Rule Britannia" instead of "O Canada". It reflected such incredible insensitivity that I wrote a blistering letter to Sir Henry Lintott, the U.K. High Commissioner to Canada. Fortunately Bill Lee persuaded me not to send it, because it lacked any of the niceties of diplomacy. I could only presume that somehow the message had been transmitted through unofficial channels, because Lionel Chevrier, our High Commissioner to London, was invited to the *Onondaga* christening, the new Canadian flag was very much in evidence, and the band had discovered "O Canada".

The brief respite provided by the British trip was good for the spirits, because the rest of the campaign was just one mad mixture of politics and precommitted official functions. On October 7, I flew to Quebec City for the nominating convention of J.-C. Cantin, in Quebec South. I accepted a flip home in the de Havilland HS-125. The defence department was in the process of evaluating American, French, and British aircraft, and each manufacturer was insistent that I should at least ride in its product. There was no time for demonstration flights, which were really out of the question during an election campaign, so in response to what amounted to almost annoying insistence, I said that I would be travelling between two points on a certain day and, if they had an airplane waiting at the point of departure, I would ride in it. That way I would at least see what the machine looked like and how it operated – and without any loss of time. It seemed like a common-sense, practical solution to an otherwise insoluble problem, but it was destined to get me into some difficulty in the months to come, when John Diefenbaker took umbrage.

October 19 saw the official opening of the army's Mobile Command at Longueuil, across the St. Lawrence River from Montreal. This represented another milestone in the reorganization of the armed forces, and I wished that the task could be a full-time effort without the diversion of an unnecessary election. A couple of hours later I took off for Truro, Nova Scotia, in a Grumman Gulfstream, another of the executive jets under consideration by the department. That night it was on to Fredericton, where I spoke to students at the University of New Brunswick before moving on to the army base at Oromocto the next morning for a hospital sod-turning ceremony, followed by an evening public meeting at Souris.

A two-day interlude in Toronto allowed me to drop into my committee room, which is never a bad idea in the course of an election. Then it was off to the West Coast for meetings in Victoria, Vancouver, Calgary, and Lethbridge. At Lethbridge, it was a Lear jet that was on the runway for a hasty exit to Regina. I admit to some nervousness riding in the Lear, based on the early controversy concerning its radical design, but I consoled myself with the thought that all of the bugs must have been ironed out by then, and that it must be at least as safe as riding in a farm wagon.

That night saw the last of my out-of-town engagements, on behalf of Bob Temple of Belleville, in a hall above the Legion. We were very late starting, a deliberate strategy of the local Liberals, which was, in my opinion, a very bad judgment-call. It was supposed to heighten the anticipation, but all it did was raise the blood-alcohol level of several attendees who were waiting impatiently in the bar for the guest speaker to arrive. When the meeting finally got under way there were several RCAF personnel from the Trenton base present. "One corporal was sloshed and started to heckle. A civilian wino did as well. An officer apologized on behalf of those present, but it was another night to remember!!"[6]

Election day was terrible, with teeming rain. It really hampered operations and put our organization to the test. Within minutes of the polls closing, however, I knew I was okay. Ted Elliott and his super team, which included regulars like Angela Canzanese,

Muriel Smith, Theresa Murphy, Marg Bulger, Kay Mansley, Gwen Vernon, Rupert Edwards, Ethye Hayden, the Michniewicz sisters, Joanna Wice, and Muriel Branton, had done their homework, and it showed on the scoreboard. Final tally: Hellyer (Lib.), 9,897; Brazill (PC), 4,375; Ragno (NDP), 2,773.

Nationally, however, we were not doing as well. We won all seven seats in Newfoundland, but only one in Nova Scotia and none in Prince Edward Island. About 7:45 p.m. EST Don Sims of CBC radio asked for my prediction of the outcome, and I forecast another Liberal minority, which proved to be correct.

1965 Federal Election Results

Liberals	131
Conservatives	97
New Democrats	21
Socreds	5
Other	11

"The Prime Minister was shattered and (according to Keith, who was there) almost resigned on the spot; but Mrs. Pearson talked him out of it. He went on television and performed admirably. Harry Hays and Watson MacNaught were defeated. Poor show – for Parliament too!"[7] We finally got to bed at 3:45 a.m. "At 6:00 a.m. dear old Mary Elizabeth decided to make herself a cup of tea and wake us all up! Bless her little heart!"[8] Later we drove her to Union Station to get the 10:15 train to Quebec City, where she was attending school, and then headed to the committee room to clean up. As always it was a horrendous job that took most of the day.

I made a reservation back to Ottawa, and returned to the apartment to pack. Just as we were about to depart the lights went out, and we could see from our seventh floor balcony that they were out all over the city. What we didn't know, until later, was that it was a general blackout, affecting the entire eastern-seabord area as far south as New York City. The power came on just in time for us to make the airport – with difficulty. It was such a close call that I didn't have time to park and had to leave the car with airport limousine drivers, who promised to cope one way or another.

Wednesday morning "the girls had a little sign on my desk 'congratulations and welcome home' as well as some petite roses.

It gave my soul quite a lift to know that someone cared."[9] At cabinet we had the usual recap of the election. Walter argued that the slippage was caused by a trip Jean Lesage had made to western Canada and by getting off on the wrong issues – defensive instead of offensive. Mitchell Sharp still insisted it had been the right time to hold an election, and I disagreed again. It was an election people didn't want, and for no apparent purpose that would make the necessity credible.

After the Remembrance Day ceremony on November 11, I learned that "Maurice Sauvé, Léo Cadieux, and Jean-Luc Pepin went to see the PM at 12:15. They insist on the resignation of Guy Favreau and Maurice Lamontagne; and that two of the big five portfolios go to French-Canadians; action by early January, or else! Poor PM, I feel for him."[10]

It seems that it never rains but it pours. One day after the ultimatum from the French-speaking ministers, Walter Gordon resigned from the cabinet. The unthinkable had happened! "Keith [Davey] said that Walter submitted his resignation on the basis of [his performance as] Liberal Campaign Chairman – and it was ostensibly accepted on that basis. In truth, however, he was fired from the Finance portfolio. Mike offered him another portfolio but he refused – as you might expect."[11] Walter was also offered the post of Canadian ambassador to Washington, but said he "had no interest in such an appointment".[12]

Three weeks later Ellen and I had a fascinating discussion with Isobel and Keith Davey over dinner at the Châteaubriand. We reviewed the entire gamut of election and post-election events, including the Liberal succession, which had been the subject of much gossip since the party failed to win a majority. "He told me that Walter Gordon had been deeply hurt because the Prime Minister had accepted his resignation and felt that deep down the PM had wanted it ever since the first budget. He thinks there is an even chance of getting WLG's support at a convention. He told me that John Matheson and Jim Walker are with me. [Jim] Coutts may be the next national organizer. He [Keith] wants to quit soon, will likely go to the Senate – and will write a book! Sounds interesting."[13] In retrospect Walter's departure from the cabinet not only ended what he regarded as a "political partnership" with Pearson, but also their "long personal friendship".[14] The wound was so deep that, with the excuse of an ice storm, Walter wasn't present at Mike's funeral seven years later.

On Sunday, November 14, I spent most of the day in bed with a miserable cold. "In the afternoon Bob Thompson came to pay a friendly visit. He was just chatting between friends and not making a proposition – he made perfectly clear. Nevertheless there was, in fact, a message. He felt both Dief and LBP would stay on at least until 1967. Either the Tory or Liberal parties would disappear eventually in favour of the NDP. Meanwhile it was important that there be no new election and that the left wing forces be held in check. He thinks Bud Olson would make an excellent Minister of Agriculture; and for himself, though he is not ambitious, he has a prestige to maintain – either External Affairs or Trade and Commerce would do. Two of his other men from B.C. should rate Parliamentary Assistants. Any contact could be made through Dave Wilson. I am not as pessimistic as he is about the future of the two old parties, subject, of course, to their leadership. [Re. the Socreds] I doubt if Sauvé, Kent, etc. will permit the PM to take them in?!"[15]

On Monday the cabinet met and decided the new Parliament would open on January 18, 1966. It was basically a routine meeting, although we discussed some important foreign-policy issues, including the Rhodesian Unilateral Declaration of Independence and the possible admittance of Red China to the United Nations. The most interesting subject that morning wasn't on the agenda. It was the change in the Prime Minister. He acted like his own man for the first time since the government had been formed. It was as if Walter's departure had removed an albatross from around his neck and he was free at last. When we adjourned, I had lunch with Jack Pickersgill. "He has been talking to LBP about the future. He told the Prime Minister that in his opinion I was the only one who could take over Transport and adequately cope with the problems. I thanked him for the compliment, but said that I must stay with Defence at least six more months to get the reorganization past the critical point. The passive resistance must be overcome. Jack said that if he steps down to another portfolio to make it [Transport] available for a French-Canadian, he would state the reason of health, which is not entirely without foundation."[16]

When Cabinet met on December 8 a number of items on defence and foreign policy were deferred to allow me time to complete my opening remarks to the Defence Research Board annual symposium. Cabinet continued all day with Paul Martin in the chair. "He and Jack Pickersgill used the occasion to clean up all the items they must have had in their baskets since last summer. Not a bad idea at that. Harry Hays told me that he would like to run again and that it would help to use the Senate as a base in the meantime. I said I would pass the word along."[17]

I fulfilled that promise when I met with the PM to discuss my own future. Messages from Hays, Bob Thompson, and others were passed along for consideration by the man who had to make the decisions. Mike asked if I would like to have a new portfolio, and I replied that the question was really academic, because there was no way I could leave Defence as it was. The process of reorganization was something like swimming across a river. We were at the mid-stream point, where the currents were strongest and most treacherous. Apart from drifting downstream and drowning in indecision, there were just two options, either continue until reaching the safety of the distant shore or turn back. For me, to turn back would constitute an unforgivable crime, so there was really no choice but to struggle on. And that's the way we left it.

On Friday, December 10, "Judy LaMarsh told me, in tears, that the PM had asked her to take Secretary of State or Solicitor General and she had refused. She was angry and hurt because she had submitted her resignation in August and he had asked her to stay until the health plan was through."[18] I listened sympathetically, because she really had been pushed around with scant consideration of her feelings, even though this was one of two big work days for getting caught up before the annual pilgrimage to NATO.

"Cousin" Paul and I spent Sunday crossing the Atlantic and were met in Paris by our ambassador, George Ignatieff, who gave us a short rundown. After trying rather unsuccessfully to grab a few hours' sleep, I joined our delegation for the usual 10:00 a.m. briefing at the Embassy. "How so many can consume so much time doing so little is the thought that crossed my mind. The briefing was as dull as it was long."[19] That evening I watched a television debate between François Mitterand and Charles DeGaulle that was probably the best entertainment in town.

When the formal meetings began on Tuesday morning, the political review was moderately interesting with reports of British and French visits to the Soviet Union being the highlights. Vietnam and Rhodesia were also front and centre. The United

States indicated it would welcome any assistance it could get for its effort in Vietnam, but the request, as usual, drew a blank. The French, in particular, had long memories, and couldn't forget that their earlier pleas to the United States for assistance in fighting the Viet Cong had been ignored.

At the end of the day Paul Martin, in his capacity as "president d'honneur" for the year, gave a dinner for everyone, including the military. The cost of $18 a plate, which included fresh Canadian salmon flown in for the occasion, seemed more extravagant than it does in hindsight. Even then, it was modest compared to the banquet French Defence Minister, Pierre Messmer, gave his opposite members. The cutlery was gold and the hand-painted plates had belonged to Napoleon's mother. They were irreplaceable, and even the cheap imitations that were substituted when one was broken cost $350 each. The thought made my hand shake each time I touched mine. After dinner half a dozen of us stood around the piano in the lounge while Messmer gave us his own chilling version of East–West relations. The French, twice burned in the first half of this century, feared the reunification of Germany more than they feared the Soviets. Also, though they had great respect for the Americans, they didn't believe U.S. assurances that they would risk a war of nuclear annihilation just to prevent a Soviet invasion of Western Europe. This underlying incredulity gave birth to the idea of an independent French *force de frappe* that was not subject to a U.S. veto.

The flight home was pleasant but very, very long. Before we lunched, we received word of the cabinet shuffle. Paul and I, along with Jack Pickersgill, were among the few senior survivors in our existing jobs. "The PM did not meet Quebec's demand for an additional one of the big five portfolios, and this will likely spell trouble in the days ahead. New ministers are Joe Greene, Agriculture; John Turner, without portfolio; Jean-Pierre Côté, Postmaster General; and Jean Marchand [was slated for] the new manpower job. Bob Winters will come into Trade and Commerce in January."[20] That meant that Bob would probably be a leadership contender, while Marchand's elevation was the beginning of the ascendancy of the three newly elected "wise men" from Quebec whose potential impact was still unknown.

Cabinet met early Monday morning with a very full agenda. "After I returned to the department I saw Léo Cadieux come out of his office. He asked me if anything special had happened. I replied in the negative. He then came to my office and told me he had sent his resignation to the PM in protest at the lack of real participation of French-speaking ministers in the new cabinet. I read his letter, which wouldn't look at all good in the newspapers. I admitted that I agreed with his point of view in principle. He spent half the afternoon talking to Guy Favreau, who persuaded him (almost) that [the proposed] Manpower [for Marchand] and Resources [for Jean-Luc Pepin] are important portfolios. Our departmental party was held in the evening and by then he had really changed his mind. Ellen and I took Léo and H. E. T. 'Pot' Doucet [Léo's executive assistant] and his wife to the Château for dinner. Léo was still deep in thought."[21]

The next day Defence Council met to consider my cabinet submission on unification. Sometimes, when I had run into vehement opposition, I wondered if there was some genuine military problem with unification that I was unaware of. Was there some technical flaw in the theory that hadn't been brought to my attention? On the basis that it is best to know all of the arguments both for and against before making a final decision, I convened a special meeting and invited all "two-star" (Major-General, equivalent) and above officers to attend and state their views. "This they did – some straightforward some equivocal. A first class discussion. CDS [Miller] was home ill, but all the 'three stars' are opposed except [Air Marshal Clare] Annis."[22] His position was somewhat ambiguous.

Most of the "two-stars" were supportive in varying degrees. It was sometimes difficult to determine which ones had an eye on future promotion and which were totally sincere, although in most cases I could guess. At least I found out what I wanted to know. There was no valid military objection to unification. The opposition was purely emotional. This I understood, although some of the comment was pretty silly. It was so silly, in fact, that the secretary, Ron Sutherland, prepared two sets of minutes: one unexpurgated version, of which there are only three or four copies, and another totally innocuous version that stands as the record. My own notes of the occasion show that Bill Anderson, for example, was primarily concerned about buttons and badges. Important though these are, one is scraping the bottom of the barrel to include them in a serious discussion of whether it makes more sense for land, sea, and air forces to operate as a single unified team or in relative isolation.

"Léo wasn't at the meeting and when I saw him later he was still having second thoughts about his position. He can't really chuck it and start a controversy and yet he is still rebellious. He will just ask the PM to 'table' his letter. It will be 'on file' in case things blow up later – in a few months."[23]

A few days after the meeting, Christmas was upon us. We spent a pleasant holiday at the farm near Waterford, "en famille". My sister and brother-in-law, John and Hazel Race, had moved out to go into the ginseng business, so the folks were building a new house in town, which we were obliged to inspect. When we arrived back in Ottawa on December 28, we were greeted by a mountain of Christmas cards and unopened mail. One parcel, from Keith Davey, contained a present money couldn't buy: a printout of the entire coast-to-coast Liberal membership list. An accompanying note suggested that he expected a leadership convention sooner rather than later. I can't remember if sending me the list bent any rules existing at the time, but I can say the gesture was deeply appreciated.

What I did not appreciate was an announcement on the CBC 11 o'clock news that the name of the new unified armed forces would be the Royal Canadian Marines. It was a complete fabrication, and it shocked me deeply to hear it on the news.

Wednesday, the cabinet met all day. "I think Leo was disturbed by the CBC 'Marines' story. He probably won't believe that it wasn't inspired."[24] It sounded like a leak from Defence, even though it wasn't.

CHAPTER 9

DAMN THE TORPEDOES

The year 1966 was destined to be a year of intense activity, pressure, and change for me. Before Parliament met, the Prime Minister announced that Lucien Lamoureux, MP for Stormont, would be elected Speaker, and Herman Batten, MP for Humber–St. George's, his deputy. Among the parliamentary secretaries the PM named two for himself, John Ross Matheson and Pierre Elliott Trudeau. Party appointments included Bernie Pilon as chief Liberal whip, Jim McNulty as deputy whip, and Russell Honey as chairman of caucus. In varying degrees these men would play significant roles in the second half of the Pearson "play", on which the curtain was just rising.

It was a critical year both politically and in the reorganization of the armed forces, one that would mould what was to come. Keith Davey resigned as national organizer of the Liberal Party. Just before he gave up full-time politics to return to Toronto and the world of advertising, he sent me a farewell letter which read, in part, as follows:

In my years here, few people were more helpful. Your co-operation and support was, of course, buttressed by a marked degree of personal interest in my own personal career. I will not forget this kindness.

Our relationship – both political and personal – predates my arrival here, and hopefully will last long after I have departed from Cooper Street. But while I was here you were, as one might have expected, a good friend and a valued political asset. Too often we fail to put such things in writing – so before I go, thank you.[1]

It was widely assumed that the Prime Minister would not lead the Liberal Party into another election, especially when he had come so close to resigning after failing to win a majority in 1965. This view was confirmed early in 1966 when he told at least three of his senior colleagues, Paul Martin, Mitchell Sharp, and me, that he planned to resign in 1967. If he were in my shoes, he told me, he would be speaking to a few close friends about forming the embryo of a campaign organization.

I took the PM at his word about his impending resignation and added "talent scout" to my myriad roles, as I began to build my team. At the Maritime Universities Liberal Federation, for example, I had been favourably impressed by the handsome young president, Peter Scheult. He looked like a comer, so at the closing banquet I made some effort to recruit him. Eventually he joined the Hellyer team as a member of my staff in Ottawa, but not before he had thoroughly tested my political acuity. His final question was whether I would be willing to spend some time in Florida or under a sun lamp if the convention were held in winter. Assured that I understood the importance of looking tanned and fit, Peter "signed in".

The publicity battle amongst leadership hopefuls was ongoing, so an invitation from Christina and Peter Newman to meet with Toronto *Star* publisher Beland Honderich at an "open house" seemed an opportunity too good to be missed. Several of the potential candidates would be there, and the publisher of Canada's number-one-circulation newspaper would be taking our measure for the top job. I had known "Bee" for years, but we had never been close, and I may have fantasized that a bit of charm would soften his air of detachment. Any illusion that the congenial atmosphere of the evening would translate into improved

rapport soon dissipated. Val Sears, one of the *Star*'s senior reporters, stated the position clearly through the alcoholic mist rising
from that winter's parliamentary Press Gallery dinner. "As long
as your boss sticks to defence," he warned Bill Lee in the wee
small hours, "the *Star* will support him. But if he gets any notion
of going for the top job, we'll cut him up in little pieces." Sears's
insight was prophetic.

Despite the constraints of an overcrowded schedule, my allocation of time was something less than scientific. Human and
emotional considerations were always a factor to be considered,
so when a young Paul Hellyer requested an interview as background for an essay he was writing about the cancellation of the
Avro Arrow, it was impossible to say no. I had heard of my
namesake, the son of a distant relative who worked at the National Research Council's top-secret facility, and naturally I was
curious to meet him. We agreed that he should come to my office
at National Defence Headquarters on a Saturday morning, when
activity was less hectic.

When he arrived, on February 5, the commissionaire at the
door insisted that he sign the time sheet, a routine procedure,
even for the minister, on Saturdays, Sundays, and holidays. No
sooner had he done so than the lecture began. "You are supposed
to sign your own name," the man in uniform scolded, "not that
of the person you are coming to see."

"But that is my name," Paul replied.

"No," said the commissionaire, "you must sign your own
name." Each exchange added fuel to the controversy, and the
impasse continued until the guard phoned Marg Bulger in my
office for an explanation and verification.

Paul was a pleasant young man, and after the interview I told
Ellen it would only be a matter of time before some of our mail
was mixed up. This happened within months when I got a nice
letter from the CBC thanking me for my participation in the
program "Teen Talk". In later years the name caused the younger
Paul some considerable embarrassment, but the confusion was
not all one-sided. When he bought the British Hotel in Cobourg,
Ontario, a reporter from the Toronto *Star* called and began the
conversation with "Hellyer, I always thought you were crazy,
but now I know it." It required considerable persuasion to convince my interrogator that, apart from Arundel Lodge, I was not
in the hotel business. According to reports, the younger Paul

turned the business around and made it a commercial success. When he sold it, however, he ran into some problems because of the name.

On Tuesday, February 8, 1966, I received a hand-delivered "secret" letter from the Prime Minister, authorizing "the preparation and introduction of the necessary legislation for unification."[2] This was in response to one from me dated January 27, indicating that in light of the progress we had made in integration, the time had come to take the next step and create a single unified force. This had always been implied, but I wanted his assurance that he hadn't changed his mind. He gave me his "blessing", but in a way that left no doubt that the burden would lie heavily on my shoulders. In his words:

> It is obvious that the successful achievement of the unification of the services, something which no western government has yet achieved, will require careful preparation, and wise and skilful handling. As you say it will have a more direct impact on individuals than integration. It will also arouse emotions and affect traditions, and give unfriendly critics a new opportunity to criticize. In this connection, I feel strongly, as I know you do, that traditions and past associations which have been a part of the organization of our Defence Forces should be recognized and retained to the maximum posssible extent.[3]

That weekend I took time out to present the Paul Hellyer Trophy, which I had donated to recognize the outstanding University Liberal Club in Ontario. I had a soft spot in my heart for these clubs because they were a great training ground for activists, and the one at the U. of T. had nurtured my own interest and that of some of my closest collaborators. The clubs were the spawning ground for future leaders and deserved all the encouragement they could get. My trophy was awarded in recognition of a job well done, and it is with some wistfulness that I often wonder in whose cellar or attic it is now residing.

In mid February I met with U.S. Defence Secretary Bob McNamara and decided to take advantage of my time in Washington to meet as well with the officers and men of the Canadian Joint Staff. It proved to be a gruelling experience. There was no objection to my address, which dealt with the principle of unification, but the questions were as tough as any I had ever faced. Why weren't leave regulations the same for the three services?

Why hadn't we adopted a common retirement age? Why hadn't the tradesmen's lists been integrated? One corporal had been in a transportation unit of eight men from the three services. The worst driver of the eight had been promoted because he was the senior man on the army list. Was that what they could expect from integration? If so, I could "shove it"!

The questions went on and on. They all related to personnel matters, and there were no satisfactory answers because they concerned the anomalies in the proposed system that Admiral Dyer, Chief of Personnel, and his staff were supposed to be working on. The problems weren't easy to solve, but they simply weren't being resolved, and all ranks were becoming increasingly resentful. Whether the snail's pace was due to incompetent management or a lack of will to cooperate was never clear, although I strongly suspected it was the latter. Either way, the hiatus was sabotaging support for the reorganization and exercising a negative effect on morale. Momentum had to be regained, and I returned to Ottawa more convinced than ever that we would have to press ahead if the war was not to be lost.

Early in March I flew to British Columbia to address the officers and men at the Esquimalt naval establishment and the staff and officer cadets at Royal Roads Service College, of which I was president. Needless to say, there was not universal agreement with my policy, but the questions were a snap compared to Washington, where an integrated staff could see how slow progress really was.

Later that same day I took my spiel to the B.C. Liberal Convention where I shared a bearpit session with colleagues Jack Pickersgill, Art Laing, and Jack Nicholson, before delivering the keynote address at the evening banquet. What I had to say about integration and unification was still very popular, and consequently attractive to most potential delegates to any forthcoming leadership convention. A number of Liberal stalwarts offered their support, including George Van Roggen, Larry Jolivet, and Alec Walton. My list of backers was growing slowly but surely, and many of those on the list were very influential Liberals.

Inevitably, partisans were influenced by the popular press. Most of the publicity was positive, some of it almost fulsome. In his "On Parliament Hill" column in the *Financial Post*, John Bird wrote "Hellyer, Martin, Sharp, Winters are advance bets." He ended his assessment with this paragraph:

Meanwhile Paul Hellyer appears to be favored in the betting, partly because of his combination of youth (42) and experience, partly because he appears somewhat closer to the activists than any other English-speaking aspirant.[4]

In March an article in the Toronto *Star* by Peter C. Newman was captioned "Paul Hellyer: Lack of Liabilities Is his Big Asset". In Newman's words,

> of all the pretenders to Lester Pearson's throne, none is attracting more attention inside Liberal circles at the moment than Paul Theodore Hellyer, a cabinet minister of handsome mien and reticent manner, who goes into the leadership race with some enviable assets and few tangible liabilities.[5]

It was the March issue of the *United Church Observer*, however, which roused the political wolves from their winter's slumber. A cover story asked "Will This Man Be Our Next Prime Minister?", and the editorial-page promo added:

> Before we go to the polls again, say most political observers, we'll have new leaders for the major political parties. Paul Hellyer looms as one of the contenders for the Liberal leadership. He discusses his family, his future, and his hopes for peace in this article by Kenneth Bagnell.[6]

It showed the best research of any story that has been done about me. Bagnell sought the opinions of numerous people who had known me well over the years, and his in-depth personal cross-examination was almost unique in my experience – not malicious but tough. The result was a flattering piece that would be any public-relations person's dream. When it arrived in Ottawa, Bill Lee observed from the Press Gallery that every third or fourth MP on both sides of the House was reading it. In the normal course it should have been a big plus, but in the long haul it may actually have hurt my chances, because it alerted and activated opponents and nay-sayers who sharpened their political knives accordingly. The negative comment was yet to come.

All of a sudden I was fighting a war on three fronts – with the military, the Tory Opposition, and those Liberals who considered me a threat to their own ambitions. It was widely assumed that I was number one in the leadership steeplechase, and Douglas Fisher put me at the top of his form sheet of twelve possible contenders with odds of 3 to 1.[7]

About the only reservation I had concerning the accuracy of Fisher's assessment was his conclusion that if he didn't run himself, Walter Gordon would wind up supporting me. I can only assume that Doug got the idea from Keith Davey, who thought he could influence Walter to that extent. I was never convinced because, of the two men, it was Keith rather than Walter who was more open to the power of suggestion.

On March 22, 1966, Keith, Bill Lee, and I got together for a strategy session over lunch. It was an enjoyable time, because both men are extroverts with zest for whatever they are doing or saying, and in this respect, they have a lot in common. There was little disagreement between them on the essentials for a winning campaign, but my political sonar detected a shoal below the sparkling waters. They enjoyed each other's company, and insisted they were "friends", but beneath the surface there was a significant rivalry – a critical factor which would emerge when we were choosing a campaign manager and would re-emerge almost two decades later in John Turner's 1984 election and post-election fiasco.

On the defence front, it was of some comfort to know I wasn't the only one stirring up a storm. A March 21 *Newsweek* "Inside Story" from London, under the heading "Britain's Uniformed Unity" read as follows: "Britain's next Defence Minister – Labour or Tory – will find himself in the middle of a new interservice war over unification of the army, navy, and air force. Lord Mountbatten, the former chairman of Britain's Joint Chiefs, has submitted a revolutionary new plan that would put all officers above two-star rank on the same promotion list, wearing the same uniform, and interchanging staff duties and commands."[8] I wished Mountbatten luck, but I feared he would not succeed, because I thought Denis Healey's jaundiced view would likely prevail, no matter which party was in control.

Keeping Parliament fully informed of changes as they occurred was a constant drain on my time. The defence estimates for 1966-67 were referred to the Standing Committee on Defence where I began the briefings on May 12 with a lengthy overview of departmental plans, including the reasons for unification. Other witnesses, at more than a dozen sessions in the following six weeks, included my associate minister, Léo Cadieux, the deputy minister, Elgin Armstrong, E. J. "Ben" Benson, Minister of National Revenue, speaking on the subject of government pay policy, as well as nearly all of my top officers from headquarters and the various commands. In addition, Brigadier L. E. Kenyon, Director General Intelligence, gave members an *in camera* briefing of the type that is routine for congressmen in Washington, but was unheard of in Canada except in wartime.

In a major departure from the long-standing and strict rule established by Brooke Claxton that officers might answer technical questions only, I applied no restrictions other than common sense. Officers were allowed to state their opinions on subjects as sensitive as government policy on unification. The following exchange between John Matheson, MP for Leeds, and Admiral William Landymore is illustrative:

> Mr. Matheson: Admiral, in comparing the presentation we had today with a presentation we received in the previous Parliament from the Chief of Naval Services, I tend to see an enormous emphasis on a specialty, a fighting capacity. Am I correct in thinking that within the navy, the senior service, there is, of course, some reluctance, to this tendency toward unification of service? Would you be frank with us on this matter?
>
> Rear-Adm. Landymore: Well, the answer to that is yes. I think there is a great reluctance on the part of the navy.
>
> Mr. Matheson: Is it love of tradition and love of the sea? Or does it actually go beyond that to tactics and strategy?
>
> Rear-Adm. Landymore: I do not think it enters into the operational field. I think that generally navies are very close to one another and their way of doing things and their manner of presenting themselves and in their identity. If there is reluctance, and there is, it is due to that factor more than any other.[9]

This kind of freedom of expression of opinion in respect of government policy was unheard of in our parliamentary system, but I gave the officers their heads because I thought a lot more openness was both possible and desirable, especially for a country next door to the United States, where there are few areas the military are unwilling to discuss. Extending this freedom of speech to the unification debate involved considerable risk, but I thought the public might as well hear, as I had repeatedly heard, that opposition was primarily centred on loss of tradition and didn't extend to operational effectiveness. In fact, the opinion expressed by Landymore at that time created few ripples, and on June 29, despite some kicking and screaming by Tory MP Marcel Lambert, the committee forwarded its report on defence estimates to the House without fanfare.

On May 18, U.S. Secretary of Defence, Robert McNamara, was speaking in Montreal. I had accepted an invitation to join him and sit at the head table. After the luncheon, I was at first incredulous but then stunned by news that a bomb had gone off in the House of Commons. Early reports were sketchy and raised more questions than they answered, but it wasn't long before confirmation came that, alas, a bomb had detonated. The good news was that it had gone off in the third-floor washroom, and the only person killed was the would-be bomber, Paul Chartier, a forty-five-year-old Torontonian. The course of history often turns on a delicate thread, and for several days cabinet colleagues speculated as to whom the intended target or targets might have been – and why – and if the bomb had exploded in the House how many would have died in the carnage. Thankfully the questions were, by then, hypothetical, and not subject to definitive reply.

The end of the month marked a milestone in the Hellyer family: my parents' fiftieth wedding anniversary. It was a grand occasion, because they were still in good health and were happy to see the hundreds of friends, relatives, and neighbours who attended the afternoon reception. My sister Hazel and I enjoyed a bit of reflected glory from our parents' popularity in the community, but there was one aspect of greeting the never-ending stream of well-wishers that wasn't easy. There were literally dozens of ex-schoolmates and ex-playmates present that I hadn't seen for more than twenty years. Many expected me to call them by name.

This is one of the most frustrating aspects of public life, at least for me. During the course of my career I have been introduced to more than half a million people, and although I can recall a few thousand of them, especially if the context is right and I am not taken by surprise, the rest have become a blur. So when someone comes up to me and says "You don't remember me, do you?" or "You can't remember my name, can you?" I tend to freeze – because it's true. Unquestionably this contributes to my image of detachment and coolness.

An early experience may have added to this problem. Towards the beginning of my career, I was standing in a receiving line, greeting about a thousand guests at a big dinner, when a man shook hands, smiled, and said, "Mr. Hellyer, do you remember me?" His face looked familiar, so I conveyed the impresson that I did. "You're a damn liar," he responded. "You've never seen me before in your life." I was crushed! I do my best not to tell lies, but I do make mistakes, and ever since, when the same or a similar question is posed, I wonder if it is another wise guy trying to trip me up.

Robert McNamara had a wonderful technique, which I sometimes copy. When he arrived at a NATO meeting after an interval of a few months, he would always greet me with "Hello Paul, Bob McNamara." It's a terrific way of putting someone at ease so they can reply instantly "Of course, Bob. How are you?" In McNamara's case I certainly didn't need reminding, but it's a nice gesture and, with me, is likely to make the difference between a blank stare and a genuinely warm and friendly greeting.

So despite the excitement of a great celebration with the senior Hellyers, it was almost a relief to get back to the battlefront where, on the surface at least, everything seemed to be under control. Beneath the surface, however, trouble was brewing. In Halifax Admiral Landymore was holding private meetings with his officers and urging them to join him in all-out opposition to the government plan. This news came initially from naval sources, for although the majority of the officers in his command were thoroughly in support of the admiral's position, there were some who were not. They thought it was highly irregular, and foreign to everything they had been taught, for a serving officer to be openly defiant of government policy.

I was told that secret meetings had begun months earlier after Admiral Landymore had attended the Commanders Conference in Ottawa and heard me say that I was fully committed to the concept of a single unified force. To his credit, and unlike some of the others, he took me seriously and worked out a strategy not unlike a political campaign. He made frequent visits "below deck" to ingratiate himself with the sailors. He volunteered to act as their agent in redressing grievances. He would be their champion. His approach to the officers was less subtle. He was offering, in effect, an open invitation to join him in a crusade against the policy laid down by Ottawa. At first I was somewhat incredulous, but after double-checking I found the account was authentic. Furthermore, the incipient revolt was well advanced and had to be stopped at once. There was no alternative but to fire Landymore. On July 12 he came to my office. He didn't seem to be too surprised when he heard the verdict; I think he may have been expecting it.

I had also come to the reluctant conclusion that Frank Miller would have to go. He was still adamantly opposed to unification, and although it was impossible to prove the allegations running through my mind, I had to face the fact that progress in some areas was intolerably slow. Inertia on the personnel front had been one common denominator in the complaints that arose during the free-for-all at the Joint Staff meeting in Washington in February. Then on our return, Bill Lee let me know in one of his succinct "Leegrams" that the dry rot was affecting other parts of the ship as well. "MND. We have a serious internal problem on the planning side. Key people, whom you know & who are with us, are absolutely disgusted and frustrated (Sample: 'Hell, it's harder to get a plan approved under integration than it was before!') Like to discuss."[10] When we did talk we were of one mind. The senior staff were stalling! No one ever said "no", because that isn't the way of bureaucracy. They just sat on their hands. The object of the exercise was obvious. If they outlasted me, the game was over. The whole project would collapse. Either I had to beat them to the punch, or capitulate.

The political risk was great and might prove disastrous. Rocking the boat so violently would create waves of unpredictable power and intensity. The waters were uncharted and the inevitable shoals would be difficult to anticipate. Yet turning back would have been a denial of everything I believed in, so I decided, in the words of Franklin D. Roosevelt, to "Damn the torpedoes; full speed ahead."

Fortunately, Miller was past retirement age, which helped. Also I had a report from the Surgeon General expressing some concern about Frank's health. While it was in no way alarming, there were indications of tension-related problems that might recur under conditions of prolonged and unusual stress.[11] It seemed to me that the risk would increase as the tension continued to mount, and I was concerned because, despite our differences, I was not without feeling for Frank as a person. It was more than respect for a truly outstanding officer; I had always liked him and still did. So when I broke the news that I wanted him to retire because I was concerned about his health, it was the truth – though not the whole truth. He was reluctant to agree, because he could read me as well as I could read him; but the resistance was short-lived and instead he took another tack.

I didn't ask him for a recommendation on the succession, but I got one anyway – Lt.-Gen. Robert Moncel. A handsome, debonair, and bilingual officer, Bob had an excellent war record and was a good administrator. Nevertheless, he was something of an enigma. He wore a lace handkerchief tucked up his sleeve – which must have been unique in the Canadian army – and his logic was a bit inconsistent. He spent several hours trying to persuade me that we should have only one Regiment of Canadian Infantry, with numbered battalions. That would have meant abolishing the Queen's Own Rifles, the Royal 22nd [Van Doos], and all the other famous Canadian regiments. The proposal was so revolutionary that it took me a while to be sure that he wasn't joking. What I couldn't understand was why he would tamper with one of the most sacred of Canadian traditions, to no apparent purpose other than administrative convenience, and at the same time be adamantly opposed to unification, which had ten times more to justify it both administratively and, most important of all, operationally. Nevertheless, he was stubbornly opposed, and whereas I had managed to outlast Frank, the reverse would be true with a younger, fresher antagonist who could scuttle the plan by simply stonewalling until I was gone.

Clearly the Chief of Defence Staff job was the key move on which the war would be won or lost, and Frank and I both knew it. Consequently, he was not pleased when I told him that Moncel's appointment wouldn't wash, and that I was looking elsewhere. My candidate was Jean Allard. He, too, was a very handsome man with a first-class war record. Fluently bilingual, Jean was an ebullient leader of men, an optimist who radiated enthusiasm. His earlier promotion to Lt.-Gen. had put him on the fast track, although there was no thought at the time that he would be in the running for the number-one position so soon. Before deciding, we had a chat about his views. He was quite enthusiastic about the appointment, subject to two conditions: that the unified force would not be named the Royal Canadian Marines, and that we would provide better opportunities for French-speaking Canadians. It wasn't clear whether his objection about the name was to the word "Royal", though I doubted that because it also belonged to his regiment, the Royal 22nd, of which he was so proud. It could have been that "Marine" has different meanings in French and English. In any event that name was not in the cards, so I had no difficulty in giving my assurances. As soon as he had reflected long enough to prove that he wasn't too eager, the deal was struck. On June 21, cabinet approved my recommendation that J. V. Allard become Chief of Defence Staff to replace Air Chief Marshal F. R. Miller, with the rank of General, effective July 15, 1966.

Prior to Frank's departure he was afforded the usual dinner for retiring officers. It was planned as a really grand affair, with the Governor General and everyone who was anyone in the military world in attendance. All appeared to be sweetness and light. Everyone said nice things about everybody; but beneath the surface there was an undercurrent of bitterness, and heaven knows what people were saying when I was out of earshot. I, of course, imagined the worst. Frank's banquet was just one of the first of what Ellen dubbed the "Dear John" dinners, which she grew to hate. There was no escape from the phoniness, pretense, and hypocrisy, both for the officers and wives who were being honoured or for some of us who were joining in the tribute. We were all trapped by the system.

This was one of the saddest aspects of the whole reorganization process. Officers who had served their country well deserved fitting tributes. Yet the unusual circumstances surrounding the events detracted immeasurably from what in other days would have been joyful occasions. At Frank's dinner I was even requested (drafted) to sing a song by way of a toast, as follows:

PAUL T.'S SONG
(Tune "Bless Them All")

Air Chief Marshal Miller is leaving tonight
For pastures more sunny and green.
In the rarified air of old Cartier Square
His figure no more will be seen.
He's faithfully satisfied all the demands
Of each Ministerial whim –
He's been so sincere that I'm now in the clear –
You can blame all your troubles on him!

Here's to Frank! Here's to Frank!
A man of the very first rank!
Here's to his courage and loyal support

Without which my Ministry might have been short.
He's the man that you all ought to thank,
When he goes you'll all move up a rank.
Let's knock back a beer to a man without peer
And join in a toast – here's to Frank!

I wondered at the appropriateness of my singing some of the words that were put in my mouth, and Frank must have done the same. It was his night, however, and there was no unpleasantness; any reservations were withheld for anti-unification battles to come.

Allard's appointment was generally popular, but not with Frank Miller and the senior officers at headquarters. Frank was really upset because he and Allard were about as opposite in temperament as two men could possibly be. One was cool and detached, and the other effervescent, wearing his heart on his sleeve. Jean wouldn't even have been included on Frank's short list. The antipathy at the top was no surprise, but I really hoped that Vice-Admiral Ken Dyer, and Lieutenant-Generals Bob Moncel and Frank Fleury would accept Allard's leadership and the posts I offered them. In each case we reached tentative agreement, and I went home thinking all the incipient fires had been put out. When I got back to the office the next morning, however, I was to see my hopes engulfed in flames. The three remaining top men had decided, overnight, to resign en masse. Frank Miller denied that he had struck the match, but I was never totally convinced. It appeared to me like a calculated attempt to embarrass me in the eyes of my government colleagues and the public alike.

Getting a crisis of that magnitude under control is not easy. I moved Air Marshal F. R. Sharp from Training Command in Winnipeg to become Vice-Chief of Defence Staff. Freddie had his MBA from the University of Western Ontario and personified the brightest and best of a new generation of airmen. He was committed to unification and was an early graduate of the "let's-get-on-with-it" school. The other airman picked for top staff, as Chief of Personnel, was Ed Reyno, a war hero with a warm heart and a winning way. Some of his colleagues accused Ed of opportunism in his enthusiasm for unification, but I never doubted his acceptance of the concept. His loyalty was broad enough to include me, the air force, and Canada. George Lilley, a solid, efficient, and conscientious army officer with a pleasant personality was named as Fleury's replacement in Materiel Command, with the rank of lieutenant-general. The only major problem in rounding out a winning team was in finding someone suitable from the navy – someone both competent and amenable – now that Admiral Dyer had gone.

Some preliminary discussions convinced me that the appointee had to be a line officer rather than someone from the technical side, and this eliminated the only rear-admirals who were "on side" in this war of attrition. The senior sea dogs were all part of the opposition, and promoting any one of them would have been just another Band-Aid solution at best. I began to think the unthinkable. The only ray of hope was a tall, good-looking officer with a commanding presence, R. L. "Spike" Hennessey. He had done a splendid job on a "Minister's Manpower Study – Men", analysing which trades were common to the three services and which were not. But, and it was a very big but, he was only a commodore and I needed a vice-admiral. To even think of promoting someone by two ranks was heresy – especially in the navy, where seniority and God were afforded virtually equal reverence. I had a long chat with Hennessey, who wanted clarification of some technical items concerning unification that were not well understood. Reassured by the response to his questions, he agreed to take the job of Comptroller General and to row in the same direction as the rest of the crew.

As I had anticipated, the announcement of Hennessey's double-jump created a sea state ten in the upper echelons of the navy. Rear-admirals who had been passed over were outraged, and it wasn't long before they abandoned ship. The press dubbed it "mutiny" as six rear-admirals walked the plank, with a golden handshake on one side and some vaguely rude salutes on the other. Despite the unquestioned loss of expertise that this represented, their departure was probably the best thing that could have happened to the navy. The old clique of admirals, all about the same age and graduates of the same school, had gone. The logjam had been broken, and the channel was cleared for some upward mobility by a new and less stereotyped generation. The desirability of a major shake-up was reinforced by the conclusions of Henry L. Stimson, Secretary of the Navy in the United States. His experience was reported as follows:

Some of the Army-Navy troubles, in Stimson's view, grew mainly from the peculiar psychology of the Navy Department, which frequently seems to retire from the realm of logic into a dim religious world in which Neptune was God, Mahan his prophet, and the United States Navy was the only true Church. The high priests of this Church were a group of men to whom Stimson always referred as "the admirals". These gentlemen were to him both anonymous and continuous; he had met them in 1930 in discussions of the London Naval Treaty; in 1940 and afterwards he found them still active and still uncontrolled by either their Secretary or the President. This was not Knox's fault, or the President's, as Stimson saw it. It was simply that the Navy Department had never had its Elihu Root. "The admirals" had never been given their comeuppance.[12]

It's little wonder, then, that someone once said that navies are like feather pillows; you can punch them or squeeze them, but eventually they return to their original shape.

I had survived the admirals' "mutiny" and was still at the helm when Landymore fired his now-famous "torpedo", in which he criticized the government's plan to unify the armed forces, the day before Allard's appointment as CDS became effective. That afternoon I was in London, Ontario, attending a Middlesex East barbeque at the invitation of James Lind, MP. It was a happy occasion, at which person after person stopped me on the street to shake hands and tell me what a great job I was doing. I even took a few minutes off to visit the hospital, where Liberal stalwart Ann Harding was cuddling her new baby daughter. The whole afternoon was a good experience and I was in high good spirits when we took off for Edmonton, where I was to address the RCAF Association annual banquet.

We were barely off the ground, when I was given the news of Landymore's outburst. My mood changed as dramatically as the weather when a black cloud blots out the sun. It didn't help that I was trying to concentrate on what I was going to say to the retired airmen – and couldn't. Instead, with Bill Lee's help and quick-witted draftsmanship, I prepared a blistering rebuttal to the admiral's charges. The issue, I insisted, was civilian control of the military. Integration was the policy of the Government of Canada, and it was the responsibility of serving officers to implement rather than oppose it.

Later, I took Edmonton Liberals into my confidence at a private meeting. It was my understanding that the press was excluded. There was one journalist present, but I was assured he was there as a Liberal and not as a reporter. However, the temptation of an exclusive story was too great, and after the meeting broke up he filed a story that produced headlines like "Integration or I Quit Warns Hellyer" and "Hellyer Stakes His Job Against Ousted Admiral". These were based on a quip I had made that I would resign if I didn't receive the full support of my cabinet colleagues. It was intended as a broad-grinned private joke. I was certainly not serious, because at that time I had solid backing from the other members of the government. A clarification – which is always embarrassing – was necessary, and was released to the press.

Some of his other points were more relevant:

> Questioned on the resignations or firings of four rear admirals, Mr. Hellyer said he had no intention of letting anyone "even if he is an admiral" tell the Government how to run the armed forces. And he revealed that not only admirals are raising storms. Some top officers of the air force and army are also bucking integration. . . .
>
> "I don't pretend that support for my integration policy has been unanimous. I never expected that it would be." [13]

The overnight ride back from Edmonton provided intermittent restless sleep, but slowly, as the lights of Ottawa first penetrated the darkness, the reality of the depth of the crisis began to sink in. Until then I had been flexible about Landymore's time of leaving, but once he had spoken out publicly, there was no alternative but to relieve him of his command – at once. That much was easy. The problem was finding a suitable successor.

Earlier in the month Bill had sent me a Leegram on the subject, recommending Admiral Welland for the job. Other advisers had reservations about the appointment, and besides, Welland was miffed about Hennessey's promotion and had already decided to walk the plank. I was told that Landymore's senior officer afloat, Commodore J. C. "Scruffy" O'Brien was the only one who could get the situation under control. Time was of the essence, because each day of delay was drawing more blood; so I called O'Brien, the man of the hour, and asked to see him in my office on

Monday, July 18. Later I recorded the events of the next few days in my diary.

"Today is absolutely critical. If O'Brien will take the command we should get everything under control soon – if not we may be in real trouble.

"I saw Ralph Gordon [the senior RCAF officer at Halifax] first. He confirmed that Landymore had been impossible. All the secret meetings were held when he was 'ashore'. . . .

"O'Brien was very nervous. I told him the reasons for unification and he was most attentive. He said there were certain points he would like clarified. It sounded like bargaining, but when I heard the substance there were no requests that were not in accordance with policy and I could agree in clear conscience. Hennessey and O'Brien to put them on paper."[14]

On Tuesday, July 19, "I saw Hennessey and O'Brien again at 9:30. They showed me the prepared statement. It contained absolutely nothing new and was completely acceptable. O'Brien agreed to take Maritime Command and to go back to Halifax tonight.

"I called a press conference for 4:00 p.m. in room 308, West Block. What an experience. More than sixty newsmen with TV cameras, a battery of microphones, etc. Notwithstanding the formidable atmosphere I managed to handle the conference reasonably well and then recorded a brief statement in French and a special 10 minute film for CBC 'Newsmagazine'.

"O'Brien should be back in Halifax tonight and I really feel the worst is over. Nevertheless one must keep one's guard up, because this is a well-organized campaign."[15]

Wednesday, July 20, "The reaction to yesterday's press conference was excellent. Bill gave me the highest marks and Elgin Armstrong described it as masterful.

"I saw Rear-Admiral Landymore with CDS. I asked him why he did it, and he replied that he had not started it. He was phoned by Canadian Press at 2:00 a.m. – but spoke out after talking to Admiral Pullen. Old admirals never die – they don't even fade away. Landymore denied calling Commander Harry McClymont. He also denied having the opportunity to retire with the 'golden handshake'. Someone has a faulty memory. I guess we should keep tape recordings. From what he said about O'Brien's statement it appeared that he would make more trouble by pretending that O'Brien got all he wanted and that, with the same 'concessions' (which were not concessions at all), he would have been content. I do not believe him!''[16]

I raised the subject at cabinet later that morning and expressed concern about public statements by Landymore and other senior officials. It appeared that for some time Landymore had been acting and speaking in a way that was undermining confidence in the integration program. I thought there was good public support for the government's program, except in Halifax, and said I didn't expect much more flak until Parliament resumed in October. As the cabinet minutes recorded: "Several Ministers confirmed that there was widespread support across the country for the government's action and congratulated the minister on his handling of the matter."[17]

The headlines that day were positive. "Hellyer Says Integration To Proceed Full Speed" began the *Globe and Mail*'s lead story.[18] The Ottawa *Citizen* led with " 'Full Speed Ahead', Hellyer Order after Admirals' Revolt". Greg Connolley's report continued:

> Defence Minister Hellyer has fired Rear-Admiral Landymore. He named Commodore J. C. O'Brien, 47, to be chief of the maritime command and Atlantic Fleet commander. Mr. Hellyer was content to fire Admiral Landymore forthwith, although he might have taken sterner disciplinary action. "In view of his long and distinguished service, I have decided simply to retire him without penalty." The defence minister insisted that Admiral Landymore, 50, contravened regulations "by publicly opposing government policy while in uniform. It is regrettable in that he set an unfortunate example for junior officers and other ranks." Mr. Hellyer added that in simply dismissing Admiral Landymore he still felt the latter's conduct was a "matter for regret".[19]

I had guessed correctly concerning Landymore's intentions, however, and he did a good job in persuading the press that concessions had been made to O'Brien. He said that, following interviews with me and the Chief of Defence Staff, Gen. J. V. Allard, he was convinced that unification wouldn't be forced upon Canadian servicemen. "To this extent what has happened has been worthwhile," he said.[20] This was enough to convince the press that we had wavered.

On Thursday, I recorded: "Things are quietening down a bit. Bill and Robbie [Robinson] are still having trouble with the press over the alleged 'back down' but they are making progress. Bill is hoarse from talking so much.

"Lunch with Bill MacDonald [Toronto Liberal lawyer]. He had a long chat with Tom Kent and guess who is his favourite candidate? I find it hard to believe but very encouraging because he may influence Marchand. He also related a conversation between Clark Davey (or George Bain) with Andy Thompson in which Andy said: 1) Walter Gordon would run for the leadership. 2) He (WLG) knew he couldn't win. 3) He would throw his influence behind the man of his choice. 4) It wouldn't be PTH. I still think Keith is too optimistic and that WLG cannot be delivered."[21]

One of the rare occasions when an issue came along that I considered of greater consequence than the reorganization of the armed forces had arisen in June when we were considering a settlement for Seaway workers. They had been demanding parity with U.S. workers, and a strike seemed imminent, so the government appointed Senator Norman Mackenzie, former president of the University of British Columbia, as a commissioner to mediate the dispute. At cabinet on June 14 the Minister of Labour, Jack Nicholson, gave this report:

> The mediator was convinced that substantial wage increases would have to be granted. The demands of the union had been reinforced by substantial increases gained by construction workers in Montreal, but although much had been made of the disparity in wages between Canadian and American Seaway workers, it was not likely that the settlement would have to grant parity.[22]

In the discussion Mitchell Sharp and I pointed out that wage increases from the current dispute would influence future civil-service and armed-forces salary levels.

Thursday morning, June 16, Nicholson reported that an Air Canada dispute appeared to be settled and that Seaway negotiations were proceeding in a good atmosphere and might be settled that day. If not, the government intended to go ahead with legislation. That night cabinet met again to consider Senator Mackenzie's recommendations, based on a settlement of thirty percent over two years. The Senator had made it clear that in his view this was the only solution that would avert a strike. Jack

Pickersgill pointed out that Mackenzie had exceeded his instructions (a twenty-five-percent limit), but he had agreed to recommend thirty percent, and this was known to the union. In his view there was no alternative but for the government to accept the report of its own mediator.[23]

Most of the ministers were incensed at having a gun put to their heads, although there is little in the cabinet minutes to indicate either the depth of the opposition or the widespread recognition of the disastrous precedent that was being set. I was the most outspoken, and the watered-down guts of my intervention was recorded as follows:

> The Minister of National Defence expressed great concern that action by the government along the lines proposed by Senator Mackenzie would have a serious effect on the price structure in Canada, particularly in a situation where Canadian productivity was not rising very quickly. The result could be a further loss of competitiveness and an eventual devaluation. The inflationary trend also imposed serious burdens on pensioners and fixed income employees.[24]

The words were prophetic, but to no avail. They fell on a deaf ear. Even though he admitted that it was an awkward and unfortunate position, and vowed that it wouldn't happen again, the Prime Minister refused to give the long view priority over a solution to an immediate crisis. He polled ministers, who were almost universally and adamantly opposed, and then settled the matter with a simple, unilateral dictum, "We can't let dear old Larry [Mackenzie] down." With this he confirmed my thesis that Canadian governments are run by "consensus", where consensus is defined as "one or more ministers of whom the Prime Minister is one."

In my opinion it ranked as one of the worst decisions made by any Canadian government in recent memory. The seeds of inflation and economic chaos were sown, and would produce their bitter harvest in decades to come.

CHAPTER 10

THE LANDYMORE AFFAIR

T he summer of 1966 marked the beginning of a dramatic change in the public perception of the unification battle. Until then the opposition, though intense, was nearly all passive and internal within the department. There was little public dissent, and this presented an image of a relatively smooth transition from the old to the new. With the retirement of Frank Miller, Robert Moncel, Ken Dyer, and Frank Fleury, plus the subsequent outburst by Rear-Admiral Landymore, the whole scene changed. Opposition MPs, taking their cue from retired officers, became increasingly harsh, even though internally the situation was finally under control and the men in charge of the forces were both willing and anxious to implement the government's policy in a workmanlike manner.

When the Defence Council met on August 2, 1966, with the new cast of General Jean V. Allard as Chief of Defence Staff; Air Marshal Fred Sharp as VCDS; Vice-Admiral Ralph Hennessey, Comptroller General; Air Marshal Ed Reyno, Chief of Personnel;

and Chief of Technical Services, Lt. Gen. George Lilley, who had been faithful throughout, the atmosphere was like the advent of spring after a long and difficult winter. The subject being considered was amendments to the National Defence Act, or as the bill was commonly called, the Unification Bill. Indeed the change of atmosphere in my diary: "What a contrast with the 'old' Defence Council. All the discussion was 'pro'. Only the details were considered at length. I gave special opportunity for objections to be raised, but there were none. The Council was unanimous.

"What a pleasant surprise to have everyone working together toward the same goals. Now, instead of standing on the Hill alone, with Bill, we have some troops behind us. It should make quite a difference in the months ahead. The decision [unification] will now be referred to Cabinet Defence Committee. Details in respect of lists, uniform, rank designation, etc., are referred to Defence Staff for consideration and advice."[1]

Being outflanked in the propaganda war was the inevitable price of the major upheaval required for victory within the department. Warned by headlines like "Stormy Session Ahead for Hellyer" on a *Dartmouth Free Press* article written by Bob McCleave, MP,[2] I opted to take a long weekend in Muskoka before the storm broke.

August 9: "Cabinet Defence Committee met at 10:00 a.m. The first item was a brief résumé of the integrated defence plan. Elgin Armstrong gave the brief. It showed conclusively that with the present rate of inflation it is impossible to keep within the defence ceiling (2% escalation) and at the same time maintain the agreed force structure. . . . I then presented the case for unification. To diminish the loyalty to, and identification with, a single environment. The practical application being related to representation, establishment, seniority and *objectivity*. The policy was approved and referred to the cabinet for approval. Good!"[3]

The following morning: "Cabinet considered the report of the Cabinet Defence Committee recommending changes to the National Defence Act. I am not sure what the decision – if any – was. The PM was as usual. However it was agreed that the legislation be prepared and that I give the presentation on unification at the appropriate time."[4] That may have been what led Frank Miller to tell a Commons committee, months later, that the unification bill was never approved by cabinet. His source may have been one of my cabinet colleagues who left the meeting as confused as I was. What cabinet decided, according to the minutes, which is the only record that counts in the circumstance, is that the proposed amendments to the National Defence Act, recommended by the Cabinet Defence Committee, were approved in principle, on the understanding that the detailed legislation be fully examined by the Cabinet Committee on Legislation and by the cabinet before introduction in the House of Commons.[5] These conditions were subsequently met, and that ended any doubt, except in Frank Miller's mind, that the legislation had full cabinet approval.

On Thursday, August 11, I saw the new uniform for the first time. It had been prepared without any direction from me, by Air Commodore Garnet Jacobsen, who worked in the Personnel Department under Air Marshal Reyno, and his group. That morning he came to my office with navy, army, and air force "models", replete in the greens. My initial assessment was quite objective. One of the strong points of the new uniform was comfort. This was not an accident. The RCAF had been interested in a new uniform for some time – one without a belt and buckle – and had pretty well settled on a modified version of the latest United States Air Force uniform. Jacobsen took that basic design and substituted green for blue, because the three services couldn't agree on any one of the traditional colours. The result was a great improvement in design and quality over the bell-bottoms and the cheap rough serge cloth worn by private soldiers and airmen, who had long been treated as second-class citizens in a country that claimed to be democratic. The new uniform was also roughly on a par with the existing army and air force officers' uniforms. But it wasn't as classy as the existing naval officers' uniform, and the more I thought about it the more it bothered me. I almost asked Jacobsen to go back to the drawing board and start again, but I was seduced by the memory of the initial impact and the obvious pride of the models in being first to be outfitted. I didn't have the heart to order a change. Hindsight indicates that I should have followed my instinct and insisted on something more glamorous.

The need for a common walking-out uniform was real. It was not, as critics suggest, just a ministerial whim. Once the medical, dental, legal, pay, supply, intelligence, and other common functions were fully integrated, more than fifty percent of total personnel no longer belonged exclusively to navy, army, or air force.

So which uniform would they wear? One solution was a fourth uniform of their own. This "pink uniform" option was soundly rejected by the integrated support services themselves. They didn't want to be visibly separate from the fighting arms. The "medicos", for example, pointed out that in wartime the need to treat wounded soldiers at the battlefront would often expose them to more danger than some of the generals at headquarters, and they didn't want to be dressed differently. It boiled down to a choice between four uniforms and one, and we opted for the common-sense solution and chose one.

As I indicated in my presentation on the issue to the Cabinet Defence Committee, there were important psychological reasons for a common uniform, and these were every bit as compelling as the case for three separate uniforms. There were also logistic considerations that couldn't be ignored. In many cases it is quite impractical to stock a range of sizes in three or four different colours. The prospect was horrendous. This lesson had been drummed into me by an early specific case. A female navy lab technician was posted to the RCAF hospital at Cold Lake, Alberta; because she wore navy blue in a light blue environment, her "pay and pantyhose" had to be driven each week from the nearest naval reserve station, at Calgary – at taxpayers' expense. It was a great waste of time and money. Still it was the kind of anomaly inherent in the separate-system plan.

Even though practical experience of this sort confirmed my belief that I was on the right track, the opposition continued to grow. On Friday, August 12: "Terry Robertson [CBC] reported that [Bob] Hilborne, [George] Penfold and [Bruce] Legge were 'involved' in Toronto. Also A/M [Wilfred A.] Curtis says that Bill and I are the Hitler and Goebels of Canada."[6] Another man who was very much "involved" in the Toronto group that I was referring to was Robert Hendy, a Commodore in the RCN Reserve. Hendy became a leading spokesman for retired naval officers, and along with Hilborne for the army and Penfold for the air force, helped found the Tri-Service Identities Organization, commonly referred to as TRIO, which became extremely vocal in its opposition to unification and active in organizing retired officers in opposition to it.

In an interview the following week, reported in the Ottawa *Journal* under the heading "Ex-officers May Get Chance To

Sound Off", I said I hoped that unification legislation would be presented to Parliament in the fall, and that it would almost certainly be sent to the Defence Committee for study. That would provide the air marshals and admirals who were opposed to unification with an opportunity to be heard. The assurance was received with some scepticism by Marcel Lambert, Tory MP for Edmonton West, who was vice-chairman of the committee. In the same story he warned "there will not be the same spirit of inter-party co-operation within the defence committee after the Liberals' fast foot-work and railroad job of June 29."[7]

The Tory pressure was building! On August 20 the Saint John *Telegraph-Journal* carried a story captioned "Harkness Urges Halt to Unification Move". The second paragraph began:

> In a letter to Mr. Pearson dated August 11 and released Friday, Mr. Harkness said he has information that Canadian Forces Headquarters recently sent a message to all commands outlining the introduction of a unified trade structure for the three services.
>
> He said he understands this would be implemented when treasury board approves accompanying pay raises, presumably to take effect October 1, the day called for in the cyclical pay review.
>
> Mr. Harkness said it would be a "complete disregard of Parliament" to put the unified trade structure into effect before Parliament approves.[8]

Harkness told the PM he was writing to him personally because he didn't know if he was aware of the proposed action. This intervention was at least enough to trigger a memorandum to me from the Prime Minister, which read as follows:

> I wish to be kept informed of the progress made in regard to "unification"; the plans that you have for proceeding in the weeks ahead, including Parliamentary discussions and consideration of these matters by the House Committee on Defence.
>
> We must be careful not to get into a position where we agree to – as we must – Committee discussion and then have to tell its members that decisions have already been taken finally on the matters that are being discussed.[9]

Doug Harkness's concern, fed by some mole in the bowels of the Defence Department, reflected a common misunderstanding of the difference between integration and unification. Rationalizing the trade structure was part of the "integration" process that he and others had been applauding. It would help resolve some of the anomalies that personnel at the Joint Staff meeting at Washington had found so irritating. As Bill Lee told the press in response to Harkness's letter, "integration of the armed forces trades would come about whether or not there was unification. . . . The main purpose was to equalize pay and rank levels for similar work."[10] No one seemed to understand that unification was simply merging navy, army, and air force under one corporate umbrella, like Cadillac, Buick, and GM Trucks.

My response to all the fuss was to repeat my undertaking that "there would be no common rank or uniform adopted by the forces until after Parliament approves unification legislation."[11] This was the assurance that a number of high-ranking officers, including Admiral O'Brien, had asked for. For me it was a moral requirement rather than a legal one. The National Defence Act already gave the minister power to dress all three services in pink or purple uniforms. The restraints were not in the law, but were the more compelling ones of common sense and tradition. So many people had come to think of the word "unification" as simply a synonym for "one uniform" that it would have been morally unacceptable to proceed before Parliament had another say.

Landymore's mid-summer outburst had opened the Pandora's Box of opposition. Retired officers of all stripes emerged with a verbal barrage. On September 1 the "Toronto group" brought out the big guns. As the *Globe and Mail* reported:

> LGen Guy G. Simonds and MGen Christopher Vokes joined the public debate over army, navy and air force unification in a joint letter mailed to about 75 persons across Canada. The generals maintain that present government policy ignores the possibility that Canada may one day be forced to mobilize the maximum military capacity to fight a major war. They argue that Mr. Hellyer's plans are aimed only toward the country's peacetime obligations.[12]

I found the criticism a bit insulting, because it was obviously a product of the rumour mill. It certainly didn't reflect the kind of analysis one expects from men who have achieved general rank. A unified recruiting system would be able to move more quickly and allocate manpower much more efficiently in the event of a major mobilization than the fractured and rigid system we suffered under in World War II. As for their suggestion that we were concentrating on peacekeeping forces, the generals must have failed to note that we had been buying armoured personnel-carriers, mechanized howitzers, helicopter destroyers, and other major items of equipment, which would not be required if peacekeeping was all we had in mind.

The most ridiculous proposition came from Gen. Vokes. "You can't have a sailor one day and a soldier the next," he said.[13] The notion was so absurd that I mentally dismissed the views of anyone silly enough to suggest it. There was no more thought of turning sailors into instant soldiers than of making cooks into pilots or doctors into dentists. I knew Simonds's and Vokes's reputations for brilliance in wartime, and I respected them for it. Some of their peacetime exploits, however, underlined their human fallibility. Simonds had insisted that the Canadian Brigade Group in Europe be attached to the British supply line rather than the American. This decision, deeply rooted in nostalgia, imposed considerable hardship on Canadian troops and caused no end of trouble. Chris Vokes, on the other hand, had long been accused of moving the Canadian Army's Central Command headquarters from Toronto to Oakville for no apparent reason. More land was available, but there was no stated military requirement. So the bottom line was that the generals' opinions had to be subjected to the same critical evaluation afforded all others.

Help came in the form of a major speech in favour of unification by General Jean Allard, the new Chief of Defence Staff. Alas, and quite predictably, this drew the Opposition's ire and led to headlines like "Allard Branded Propagandist for Unification" and "MPs Question Allard's Role."[14] Questions in the House concerning which serving officers could express opinions in public and under what circumstances created a Donnybrook and was inconclusive. In a way it was a pleasant change to have the CDS publicly in support, but the obverse of the coin was the necessity of expending considerable time and emotional energy in his defence. "The Chief of Defence Staff made a speech on his own responsibility, and he has the prerogative under the standing orders to do that," I explained.[15] The Opposition was unimpressed.

The *Victoria Daily Times* of September 8 ran a four-column article entitled "Opposition Accuses Hellyer of Contmpt". It continued,

The Conservatives mounted their second furious Commons attack in two days on Defence Minister Hellyer Wednesday. They accused him of contempt of Parliament for going ahead with unification of the armed forces before putting any unification legislation before the Commons.[16]

The Opposition still didn't understand, or for political purposes pretended not to understand, the difference between unification and the integration they had enthusiastically endorsed for more than two years.

The same article in the *Victoria Daily Times* reported that Speaker Lucien Lamoureux had ruled out-of-order a motion by Michael Forrestall, MP (Halifax), charging that I had made textual changes in the statement that Rear-Admiral William Landymore had presented to the Commons Defence Committee at the outset of his testimony in June. This accusation had first come up when I was in Paris for the NATO meeting, but I had dismissed it out of hand because, as far as I could remember, any suggestions from me had been too insignificant to be taken seriously.

As the battle lines were drawn, it became clear that, apart from partisan politics, itself a blood sport, opposition to unification was primarily a function of age, rank, and the military mind. This is not surprising, because most of us become more set in our ways as we get older. There was a special category that included majors who had not been promoted to lieutenant-colonel and who attributed this bad luck to integration rather than to their own relative abilities. Other opponents included any of those high enough up the ladder to perceive themselves as ultimate heads of their services. Their vehemence was understandably severe. After fantasizing about the changes they would effect as chief of staff, it must have been soul-wrenching to see their dreams evaporate.

The bulk of the opposition, however, came from the most senior and retired officers – the natural custodians of the "military mind-set". May it be abundantly clear that I am not using the term in the pejorative. It is simply an acknowledgement of the centuries'-old truth that men who have served with distinction,

even brilliance, in one war may be singularly incapable of innovation preceding or during the next one. Their minds are monu-
ments to their earlier experience, frozen in time. The phenomenon affects us all in one area of experience or another, and
for that reason should be regarded as the norm rather than the
exception. Still, in the military, as in other walks of life, failure to
accept change can prove disastrous. In retrospect, as Jean Allard
used to say, it is the stuff of comic opera.

Quaint notions were recorded as far back as the first century
A.D. when Julius Frontinus, chief military engineer to the Ro-
man emperor Vespasian, remarked, "I will ignore all ideas for
new works and engines of war, the invention of which has
reached its limits and for whose improvement I see no further
hope."[17] Almost two thousand years later, at the outbreak of
World War I, British Field Marshal Douglas Haig was convinced
that "[The machine gun is] a grossly overrated weapon."[18] This
was less than two months before it became apparent that the
machine gun, almost by itself, had rendered the frontal assault,
the centrepiece of French and British military tactics, all but
impossible.

The naivety was not restricted to the experts in land warfare; it
extended to the other elements as well. In 1911 Maréchal Ferdinand Foch, Professor of Strategy and Commandant of the École
Supérieure de Guerre, remarked: "[Airplanes] are interesting
toys but of no military value."[19] Three years later, reacting to the
1914 story "Danger!" by Sir Arthur Conan Doyle, in which the
author warned that England was susceptible to a submarine
blockade, Admiral Sir Compton Dombile replied: "Most im-
probable and more like one of Jules Verne's stories."[20]

As far as the navy is concerned, the "admirals' " affinity for the
status quo is so strong that it attempts to smother the creative
genius of the occasional maverick who succeeds in infiltrating
their ranks. The life story of the late Admiral Hyman George
Rickover provides silent witness. The father of the nuclear submarine that can operate silently, at great depth, even under the
polar ice cap, succeeded in dragging the U.S. Navy kicking and
screaming into the twentieth century, but only after winning a
prolonged and bitter private war with his fellow admirals.

The military mind has invariably reacted passively or nega-
tively to changes in technology, and that was precisely the situation I faced. Technology had erased the neat divisions between

land, sea, air, and space warfare to the point at which the institutional arrangements, based on the old order, ceased to be valid. This proposition is general and axiomatic: Technology changes first, and the consequent institutional changes follow decades or even centuries later. For example, urban design and urban forms of government are still in the process of catching up to the impact of automobiles, airplanes, and other innovations in communications and transportation. Similarly, the impact of agricultural and medical technology on life expectancy and world population has not yet been fully reflected in institutional concerns about birth control. Attitudes in some of these areas change as slowly as with the military.

A visit to the RCAF electronics school at Clinton on September 16 gave me fresh insight into the speed with which technological change was taking place. The school was impressive and gave me a worth-while exposure to the excellent training facilities available to our tradesmen. Another impression was equally indelible. My pilot that day, a flight-lieutenant, had asked for the assignment because his father was an NCO instructor at the school, and the opportunity for a visit was too good to miss. Their mutual pride and affection was readily apparent, but the difference in the quality of their uniforms stood out like a sore thumb. The son's was a fine worsted, while his father's was coarse serge. Judging from their clothes alone, they were prince and pauper. It didn't seem right. There wouldn't be that distinction if they were going to church together, in civies, and I resolved that whatever the ultimate decision on uniforms, we would abandon the tradition imported from a class-conscious society and have just one quality of cloth for all ranks.

The legacy of class consciousness was most visible in the navy, where I was scheduled for a three-day visit from September 21 to 23. Admiral O'Brien's return to Halifax had brought the situation there under control, but he strongly recommended that I pay a visit and face the officers and men under his command "eyeball to eyeball". I accepted – not without some trepidation, mind you, because I was fully aware of the "warmth" of the reception I could expect. I also knew that facing that particular emotional barrage was part of the price that had to be paid to win the war.

On September 22 the *Globe and Mail* correctly reported that I found the three separate face-to-face meetings with the five thousand officers and men a most rewarding experience; but I had no intention of changing the unification plan. My reception varied considerably from one group to another, but the problem of getting accurate assessments can be seen from the diverse comments in the *Globe* story:

> Several seamen said the Defence Minister was booed at various intervals during the first session. Another said there were murmurs, while another said he felt Mr. Hellyer had entertained every question and answered as honestly as he could.
>
> Able Seaman John MacLeod said: "He explained [sic] a lot of things which were just rumor. He was cheered at most everything he said."
>
> Other seamen also dismissed claims that Mr. Hellyer was heckled.
>
> Petty Officers and officers who attended the other two sessions described Mr. Hellyer's reception as courteous but cool.
>
> One officer, however, said that during an address to the officers it was only the good offices of the admiral Rear-Admiral J. C. O'Brien, sea operations chief – which restored order when the Defence Minister, literally speaking, insulted the officers. . . .
>
> A leading seaman said the only round of applause the Defence Minister received while addressing the lower ranks was when he granted a make and mend – a naval term for a holiday. The seaman added with a grin that Mr. Hellyer had to ask what a made and mend was before giving the go ahead.[21]

As I recall, the ordinary seamen listened politely and asked questions about matters that concerned them. The petty officers gave me the best reception and asked the most intelligent questions. The officers were the worst, by far! This wasn't too surprising, because they were the ones Landymore had been working on for so long – almost from the time he had been posted to Halifax to replace Brock. When newsmen asked at the press conference afterward if the men had booed me, I interpreted the question literally and said "no", which was the truth. But when the Halifax *Chronicle-Herald* subsequently branded me a liar, it taught me a lesson about hiding behind a technicality. It wasn't the men who had booed; it was the officers. What about that old cliché "an officer and a gentleman", I had mused as I watched the incredible spectacle that brought Admiral O'Brien bouncing to his feet to bawl the bejeepers out of them. After that they at least listened, which was a very small step in the right direction.

While I was busily engaged in pouring oil on troubled waters in Halifax, another storm was brewing that would rock the old Tory boat and threaten to capsize it. The essence was contained in a Canadian Press dispatch picked up by the *Simcoe Reformer*.

> A dispute has flared in the top echelons of the Conservative party over the leadership of John Diefenbaker. Though there is no open dump-Dief campaign as in former years, Dalton Camp, national president, has proposed that the party examine the leadership and either confirm the seventy-one-year-old chief or replace him.
>
> Mr. Camp's proposal is to be aired from platforms across the country in preparation for the Progressive Conservative Annual Meeting, November 13th-18th.
>
> The Diefenbaker supporters struck back Wednesday demanding Mr. Camp's resignation in a telegram over the signature of Gordon Churchill, a former Diefenbaker cabinet minister and probably the leader's closest political ally.
>
> Mr. Churchill, MP for Winnipeg South Centre, said Mr. Camp "flagrantly abused" the privilege of his position in making a public attack on his leader.[22]

I felt sorry for the old "Chief", even though he had been giving me a very rough time. In a way his problems spilt over on me, because the war against unification was about the only thing on which the Tories were united, and increasing the ferocity of the campaign was one means of rallying internal support for Diefenbaker's leadership. Once the "anti-Dief" cabal became public, it was easy to understand why I had recently become a principal target for some of the ex-ministers wishing to succeed him. One of the most bombastic of the old soldiers was George Hees. His speeches produced headlines like "Hees Raps Unification – 'Forces' Morale at Stake' ", which appeared in the *Vancouver Sun*.[23] A day later it was "Forces Unity 'Doomed' " in the Vancouver *Province* and "Unification Seen as Loss to Armed Forces" in the *Globe and Mail*.[24]

I knew that the constant appearance of negative headlines was taking its toll. Bill Lee and I had discussed the propaganda aspect of the operation in its early stages. When I thought he was overdoing the efforts at positive press in 1964 and 1965, he had said I should take all I could get, because it was just like putting money in the bank. The day would come when our fortunes would turn, and withdrawals would exceed deposits. Without a substantial capital of goodwill, we would be out of business. Bill was right. Every critical headline was a withdrawal, and new deposits occurred with diminishing frequency.

Editorial support had held up quite well, but we needed all the help we could get, and I was concerned about the power and influence of the Toronto *Telegram*, published by George Hees's friend and wartime buddy John Bassett. When I phoned for an interview to make my pitch, Bassett suggested dinner on Friday, September 23, at the prestigious old York Club at the northeast corner of Bloor and St. George streets.

On arrival I was somewhat nonplussed to be greeted not by the publisher alone, but by a battery of his top staff, including Bassett's son John; Douglas MacFarlane, editor-in-chief; Arnold Agnew, executive editor; Andrew MacFarlane, managing editor; and Ron Collister, Ottawa bureau chief. The discussion began over drinks, continued through soup, fish, and meat courses, and was still going strong with dessert, coffee, and liqueurs. Seldom had I done so much talking and answered so many questions in one evening.

It must have been after 11:00 p.m. when Bassett decided to poll the group. The younger men, Agnew, Andy MacFarlane, Collister, and John, Jr., were all favourable. Doug MacFarlane, who had served overseas, was not, and his despondency showed. Bassett, Sr., a wartime major, put his arm gently on his editor-in-chief's shoulder and said, "Let's face it, Doug, you and I are a couple of old farts." In any event "Mr. Telegram", as Bassett was sometimes called, must have been sufficiently convinced that the idea had been carefully thought out, because he didn't overrule the majority, as he had been known to do on occasion. Instead he opted to ride the wave of the future and ordered Ron Collister to take out his notebook and record the outline of a series of articles, as he dictated the points to be covered. I don't mind admitting that I was impressed. I knew people who could do what he did in the morning, when they were bright and alert; but at that time of night, after good food and fine wine, it was a feat of extraordinary mental agility. Bassett also asked Arnold Agnew to write an editorial explaining the paper's position. Collister's series of articles appeared opposite the editorial page, and the series was subsequently distributed in pamphlet form, a big plus for our side. The *Tely*'s editorial support was good for morale.

One of Collister's articles contained one of my favourite true stories about the NATO military attaché in Ottawa, who had to keep his government advised on unification.

> The occasion was a banquet in the capital, and a Canadian colonel had introduced Mr. Hellyer to the attaché, who praised Canada's peacekeeping efforts.
>
> "You will be interested to know," said the colonel, "that the attaché has orders to report every two weeks on the progress of integration."
>
> "That's interesting," Mr. Hellyer replied. "It's too bad he can't wait until the spring, until we have more success to report."
>
> The NATO attaché looked Mr. Hellyer straight in the eye and said: "It isn't your successes I'm supposed to report."[25]

I took the message to anyone who would listen. On Wednesday, September 28, one of my new assistants, Michael Barry, drove me to a meeting at Queen's University. As I recorded, "We arrived at Kingston eight minutes late and the hall was packed. People sat in the aisles, on the stage, stood at the back, and about fifty went to Stanley Knowles' meeting when they couldn't squeeze in. It was a responsive audience but loaded with RMC, Staff College and naval reservists. The questions were really tough but the response was favourable."[26]

We got home about 2:00 a.m. and I started the next morning with a look at the draft legislation, which seemed to be coming along all right. this was followed by a briefing on the annual pay raise. "Brigadier George Spencer [former commandant of the Royal Military College] was very helpful. Ed Reyno tells me he is coming along just fine. What a surprise.

"The press conference took place at 11:15 in my office. It was difficult – but not too bad. Two TV interviews followed, including a ½ hour for the Hamilton station. Initial reaction to the pay raise was pretty good. Only time will tell what effect it will have.

"At 3:00 p.m. the cabinet met with John Nichol, Paul Lafond, and Al O'Brien [Keith Davey's successor] to discuss the Liberal Conference. After listening carefully and learning that Rick Cashin and Jean-Pierre Goyer are proposed to chair the defence committee, I sensed that trouble is brewing. It looks as if Allan MacEachen and the clan are going to gang up."[27]

Confirmation of an ill-wind from the east was provided in a note from Bill Lee the following day:

MND:

Rod McIsaac was approached by a middleman on behalf of Gerry Regan to team up with him (& he claims P.E.I. & N.B.) at the rally to "kill Paul Hellyer's leadership hopes over the unification issue." Rod told him what to do with the suggestion ... but the warning is passed!"[28]

Saturday morning, October 1, Marc Favreau and my driver Walter Villemaire arrived at 7:45 a.m. to take me to Kingston for the fall convocation at the Royal Military College. As usual it was a good show, with Dr. Roger Gaudry, Dr. Seraphin Marion, and General Sir Charles Loewen receiving honorary doctorates.

One "discordant note for the day was provided by Lt.-Gen. Simonds. Mr. Gordon C. Trent, of Toronto, gave the college a clock for the tower. It cost him $19,000. He is self-effacing and suggested that the senior graduate of his year – Gen. Simonds – present the keys to the clock on his behalf and on behalf of the class. Gen. Simonds refused to make the presentation to me. His attitude embarrassed the Commandant, the Director of Studies, and others – considerably.

"The parade was excellent! One of the best ever. The Wing Cadet Officer was a young French-Canadian Naval Cadet. Two more firsts. He was absolutely outstanding and obviously the type who could go right to the top."[29]

Meanwhile the storm signals in advance of the upcoming Liberal convention went far beyond the defence issue and involved the predicted leadership contest. The concern of Nova Scotians like Gerry Regan and Allan MacEachen was understandable. From their vantage as Nova Scotian politicians, the defence policy was more hurtful than helpful: also there may have been undisclosed considerations, because Allan was planning to run for leader, and the unification issue was a perfect cover for applying a little heat to one of the front-runners. When the October 10 - 12 convention finally got under way, the defence workshop, as predicted, did require a lot of attention in order to sidetrack embarrassing resolutions. Still it was little more than a sideshow compared to the main event.

The centre ring was occupied by two other undeclared leadership aspirants, Walter Gordon and Mitchell Sharp. The issues included medicare, which Sharp wanted to postpone because he thought it would be inflationary; free trade, which was strongly advocated by Western delegates; and its antithesis, economic nationalism, the perennial child of Walter Gordon. Walter had asked some of his friends, including Andy Thompson, to drum up delegate support, but for various reasons, the effort was haphazard. In contrast the delegates from the West, led by BC's Ray Perrault and Manitoba's Gil Molgat, turned out in full force ready to flex their muscle. They put through a North American free-trade resolution, which was subsequently denied by the leader and by Sharp, who refused to be bound by it; but on most issues, including the key question of economic nationalism, where they strongly opposed the Gordon position, they were solidly in Sharp's corner.

The ensuing floor-fight was quite embarrassing, because it revealed deep divisions within the party. There were ideological, regional, and leadership undertones. The Gordonites did everything possible to muster support, but it was a clear case of too little, too late. They were outflanked and outnumbered. An attempt was made to agree on a comprehensive, compromise resolution, but this allegedly fell apart, as Gordon suggests in his memoir, through the interference of Sharp's executive assistant, Michael McCabe, who subsequently persuaded newsmen that Sharp was the winner.[30]

In Walter's words: "The press generally agreed that Sharp had emerged as the strong man of the Liberal Party and, hence, as a major contender to succeed Pearson. But a poll of 150 delegates at the end of the conference named Paul Hellyer, who had not been particularly prominent during the discussions, as the man most likely to win the leadership when the time came."[31] This result confirmed another poll taken by the *Toronto Star* just prior to the convention.

No doubt the favourable nature of the polls explained, in part, why I was fighting a war on so many fronts. No sooner had I doused the little fire members of my own party had lit for me over the unification issue, than I found myself engulfed in a conflagration of indescribable magnitude. Wednesday afternoon, October 12, I left the convention in time to get to the Commons for Question Period. Actually I was a couple of minutes late and, as I poked my nose through the curtain that divided the chamber from the smoking area along the exterior, I heard my name being mentioned. Terry Nugent, the PC member for Edmonton Strathcona, was on his feet demanding an emergency debate to discuss "a definite matter of urgent public importance, namely, the charge that the Minister of National Defence had breached the privilege of this House by tampering with a witness."[32] It was the same old rumour concerning my alleged changes to the Landymore statement of the previous June that had been floating around for weeks, but I sensed instantly that it was being raised in a far more menacing vein than on previous occasions. "The urgency of the debate," Nugent intoned in his most pontifical manner, "is that the charge which has been made and the facts, if proved, go to the very heart of responsible government."[33]

I was thunderstruck, and my heart went through my boots as I walked weakly to my chair in the front row. The Press Gallery was packed, and my instinct told me at once that I was faced with equally impossible options. If I looked solemn, the reporters would say "he was visibly shaken", and any hint of a smile would result in "while the serious charges were being made, the idiot laughed". I did my best to steer a steady, if still unsatisfactory, course midway between the two extremes.

When Nugent ended his plea for an emergency debate, Andrew Brewin, NDP Greenwood, rose to the attack. He said he couldn't imagine anything more urgent, and insisted that it should be debated forthwith. H. A "Bud" Olson, Social Credit, Medicine Hat, expressed a contrary view. As five or six weeks had gone by since the question was first raised, he said, it didn't qualify as a matter requiring urgent debate. There were other ways of dealing with the subject after proper notice had been given. Stanley Knowles, acknowledged repository of the rules and precedents, supported Nugent, as did G. W. (Ged) Baldwin, PC, Peace River.

In reply I said that "obviously no one is more interested than I in having these slanderous insinuations dealt with in a proper fashion and in a proper forum." Subsequently I suggested that the proper place "is before the standing committee on national defence following the introduction of legislation."[34] That brought the pugilistic Cape Bretonner, Don MacInnes, to his feet, charging that I hadn't addressed the question of urgency.

The exchange was turning into a free-for-all with Gilles Grégoire (Socred, Lapointe), J. M. Forrestall (PC, Halifax), John Diefenbaker, and others joining the fray. The Prime Minister's reaction to all this was not particularly helpful:

> I think it has been agreed by all members of this house that this charge is a very serious one which impugns the honour and honesty of a minister of the Crown and that it should be formulated in an appropriate resolution and submitted to the appropriate committee of the House of Commons, which is the committee on privileges and elections. In fact I cannot imagine any matter more serious.[35]

His tone made it sound as if I was accused of a crime only slightly less heinous than murdering my mother.

The barrage continued for more than two hours while Tommy Douglas, Jack Pickersgill, and George McIlraith, to mention only a few, got into the act. Then with only fifteen minutes remaining before the commencement of private members' hour at five o'clock, the Speaker ruled that the business of the House should not be interrupted for an emergency debate but that Mr. Nugent should consider drafting a motion in which he would set out his charges and the Speaker would be glad to discuss them with him. With that we went on with routine business and the afternoon, which had been designated for discussing the medicare bill, was shot.

Instead of taking the Speaker's advice, Terry took a different tack on Thursday. He attempted to raise a question of personal privilege on the basis that I had described his Wednesday motion as "spurious" rather than "serious". "He had looked it up in the dictionary and he hadn't liked what he found."[36] I said I was sorry he had taken offence. I didn't think the word "spurious" was unparliamentary, but if it was I should be informed, because "after looking it up in Webster's *Seventh New Collegiate Dictionary*, I was surprised to find I had hit the nail right on the head."[37]

Terry was no more pleased with my sarcasm than I was with his rapid fire from the lips, so the argument raged until the Speaker ruled that there was no question of privilege and that if the honourable member wanted to pursue the matter he had raised the previous day, he would have to follow the rules and submit a written motion in the proper way, to which Nugent responded, "May I give notice, Mr. Speaker, that I shall be moving a motion?"[38]

On Friday there was no sign of a motion, and it was very nice to have one day pass when I was not the centre of much unwanted attention. On Saturday an article by Victor J. Mackie in the Ottawa *Journal* said "May Shelve Motion, Nugent Hints."[39] That might have been the end of it, if I had let sleeping dogs lie and not contracted a mild case of foot-in-mouth disease. I told reporters that Nugent appeared to be backing off, and this only confirmed my allegation that the charge had been spurious from the outset. My remarks had the same effect as poking a hornet's nest with a stick. Nugent was back on the attack on Monday with a new question of privilege, based on the newspaper article that reported my remarks.

Mr. Speaker reserved his judgment until the next day. When the matter came up again on Tuesday, October 18, Nugent moved a motion which broadened the question to include both the privilege based on my statement to the press and the original charge concerning Landymore's testimony. This complicated the situation for the Speaker, who invited me to make a statement. I quoted the dictionary to show that I wasn't imputing motives. After due consideration, while listening to arguments from both sides of the House, the Speaker ruled there was no valid question of privilege and the battle seemed to be over. I was mistaken, because the calm didn't last long.

On Thursday, October 20, Nugent was back on his feet, but this time his wrath was directed at Marcel Pépin, of Ottawa's *Le Droit*, who was accused of "the worst kind of journalism". Among Nugent's objections were Pépin's allegations that, in his attack on me the previous week, Nugent had been directed from the public galleries by "one Admiral Brock" and that some admirals wanted "to Preserve the Anglo-Protestant Character of the Navy."[40] Nugent added:

There is, however, a more serious allegation against myself. The article says that Admiral Brock not only directed me from the gallery, but that witnesses have confirmed that Admiral Brock, who retired three years ago, made a negative sign when the Minister of National Defence challenged me to risk my seat by making a definite accusation of misconduct.[41]

Not true insisted Nugent, who went on to move that Pépin be brought before the bar of the House – a most serious proposition. The following Monday, October 24, Mr. Speaker advised that only twice in the history of the Canadian Parliament had journalists been brought before the bar. Concerning both precedents "they were cases of flagrantly libellous allusions to members of the house."[42] For about two hours MPs argued the pros and cons, with Mr. Speaker Lamoureux acting as referee. When the motion was finally put, it was defeated 103 to 47 with only the Tories backing Nugent.

On Friday, October 28, I tabled two copies "of the text of a draft prepared by Admiral Landymore for presentation last spring to the special committee on defence, together with the actual presentation, the differences between the two texts being underlined."[43] I felt then and I still feel that the charge of "tampering" was "spurious". At the outset I had only a vague recollection of making a couple of suggestions where I thought the admiral's text was not totally factual. But I was never seriously concerned about it, and certainly not enough to indulge in "tampering" or "censorship". After all, I was the one who decided to let serving officers speak, which was contrary to Canadian tradition. Furthermore, at the actual hearings, the admiral was allowed to answer questions freely, including some on the subject of unification that were not helpful to my cause. There was no attempt to muzzle him, either directly or indirectly, which is why I thought the charge of tampering so grossly unfair.

As for the actual text, there were more editorial changes than I had been aware of at the time. I knew that my staff were going to review the admiral's draft, which was fair enough. What I didn't know, until weeks later, was that John Grant, of parliamentary returns, had rewritten a number of paragraphs to make them a bit less negative.[44] When I was handed the revised version late on the day before the committee session, I simply skimmed it and said it was okay with me if it was all right with the admiral.[45] Apparently this condition was lost between the Commons and the admiral's hotel room, and he was allegedly angered that some of the references to personnel matters had been altered.[46] That was unfortunate, but Landymore never told me he was upset, either before, during, or after the committee hearings, at which he had ample opportunity to elaborate on his concerns about personnel and other matters. His indignation was manifest only after he had been fired and had spoken out publicly, and after the Toronto group had been formed and retired officers across the country had banded together to stop unification. In this they had the cooperation of the Opposition, which opted to make the anti-unification stand an all-out campaign. Landymore had arrived in Ottawa with fresh ammunition at the behest of Admiral Brock at the very time that the Tories' sensors detected a whiff of blood – my blood.

On October 31 interim supply – the parliamentary authority necessary for the government to pay its bills – was called, and the Opposition used the occasion to continue the attack against unification and against me personally. There were charges and counterchanges and the "gravity" of it all was a bit hard on the nervous system. So, near the end of the debate, I sounded a slightly mischievious note by reading from the transcript of a radio broadcast which suggested that Nugent's charges and much of the Tory operational strategy was being orchestrated by Admiral Brock. Furthermore, Brock had been largely instrumental in preparing a paper on defence policy for the PC Party, and when they had twigged to the potential embarrassment if the paper became public, they had destroyed nineteen of the twenty existing copies.

When I asked Nugent if there was, in fact, a memo prepared by Admiral Brock, he replied, "I have no idea of such a document."[47] I didn't believe him, but I wasn't surprised at his answer. I was, however, astonished a minute later when Mike Forrestall, the junior member for Halifax, rose on a question of privilege to say

> My hand lies very deeply in that document and I am very concerned with it. The Minister talked about drafts that were changed and one thing and another. The first 19 were destroyed; indeed the first 19 were burned. What came out of it, I hope, will be presented publicly at the right time to the Canadian people and will represent a viable, reasonable and worthy alternative to the utter nonsense we have listened to over the last 20 minutes. It is a very solid document.[48]

Well! It was October 31 but no one expected the youthful MP to be playing "trick or treat" with the Commons, and Forrestall himself was blissfully unaware of the consequences.

An article by Eric Dennis, which appeared in the Halifax *Mail-Star* of November 3 was captioned "What Happened? Forrestall 'Perplexed' by Ottawa Cold Shoulder". The story continued:

John Michael Forrestall, the 34 year old novice Tory MP from Halifax, was a lonely and perplexed figure walking around the halls of Parliament here yesterday asking "What happened?" as fellow members of his own party cold shouldered him for associating them with a proposed Conservative "policy position paper" on defence basically prepared by Rear Admiral Jeffrey Brock and government MPs heaped ridicule upon him. He pleaded with newsmen and anybody else prepared to listen:

"All I was trying to do was to be helpful and when you do the roof caves in!

"You give an honest answer in Parliament and to the press and you end up catching hell for it!

"If you can't come here and get better treatment for trying to be fair and honest as to what is going on around you then it becomes plain that Parliament is sicker than sick."[49]

Forrestall was just learning the hard way, as Nugent and the rest of us had already learned, that under our political system, with a free press, one has to be constantly on the alert. When faced with a dilemma from which there is no reasonable escape, remember the wisdom of Paul Henri Spaak's cynical but realistic admonition: "You can note with concern, or view with alarm, but for heaven's sake don't blurt out the truth."

CHAPTER 11

BILL C-243
1966-67

A s November rolled around, defence was still in the spotlight. I was still under heavy attack in the House and in the press. Columnists like the *Globe and Mail*'s Scott Young were particularly damaging, and the criticism hurt. On November 3, I drafted a letter to Scott, a former naval officer, pointing out that I thought his column "The New Colonel Blimps" was hitting below the belt. His proposition, in brief, was that those of us who, for whatever reason, did not have brilliant military careers, were automatically disqualified from criticizing officers who served gallantly, like Admiral Brock, no matter what they said or did. I sent my draft to Bill Lee to censor. His reply: "MND, know how you feel but do not advise on grounds it will (a) do no good (b) end up in derision in his column. Let G&M gang take care of him."[1] I accepted Bill's sound advice.

On November 4, 1966, I introduced Bill C-243 – the unification bill. The text had been considered by cabinet on October 18 and approved at that time.[2] Even on first reading, which is usually just a formality, there was some rumbling from the Opposition benches, and the motion was only carried "on division". Although the motion was carried without a recorded vote, which would have been extraordinary, the cries of "on division" signalled an unusual level of dissent.[3] The next item of business was a question from Mr. Diefenbaker "concerning alleged Canadian participation in the execution of German War Prisoners, which I took as notice, agreeing to make a statement later.[4] It was one of the strange ironies of politics that one day I was being maligned in the newspapers for not serving overseas, and the next day was being held accountable for the actions and conduct of Canadian officers who had – twenty years earlier.

Later that same morning Mr. Diefenbaker asked another question. Would I consider submitting the unification bill to the Defence Committee, or another appropriate committee, for detailed consideration. I replied that it was the intention of the government to refer the bill "to the standing committee on defence immediately after second reading. There will then be ample opportunity to hear all outside witnesses who wish to give evidence or express their views and there can be the most thorough and thoughtful consideration of the details before the bill becomes law."[5] That would allow MPs the opportunity to hear and cross-examine retired officers, which would not have been possible if the bill had been referred to the committee of the whole House. That wasn't what the Tories wanted, of course. Their strategy was to have it referred before second reading and approval in principle, and it soon became clear that they would try to bring the government to its knees by holding up interim supply so the government could not pay its bills. That is exactly what they did, with speaker after speaker hammering the defence issue all afternoon on the 4th and again for four days the following week.

Wednesday, November 9, 1966, I noted "The filibuster continues. It was really a war of nerves. Who will capitulate first? At caucus the subject was only given reasonable prominence but I decided to speak to the several issues to keep the troops' morale up. By and large, the party is united – more so than on any other issue! The only exceptions are a few of the ambitious . . . who would like to see me fall flat on my face."[6]

Thursday, November 10: "To-day is critical. It will probably be the turning point. I said nothing – just sat and took it all day.

George Hees joined the chorus in lambasting me and then sent me a note 'no offence, Paul, just a good old rough house we all enjoy from time to time – George!' I don't want to be so sanctimonious as to suggest that I wouldn't do the same thing in Opposition, but it is the kind of tactic which is offensive both to the participants and the public at large.

"The PM spoke at night in full support! He was great! He backed me up all the way and then told the House that we had enough money to pay the mid-month salaries and that the debate could continue as far as the government was concerned, although he pleaded with the Opposition to get on with legislation. He really pulled the rug from under *them*! They are wild. I left at 10:00 p.m. for a television show with Charles Lynch and Donald Gordon, Jr. Bill [Lee] was delighted with the performance and the day!"[7]

In any war not all the news is bad. The day had ended well in the House, and I was getting some good editorial support as well. The lead editorial in the *Toronto Star* was captioned, "Call Diefenbaker's Bluff on Unification." It continued:

> In threatening to force an election on the issue of armed forces unification, the Conservative Opposition in Parliament either is bluffing or has finally been driven mad by its inner tensions over leadership.
>
> In either case, we hope the Pearson government will not flinch for an instant in marching up the trail that Defence Minister Hellyer has blazed.[8]

Another plus was the public support of retired officers in favour of the reorganization. At the end of July a retired vice-chief of the Canadian general staff, Maj.-Gen. Churchill Mann, told the twenty-fifth anniversary reunion banquet of the Eighth Canadian Reconnaissance Regiment, including many men he had once commanded, "I am absolutely in favour of integration and of all steps so far accomplished in the government's present program."[9] A month later retired Maj.-Gen. Arthur E. Potts sent a letter to the *Globe and Mail*, which was captioned "Defence Squabble" and began as follows:

> "The excellent letter of your correspondent Peyton V. Lyon prompts me to write and to state that all senior officers are not against unification of the services. I, for one, am heartily in favour and I find it difficult to understand why no one has had the courage to do something about it years ago."[10]

General Potts's letter led to another one with the same caption from RCAF Wing Commander Y. K. Carter, which read:

> Regarding the defence squabble and the Men from UNCLES, a lot of us old Second World War types have had quite a giggle out of the Toronto-based TRIO, we have dubbed these old chaps as Totally Removed, Immensely Outdated.
>
> We have gone a bit further to form our own unofficial group, known as the Men from UNCLES (Unification Now Can Legislate Effectiveness Soon).
>
> Our only argument against unification is the same as Gen Arthur Potts': It should have taken place 20 years ago.[11]

Now that the battle in the Commons was raging at fever pitch, Bill Lee circulated three new statements by retired officers. Excerpts in the *Ottawa Journal* included the following:

> Air Vice-Marshal J. A. Sully of Goderich, Ont., in charge of RCAF personnel during the war, said he finds it hard to understand how "any rationally minded man" could oppose unification. Inter-service jealousies and overlapping were appalling. "I have met Mr. Hellyer only once, but I have a great regard for his courage. He is the first minister who had the guts to tackle the unification of our services, though everyone must have known that something had to be done."
>
> Maj.-Gen. Arthur E. Potts of Kingston said unification would have prevented "unnessary loss of life in Italy" during the Second World War. A "shocking" lack of co-operation between the three services had reduced efficiency and prevented the dispatch of badly needed reinforcements to Italy.
>
> Group Captain Ken Patrick said "sitting on the sidelines it seems to me Parliament is attacking Hellyer more than unification!"[12]

Balm like this helped me to face Remembrance Day, which I dreaded because I kept wondering what all the faithful old veterans were thinking. As I recorded: "Started the day at Knox Church. I read the lesson – the same one about 'wickedness in high places', from Ephesians. Marc Favreau found out that it was Brooke Claxton's favourite and probably has been used ever since. That is the way traditions are born! At least Paul (Saint) was referring to the people who had accused him falsely and put him in prison. I must admit that rightly or wrongly I felt a bit the same way about the Nugent–Diefenbaker tactics of the last two weeks.

"The ceremony and parade went well even though the marching, other than the Guards, was lousy. I must do something about that next year.[13]

Saturday, November 12: "Arrived at the Toronto and District [Liberal] Annual Meeting just before lunch – and time to make a 10 min. fighting speech! It was well received but Mel McInnes and others were up to their usual tricks. Rumours were circulated that I was a machine, not a man – arrogant, etc. It doesn't take much Tory propaganda to set them off, aided and abetted by the Executive Assistants to the hopefuls.

"After lunch I went to see Royce Frith to ask him if he would be interested in one of the two top CBC jobs. He will think about it and advise."[14] It was Judy La Marsh's responsibility, as Secretary of State, to make a recommendation to cabinet, but appointments of that kind were of interest to a number of ministers – and I was one of them.

Royce was my only serious candidate to replace Alphonse Ouimet as president. Two or three others had asked for my support, in passing, but the surprise was Patrick Watson, the maverick CBC star broadcaster, who had sent me a long letter months earlier, in February. He appealed to my "kind of enthusiasm and imagination for changing the world with the changing times" and made a cogent case for an equally radical change in the CBC hierarchy which, he argued, would not come through reorganization or legislation but through people. He wrote:

> Anyway, Paul, I have thought about this long and prayerfully, and I think I am uniquely equipped to take the thing on. You'll agree it would be a surprising appointment – at least in some circles I think that's an advantage. I know that it would be hard to sell to some cabinet members; but I think not impossible (I've spoken to Judy [LaMarsh], already, and she asked some good hard questions and went away to think about it.)"[15]

Later, I agreed to meet him in my office. In the course of a lengthy conversation, Patrick made two cardinal errors in judgment. He played on the religious angle. Well-briefed on my roots, he may have believed this was a clever tack. Instead, he gave the impression he was trading on the issue, and the effect was negative. A while later, in discussing the influence of the media, he said that the CBC's highly controversial Sunday-night TV program, *This Hour Has Seven Days,* had more power than any government. All of the show's merits aside, the mere words were deeply offensive to a dedicated democrat. I was silently appalled. These two "revelations" dampened my enthusiasm, and I didn't pursue the matter further, except to let Judy know that I had spoken to him. Subsequently Royce bowed out of the contest, and I have sometimes wished that Patrick had chosen his words more wisely. He would have been hard to sell in political circles, but if he had made the grade, it is just possible that he might have been able to work the miracle he dreamed of. (Little did I dream that twenty-three years later he would be appointed chairman of the CBC and would finally have the opportunity he had hoped for through the years.)

My interest in television was more than academic as the Tory convention got under way in Ottawa on Monday, November 14. I recorded events in my diary: "Everyone is most interested to see how it is going to turn out. Will Dalton Camp win or will Arthur Maloney hold for Dief?

"The filibuster continues in the House of Commons, but the pressure is shifted to Ben Benson and the question is where he got the money for the Civil Service payroll. It sure is nice not to be the 'centre of attention.'

"For the first time in days I looked at the 'in' basket and started looking for new 'bombs'. The backlog is incredible.

"I saw a few minutes of Dief's appeal to the Tory Convention on television. It was fantastic! He was booed and hissed. The Camp followers had loaded the front aisles. It was a spectacle 'such as I have never seen.' No doubt it will be widely interpreted as the political death of the Dief – on television. It was sad. How could a politician and a party do that to each other?"[16]

On Tuesday evening, I joined Jack Pickersgill for a flight to Quebec City, where we were to attend Mrs. St. Laurent's funeral the following morning. While we were there, Jack reported that the interim-supply debate had ended and the appropriation bill, which the Tories had been delaying, had been given first reading. It was good news; one more major hurdle had been overcome.

With the pressure off in the Commons, I began to prepare my speech to kick off the second reading debate on Bill C-243. It was a major effort and, as with the White Paper three years earlier, I did the first draft myself in longhand. It was then referred to various people for advice and comment. When my deputy minister, Elgin Armstrong, phoned for an appointment to discuss it, I sensed some uneasiness, but I was not prepared for the reality. He was extremely nervous as he sat down opposite me and finally, ashen-faced, told me clearly and unequivocally that the second, and central, section was unacceptably bad. My instant inward reaction was totally human – simple outrage. But I held my tongue, and within seconds reason conquered passion. "In that case," I said, "we will have to do it over again." He was absolutely right, and the fresh draft was infinitely better. My appreciation of Elgin skyrocketed. He could have said nothing and just let me fall into a swamp of my own making. Instead he chose the courageous but risky course and achieved a new high in my esteem.

Refining the text became a team effort. Monday evening, December 5, "Elgin, W/C L. C. "Mo" Morrison and Bill Lee came to my House of Commons Office to go over the speech with me. We finished at midnight with only two or three minor points to be reconciled in the morning when we are fresh. What an ordeal."[17]

Tuesday, December 6, at cabinet, House Leader George McIlraith advised that Defence would be called on Wednesday for one day only. I suspect that my speech, which was just being typed for the last time, reflected more effort by more people than any speech given by any Minister of National Defence in recent history. It was checked more times by more serving officers than one would believe. The final result looked to me like a well-rounded document.

Wednesday, December 7: "Early morning cabinet re. West-Coast longshoremen's strike or lockout – or what have you. We agreed on emergency legislation but they can't get it ready in time for this afternoon, so it looks as if I will be able to get on with my speech as planned.

"Someone tried to move the adjournment of the House, but the Speaker ruled the motion out of order. Okay to go at last.

"One hour and forty-five minutes of reading a speech. A few brave souls managed to stick it out to the end, including Paul Martin who stayed for most of it – bless him! Marcel Lambert replied for the Opposition. He seemed to me, and to the staff, to be floundering. I had the staff who had helped with my speech up to my room for drinks in the afternoon. This one was a real team effort. CBC news only said 'Mr. Hellyer said unification is right for the forces and right for Canada.' That is all!"[18]

Thursday, December 8: "The popular press never ceases to amaze me. Just because my speech didn't refer to any fired admirals, it was virtually ignored. Landymore got equal space for his new blast. The timing, incidentally, was obviously arranged to coincide with my speech. TRIO's pipeline into the department is pretty good."[19]

On Monday, January 2, 1967, I phoned the PM for an appointment to discuss rumours that Walter Gordon would be returning to the cabinet. He agreed to see me on Tuesday, at 9:45 a.m. That day was to be memorable in more ways than one. Early that morning, I received a plaintive call from Celia Franca, artistic director of the National Ballet of Canada, advising that she was in deep trouble. The company had finished its holiday run of *The Nutcracker* in Toronto and was scheduled to open in Vancouver on January 4. To her dismay, however, a computerized switching system had sidetracked the baggage car containing their sets and costumes in Winnipeg. She had checked with all the commercial air-carriers, but none of them could meet the emergency. Would I help? I was quickly assured that we would get paid, as the CNR had accepted full responsibility for the error. Therefore I told her that, if the RCAF had a Hercules available, it would fly to the rescue. One from Edmonton intercepted the tardy but reconnected baggage car in Saskatoon and delivered the goods in time for the National Ballet to be on-stage when the curtain rose.

Miss Franca was ecstatic and told the press, which was generally favourable. The Ottawa *Citizen* captioned its editorial "Mr. Hellyer's Gallant Gesture",[20] while the *Toronto Star* wrote:

> "Mr. Hellyer saves the ballet. . . . Flying theatrical costumes about is not part of the normal duties of an air force. But this helping hand to a distinguished Canadian institution in an emergency is an example of official imagination which deserves praise."[21]

Only the Edmonton *Journal* was churlish. An "Abuse of Ministerial Responsibility" it called it. The editorial concluded:

> Mr. Hellyer's action in ordering the RCAF to do the job was highly improper. How readily do politicians in office abuse their power and waste the long-suffering tax-payers' money.[22]

As they say, you win some and you lose some.

When I met with the PM, "I told him I thought Walter Gordon's return to the cabinet would prove to be divisive; that the

NDP popular support increase was a 'protest' and had nothing to do with the Liberal Party's place in the political spectrum (as alleged); that other faction leaders were flexible enough to cooperate in a middle-of-the road party, but that Walter is a loner who must be top dog or he won't play. He replied that some of my colleagues had made passionate appeals on Walter's behalf and some had been opposed, but none as forcefully as I had been.

"He also told me 'not to pay any attention to press reports that he would be wishing newsmen Happy New Year, next year', and then added that he might announce in November a convention called for January '68. (This is directly contrary to what he told me a few days ago). The interview ended as 'our friend' [Walter] would be arriving in five minutes."[23]

The announcement of Walter's reappointment came as a big surprise to many. "LBP said nothing at the cabinet meeting – at least as long as I was there – although Larry Pennell, Joe Greene, Allan MacEachen, and Ben Benson were waiting for him after cabinet, which must have been significant. The afternoon press carried the speculation and the PM confirmed the appointment at a press conference later in the afternoon.

"Léo Cadieux phoned me soon after he heard the news on the Fr.-radio and expressed his surprise, and regret. Ron Collister on CBC-TV listed all Gordon's incredible blunders and then said he was delighted to see him back.

"What a paradox this man is. It shows the power of the *Toronto Star*, Peter Newman, good press relations, and the Toronto 'rat pack'."[24]

Thursday, January 5: "Reaction [to Gordon's return] still mixed but not as violent as anticipated. Gil Molgat and Ray Perrault spoke out in opposition, but everyone else is mum.

"Peter Newman ran another of his sickening columns. In it he mentioned the promoters and then singled out my name as being most sharply critical. This *leak* must have come from the PM himself, *directly* or *indirectly*. He only was privy – *no-one* else! This is the second time he has betrayed information given to him in confidence. [Jack Pickersgill says that betrayed is too strong a word. Mike didn't do it deliberately, but never learned how to keep a secret.]

"On a positive note I got two important submissions out of the way at Defence Council, the Reserve Organization and Base Consolidation. When we get the planning guide out on the 19th, I hope everything of major importance will be caught up. I can then concentrate on the Bill, the Centennial, and politics – some dream!"[25]

Monday, January 9: "Cabinet to decide order of business for the session. Walter sat opposite Mike at foot of table. In the House, WLG's reception was good but not terrific. He will have a tough row to hoe, too.

"Bob Winters told me he had been to see Mike and relayed the sad message about the reaction of the business world. His contacts for raising money had bowed out and the committee to work on trade promotion had called the whole thing off. . . . Bob is not happy!"[26]

Tuesday, January 10: "I saw the PM briefly after the intelligence briefing and before cabinet. I told him I was *very* disappointed that on both occasions when I had given him advice that was important but that wouldn't please him, it wound up in the newspapers within a few days. He denied having seen Peter Newman. I said he must have told Walter, to which he replied that Walter had asked him what the reaction of his cabinet colleagues was to his re-entry. I said he had no right to give this kind of information, which had been given to him in strictest confidence. He said he hadn't taken my advice, and I said that was correct; he took Walter's, and that was the reason he didn't have a majority. It was a very frank talk. It wouldn't win me any prizes, but it made me feel better.[27]

The emotional teeter-totter took a dramatic turn for the worse at noon January 26, when Bill Lee reported a telephone conversation with Al Scott, of the Toronto advertising firm of Vickers and Benson, which I recorded as follows: "Bumped into Keith Davey last week who said he thought WLG should be PM. Al said 'You're kidding?' KD said 'not at all, quite serious.' Scott was astonished. I am not astonished, just hurt like I have seldom been hurt, if ever, before. It is tough to have a man you consider your closest friend do a flip."[28]

That same evening, while I was attending a Technical Services Branch mess dinner at the RCAF Rockcliffe Mess, George McIlraith phoned to say that the Tories would put Jack Pickersgill's transportation bill through committee stage before adjournment that night and give it third reading the next day, if I agreed not to go on with defence at that time. The bill, encompassing a new transportation policy for Canada, had been the subject of extensive debate, and I knew Jack was very anxious to see the last of it, so I agreed. The debate on the bill to set up the Canadian Transportation Commission ended and the bill passed on Friday. The balance of the afternoon was spent on second reading of a bill to establish the Canadian Film Development Corporation.

The net effect of giving in to the Opposition proposal was negligible, because the debate on Bill C-243 was resumed the following Monday, January 30, 1967. Marcel Lambert was the lead-off speaker for the Tories. He covered the same old ground. It wasn't up to the Opposition to prove that I was wrong about unification, it was up to me to prove that I was right – a difficult task when we were leading the world and there were no precedents to use in evidence. Marcel said unification of command was possible without a single service and that Canada was moving away from its defence commitments in the direction of peacekeeping which, to my ears, was the same old nonsense.

As the debate droned on into January 31, speakers who ran out of quotes from disgruntled retired officers loaded their remarks with jibes of a more personal nature. Terry Nugent considered that my main motivation was purely political. "His prime purpose is to ensure his own greatness,"[29] he claimed. Harold Winch of the NDP and Gordon Churchill put it somewhat differently. Churchill, who admitted he had once been a corporal himself, quoted Winch as follows, " 'History would show three main troublemakers, one was Corporal Napoleon, one was Corporal Hitler, and now it is Corporal Hellyer.' They certainly have been troublemakers," Churchill observed, "but I would not want any reflection to be cast either on present or past corporals, with the sole exception of those three."[30]

Being lumped in with Napoleon and Hitler was not one of my proudest boasts, but historians did ease the pain somewhat with a critical analysis of Churchill's charge. Napoleon was an officer cadet; my highest rank was lance-bombardier; of the three, only Hitler was a corporal. That gave Churchill a thirty-three-percent mark, which wasn't too great for a high-school history teacher.

The irascible Don MacInnes spread his net of invective to include Bill Lee. At first he complained that I had put together a propaganda team, and then he reversed himself to say he was all wrong. The propaganda team had done a snow job on the minister and "He is the Charlie McCarthy of the Bergen–McCarthy team."[31] Lee was the villain, and I was merely the dupe.

MacInnes was followed by my colleague Léo Cadieux, Associate Minister of Defence, who made a very reasoned speech to the effect that he wanted the best men to be picked for the top jobs no matter whether they be army, navy, or air force. This, he maintained, was one of the principal objectives of unification, the best use of our manpower resources. I listened intently to Léo, a prince of a man, who always seemed to make sense. It was such a pleasant relief from the Opposition. Every time one of them stood, I had that sinking feeling that one might have if required to listen to the same sermon or homily forty times over a span of a few weeks.

When the debate on the bill began, everyone predicted it would last two weeks. But there was little interest in the Commons and less in the country. House attendance fell, and, after only two days, the Tories concluded that they would be better off to let the bill go to committee, where they could call outside witnesses to revive the controversy. Before allowing it to be read a second time, however, Alf Hales moved, seconded by Mike Forrestall, that instead of the bill being read a second time, "The further consideration of Bill C–243 be deferred until the principle thereof has been examined by the standing committees on national defence and external affairs meeting together."[32] The vote was called, their amendment was defeated 88 to 75, after which my motion, that the bill now be read a second time, was adopted 98 to 62. That meant that, at long last, Bill C-243, authorizing the unification of the armed forces, was approved in principle.

CHAPTER 12

THE WAR OF WORDS IS OVER

T he following Tuesday, February 7, the Commons Standing Committee on National Defence met to consider Bill C–243 in detail. At least that's what the notice said, but I didn't need a tea-cup reader to know that it was going to be a long and nasty ordeal. David Groos, a retired RCN captain, was chairman of the committee, with Marcel Lambert, from the Tory bench, as vice-chairman. The twenty-four members were about equally divided between government and Opposition MPs, including a number of heavy-hitters from each side.[1]

In spite of my premonition of the ordeal to come, and against the strenuous objection of former defence minister Doug Harkness, who wanted to hear the high-profile objectors first, I proposed that we begin with a serious review of the rationale for unification. I kicked off, followed by Air Marshal F. R. Sharp, Vice-Chief of the Defence Staff, who made a two-and-a-half-hour detailed presentation in which he reviewed pre-integration and post-integration command structures, major equipments, and how unification would affect personnel management and careers. Questions from MPs began that evening, and continued through the following day.

On February 9 I introduced other officers, who presented exhaustive briefings on personnel policy, the reserves, and such topics. I had to assume that the committee was interested in a serious and comprehensive discussion of the theory, but it soon became painfully clear that this was not the case. Positions had already hardened. Unification had become a partisan issue. Liberals wanted to get the bill approved and were impatient with any delay, while the official Opposition wanted to stop it in its tracks. The NDP and Socreds were somewhere in between, more or less favourable in principle, but critical of our alleged "strong-arm" methods. The only thing the Tories wanted to get on with was the critics.

The dissenters got their first inning on February 10, when the Tri-Service Identities Organization, commonly known as TRIO, was heard. Representatives included Robert H. Hilborne, Robert I. Hendy, and George Penfold – one each from the army, navy, and air force. TRIO presented a carefully prepared brief, which outlined all the conventional concerns. It raised doubts about our future ability to cooperate with our allies, and quoted extensively from publisher Richard S. Malone to the effect that unification wouldn't work. The brief also argued that it was imperative to hear the testimony of departed officers. Monday, when the Defence Committee resumed its hearing, Bob Hendy presented a long and detailed brief in support of navies in general and the Royal Canadian Navy in particular. At the end he tabled copies of every negative newspaper report and editorial that had appeared since the controversy began.

Tuesday, St. Valentine's Day, the committee started on the Opposition list of "heavy hitters". Rear-Admiral Jeffry V. Brock (ret.) was first. In reply to questions from Tory MP Jack McIntosh, Brock said that he didn't understand what the term "unification" meant. "No one seemed for a single moment to believe that the one reference in the White Paper could be anything but an odd expression,"[2] he claimed. This was exactly the same argument Bob Hendy had made in a letter to the Prime Minister, and I found it quite incredible that senior officers wouldn't understand what the sentence "This is the first step toward a single unified service for Canada" meant – especially when most of them had attended briefing sessions at which I had explained the plan in considerable detail.

In fact most of them did understand. That was true of Rear-Admiral C. J. Dillon, one of the few admirals who supported the concept, when he gave evidence with special reference to the financial and materiel functions. It was also true of Rear-Admiral William Landymore, who appeared on February 15. When the same Jack McIntosh asked Landymore if he understood what unification meant, he replied "one service, one uniform". While this definition is an oversimplification, it left no doubt that Landymore understood the game plan from the outset. It was, beyond question, the reason he had opposed each move so vigorously.

His testimony was diminished when he fell into the trap of exaggeration. He implied that it would be possible for the Minister of National Defence, in collusion with the Commander, Mobile Command, to set up an overnight dictatorship in Canada. This argument amounted to overkill and hurt his credibility, as I recorded in my diary for February 16. "I watched Landymore give testimony in the afternoon. He was not too ferocious. Actually he 'bombed' yesterday by suggesting that the Commander, Mobile Command, and the Minister could set up an instant dictatorship. Public reaction is that he must be out of his mind."[3]

Notwithstanding the outrageous nature of the suggestion, it sparked headlines like "Landymore Blasts Merger as Way to Dictatorship" in the *Montreal Star* of February 16, and "Landymore: Dictatorship Possible Under Hellyer Plan" in the *Toronto Star* of the same date. Editorial comment was appropriately sceptical. Under the heading "The Admiral's Spyglass", even the Conservative-leaning *Ottawa Journal* opined:

> Holy Torpedoes! Admiral Landymore has said a dictatorship could come to Canada overnight if a minister of national defence and the commander of Mobile Command got together. Maybe Parliament should pass a law to go with that armed forces unification bill making it illegal for a defence minister to talk with any of his top officers. Why take chances?
>
> The good admiral doth protest too much. To paraphrase Churchill, what kind of people does he think we are? A two-

man Canadian coup d'état would apparently be under some sorcerer's spell: Parliament, the civil service, all of us asleep except the two plotters and our new masters. . . .

No disrespect intended for Admiral Landymore's integrity. He has taken a courageous stand and raised many useful questions. But he should spare us Orwellian spectres.[4]

The original charge had been bombastic enough to attract attention in the foreign press. Landymore had said: "If a Minister of National Defence and Commander Mobile Command got together, we could have a dictatorship overnight. As members of Parliament you should contemplate this organization with some alarm,"[5] and this had been reported in *The Times* of London.

One *Times* reader, who was not favourably impressed, sent me the clipping with the notation "Where was admiral 'know-all' Landymore when we were winning the last war with 'combined' operations?" The accompanying letter read as follows:

Dear Mr. Hellyer:

I enclose cutting from the London (Eng.) Times of February 18th inst. Can no-one stop this silly owl making an ever-greater fool of himself?
You have my sympathy.

Yours sincerely,

Jean I. Hall
(Mrs. Landymore's mother!)[6]

Thursday, February 16: General "Charles Foulkes (ret.) started at night. He is for the principle, but was very critical of the methods. Rayner and Brock have been working on him and, besides being sore that he wasn't appointed to the Permanent Joint Board on Defence, he is trying to prove to his admiral neighbours that he is not a Liberal hack. He of all people should know how difficult the whole process is – the reason it wasn't done years ago."[7] I was particularly resentful that his testimony produced damaging headlines like "Airborne Brigades Useless? Gen. Foulkes Fires on Hellyer Plan" in the *Ottawa Journal* and "Foulkes Raps Hellyer Plan" in the Regina *Leader-Post*. It was ironic coming from someone who had espoused unification from the day I first met him.

Foulkes continued on Friday morning. He explained how Brooke Claxton had intended to unify the services, but backed off when he found out that Mackenzie King had no intention of moving him to another department once the deed was done. Claxton decided to make his peace with the service chiefs. "That is when the committee fever started; in other words integration by committee and the start of committee hearings."[8]

Despite the General's annoying ambivalence, Bob Andras, who was doing the questioning for the Liberals, really pinned him to the masthead concerning his continuing support for the principle of unification:

> In your presentation of 1961 you said:
> "After my nine years as Chairman of the Chiefs of Staff, trying to coordinate the rival services, I am convinced that we can't achieve much more by the present road. Attempts to integrate the three services by persuasion have been going on ever since 1945. They have woven a huge spider's web of committees which are rather like foreign ministers' meetings where rival powers try to reach a compromise."
> Then you go on to say:
> "The problem can only be solved by complete unification of the three services, with one chief of staff, one chain of command, one ladder of promotion and one uniform."
> I know this is a leading question but, generally speaking, I presume you would still agree with that statement of policy conviction at least?
>
> Mr. Foulkes: That is correct.[9]

It was good to have this reaffirmation on the record, but regrettably it was ignored by the press.

"After the hearing, Jeff Brock came over for a drink. He noted that he sat in the same chair as before, etc. [the day he was fired] but was most cordial. He made two suggestions.

(a) An adjustment in pensions for those retired early to bring them to the level they would have had otherwise at normal compulsory retirement age;

(b) to reduce Mobile Command 'to a small "green-suited" special force while leaving the army, navy, and air force otherwise intact.'

"He thought this compromise would please everyone and not be considered a 'retreat'. He is willing to provide details if required.

"He admitted I could get the Bill through, but is quite pessimistic about the consequences. A very interesting chat! Incidentally he paid some compliments re. vigor, imagination, etc."[10]

Saturday's papers conveyed a very different impression of the relations between me and the admirals. Banner headlines announced that Admiral Rayner and the Minister of National Defence had engaged in an angry shouting match at the end of the Friday sitting. Anyone who knew the admiral well would know just how outrageous the allegation was. He could be very angry, and he was, but shout at the Minister? Never!

"I have asked CP for a retraction and Rayner agrees."[11]

My impression that David MacIntosh, the reporter who had written the Canadian Press story, was totally opposed to unification, had been confirmed in a conversation with Jack Pickersgill. At a cocktail party, MacIntosh told a group of bystanders, including Jack, that he was just as anxious to "kill" the bill and the minister as the Tories were. This was the second occasion on which I had heard this alleged statement, and I had no reason to doubt its authenticity. The galling reality was that, because of his special position as the recognized press specialist in defence matters, MacIntosh's material was the source for nearly all newspaper reports on the subject, plus a high percentage of those used by the electronic media. He moulded editorial reaction, which was highly critical of scenes like the alleged shouting match. He was ideally situated to achieve his objective.

On Monday, February 20, 1967, "LBP called me down for a talk. For one thing he wished to explain why he hadn't told me about his meeting with Landymore last summer [news of which had just been broken in the press]. He also wanted to know the plans for the committee and when I would be replying to the critics. I was very cordial – for a very tired man.

"I asked him about the cabinet shuffle [which had been mooted for some time]. He said that it would not be as reported in the newspapers. If Guy Favreau resigned, and possibly Lucien Cardin, there would be two changes in Quebec before Easter. In the fall there might be a shuffle involving five or six ministers. That would be his swan song. He wanted to get Paul Martin out of External Affairs. He has been there too long and is getting too involved in the Vietnam thing to the exclusion of our overall relations with the U.S. He might also move me – I had earned it. Tony Westell's article [in the *Globe and Mail*] was accurate and the convention would be about January 7, '68."[12]

That afternoon, "In the Defence Committee, Bob Moncel clobbered us."[13] He had been a very effective witness. He said he wasn't opposed to unification, *per se*, if there were a change in Canadian commitments. However, with our existing commitments, unification was unwise because it would affect our close working relationship with the U.K. and U.S. Services. This was a bit of stuff and nonsense, but it sounded plausible to anyone who wanted to believe it. His other argument was even more devastating, as reported by the press: "I became distressed because we were moving too quickly, without an adequate plan, into the final stages of unification."[14] This was the argument that hurt most, because there was no straightforward rebuttal. No one would believe that the need to press on was because of the passive internal resistance of some officers, and that the urgency of parliamentary approval was caused by the need to send a strong, positive signal to these holdouts. Oblivious to the inside story, editorial reaction was predictably harsh.

On February 21 the committee heard Air Marshal Clare L. Annis and Air Vice-Marshal M. M. Hendrick, followed on the 22nd and 23rd by Lt.-Gen. F. J. Fleury. On day two, "I talked to senior staff and told them I was about to go on – after Fleury. I appreciated their support but did not want them to say anything they didn't believe.

"Fleury finished at one and I got started about 3:30. My statement was first class and made a real impact. Churchill floundered badly when the questioning started.

"All went beautifully until about a quarter to ten. Then Mike Forrestall said I had apologized to Fleury [for saying he had been part of the roadblock], did I wish to say when Landymore had been fired and apologize to him. By 9:45 I was physically and emotionally exhausted. I asked Forrestall if he was willing to accept responsibility for the question, and when he said yes, I blurted out the truth. I said Landymore was fired for eighteen months' consistent disloyalty to the policy of the people he was paid to serve. The audience was hushed, but also the fat was in the fire."[15] I should have known better. The words had been on my lips for weeks, but until then I had been prudent enough to keep my mouth shut. It's the kind of thing one is allowed to think, and believe, but never to say, unless there is some overriding purpose to be served – which in this case there wasn't. Quite the contrary!

February 24: "One session only. I was the witness. The questioning was not too bad, but at three minutes to eleven Harkness returned to the Landymore thing. It really was too bad that I opened my big mouth last night – otherwise I think we had them licked. Now the news is all Landymore, and we have a first-class diversion.

"Later in the afternoon I gave a clarifying statement to TV, saying that I didn't believe Landymore had been disloyal to Canada, but merely to the policy I had introduced. If he will say that he did not hold meetings at which he invited naval officers to support him in his opposition to government policy, I will apologize.

"Landymore evaded by saying he will swear he was not disloyal (his interpretation) but he doesn't want a court martial and is willing to drop the whole thing. I think he is wise."[16]

Saturday: "I spent nearly all day at the office. . . .

"Bill is all in. We are both exhausted, but I think he is in worse shape than I am. His mother is very ill, and he got a call Wednesday night just at the time he was working on the statement. It never rains but it pours.

"At 5:00 I did an interview with Peter Stursberg for *W5*. He was pretty rough, but I managed to struggle through."[17]

Sunday: "We took Bill Lee and the children to the Green Valley for dinner. Chatty is in Hamilton looking after Bill's mother and I thought it would be nice for everyone not to have to do supper dishes. He has lovely children and we all enjoyed ourselves.

"The *W5* thing didn't look too bad! On the news Forrestall suggested that Landymore re-appear before the Defence Committee."[18]

On Monday, February 27, David Groos resigned as chairman of the Defence Committee. His reason was failing health, and there was little doubt that the intense pressure from fellow naval officers exacerbated the problem. The heat from them had become increasingly unbearable. David was replaced by Grant Deachman – a tough, no-nonsense Liberal colleague from Vancouver, who steered a steady course past the reefs guarding the port.

I was back on the stand before the committee. "It was a bear pit. The opposition was quite rough and grilled me on the Landymore statement. Unfortunately we are off on a tangent, and it will almost certainly hold up passage of the bill if it continues. I repeated my statement of Friday night that I didn't think there had been any conscious disloyalty to service or country. I said that if the admiral would say that he did not call meetings of his officers at which he invited their support in opposition to government policy, I would accept his word and apologize.

"The committee is extremely partisan and extremely nasty and it is difficult to say what the outcome will be. I think we had better get Landymore back on the stand and clear the matter up somehow."[19]

On February 28, Landymore was back on the stand. The Judge Advocate General, Brigadier W. J. Lawson, had given me a written opinion that the Admiral had been in breach of regulations and, technically speaking, disloyal.[20] However, I had no intention of making that public and digging myself in even deeper. My hope was that we could get an admission on the narrow question of soliciting opposition to government policy, and let it go at that. Unfortunately it was a morning when our chaps on the committee were insufficiently precise in their questioning, and Landymore was very adroit with his answers.

"By noon the Tories were getting the best of the fight. Harold Winch (NDP) asked Landymore if he had been disloyal, and he said 'no'. Winch then threw the ball to me. Of course Landymore didn't say he hadn't called meetings of his officers and invited their support etc. – because he had. He merely said he hadn't been disloyal, period.

"Our chaps wanted another round at him, but on the basis of their [lack of] success the first time around, the situation appeared hopeless if we wanted to get on with the job. When the opening came, I sat beside Landymore and withdrew the charge of disloyalty. I think it was the right thing to do because of the military connotation of the word disloyal and also the only way to get back on the rails. The episode was ended and Gen. Allard began his brief in the afternoon."[21]

What he said was upbeat and positive and produced the first positive press in days. The tone of the General's testimony was reflected by a report in the *Quebec Chronicle-Telegraph*:

Gen. Jean V. Allard, Chief of Defence Staff, has pleaded for quick passage by Parliament of the armed forces unification bill. "Uncertainty is our worst enemy," the general told the Commons defence committee Tuesday. . . .

Being greeted by Rear-Admiral William Landymore upon arrival in Halifax. (National Defence Photo)

A tête-á-tête with advisor Bill Lee.

Reviewing briefing notes with Bill Lee aboard government jet.

The Pearson government after the 1965 election. Left to right: (Front row) A. MacEachen, A. Laing, M. Sharp, J. Pickersgill, P. Martin, L.B. Pearson, R. Winters, P. Hellyer, G. McIlraith, L. Cardin, H. Robichaud; (Middle row) J-L. Pepin, L. Cadieux, M. Sauvé, G. Favreau, J. LaMarsh, R. Teillet, C. Drury, J. Nicholson, E. Benson, L. Pennell; (Back row) J. Turner, J. Greene, J. Marchand, J. Côté. (National Film Board Photo)

Watching a flypast with U.S. Secretary of Defence Robert McNamara.

At a NATO meeting with U.S. Secretary of State, Dean Rusk. (NATO Photos).

Rear-Admiral J.C. "Scruffy" O'Brien presenting me with the first casting of the new Canadian Armed Forces crest at my farewell mess dinner October 24, 1967. (National Defence Photo)

With Air Marshal F.R. Sharp (left) at the Rockcliffe Mess, October 24, 1967. (National Defence Photo)

Discussing the Quebec position with Premier
Daniel Johnson at the Federal Provincial
Conference, February 1958.

Sharing a lighter moment with broadcaster Jack Webster. (Ray Stone)

Huddling with Bill Lee, Ellen, and campaign manager, Bob Andras, MP (front), at the 1968 Liberal Convention.

Marching with the Hellyerites at the 1968 Convention.

Reflecting on the disappointing vote with Ellen and Judy LaMarsh.

Relaxing with the family at Arundel Lodge, Muskoka, Ontario.

> Gen. Allard said morale in the army and air force now is as good as it has ever been and that with "half a chance" it will be equally good in the navy.
>
> At one point during an argument with Marçel Lambert (PC – Edmonton West) the general said: "If you don't want to understand, I'm afraid I can't help you."
>
> Rod Webb (PC–Hastings Frontenac), sitting in the audience, shouted: "Just like the minister, very arrogant."[22]

Allard was certainly not a man lacking in confidence, but he had been most conciliatory in accommodating the customs of navy and army when the details of unification were being worked out. He would have preferred the army practice of locating the rank designations of commissioned officers on their epaulettes, but readily agreed to a compromise. Those rank designations up to full colonel (navy captain equivalent) appeared as stripes on the sleeve, while those of general rank (navy commodores and admiral equivalent) were identified by a single wide band on the sleeve and the appropriate number of maple leaves on the epaulettes.

It was never intended that admirals would be called generals, except for pay purposes; but the air force enthusiastically volunteered to abandon their traditional British nomenclature. Their day-to-day contacts were primarily with the United States Air Force and they preferred to adopt the American style, which was identical to the army, in preference to the British system that few people understood.

A more difficult problem arose in reconciling the army and air-force rules concerning noncommissioned officers. In the army, corporal was a rank with command responsibilities. The air force, on the other hand, promoted their trained mechanics and flight stewards to corporal in order to increase their pay. Allard knew that these air-force corporals would not want to revert to the rank of private, so he bent over backward – too far backward – by imposing the RCAF system on the army. In future all fully trained private soldiers would be promoted to corporal.

My intuition rebelled at the proposed distortion of the rank structure; but when the crunch came, I capitulated. As with the issue of the uniform, I didn't wish to be constantly overruling staff recommendations, so I concurred when I should have said no. It was a gross mistake, and led to the current bizarre ratio of NCOs to private soldiers. It is a mistake that should still be rectified, when we have a minister courageous enough to grasp the nettle.

In his plea to the committee, Allard was dead on when he said that uncertainty about the passage of the bill was our greatest enemy. "The PM had already called me in and told me there was some question of the bill being put through this session when Marcel Prud'homme told me he had picked up the rumoured 'deal' from Mike Forrestall at the airport."[23] It was, in effect, that the House would prorogue without passing Bill C–243, which would then be reintroduced in the new session. I was both sick at heart and furious. It appeared that the Prime Minister was willing to throw me to the wolves, just as he had abandoned Guy Favreau and Lucien Cardin. There was some consolation at caucus that morning when Marcel and the boys – Bob Andras, Grant Deachman, Joe Macaluso, Jim Byrne, and one or two others – gave House leader George McIlraith and the PM quite a going over. They took a very hard line about putting the bill through before the end of the session, and it seemed to have some effect.

Cabinet met early the next morning to consider the matter. "I was surprised at the support. Paul Martin, Bob Winters, and Bud Drury, as well as Léo [Cadieux] were all solidly behind finishing the bill before the end of the session."[24] Joe Greene and Allan MacEachen wondered if we shouldn't hear more witnesses to satisfy the public, even if it meant postponing third reading. In summary, the PM said the consensus seemed to favour pressing ahead, but that this might mean a shorter Easter holiday. As if to underline the continued uncertainty, he recited a long list of important legislation that had to be passed before prorogation. Cabinet agreed in principle that my bill should be concluded before the session ended, but subject to a review of developments.[25]

Thursday began with Hartley Zimmerman coming in to say goodbye. He had earned his retirement, but for me there was more than a tinge of sadness in his departure, because he had been a friend as well as a colleague. Hartley embodied the dual characteristics of gentleness and effectiveness – a rare combination that one might hope to emulate. My thanks were heartfelt and profound. Minutes later his successor as chairman of the Defence Research Board, Dr. Robert Uffen, and the new associate chairman, Dr. "Hap" L'Heureux, came to pay their respects. Hartley considered them worthy and promising appointees, and so did I.

Their enthusiasm at the outset of greater responsibility was the highlight of my day, after which it was all downhill. The Defence Committee did nothing but wrangle over a motion to get on with a clause-by-clause consideration of the bill.

Saturday Bill Lee and his daughter Cathy went to Toronto with me for a presentation of scrolls to three centenarians at Lambert Lodge, the well-known Toronto home for senior citizens. Joe Carenza, one of my most faithful Toronto supporters, brought a huge birthday cake, which contributed to a very nice party. Afterward we went back to my apartment "to talk to Al Scott [of Vickers and Benson advertising] about advertising policy after unification. We suggested playing up the world's first unified service, etc. – a pride for young Canadians."[26] That evening I spoke at the founding dinner of the Hamilton-Wentworth Liberal Association on the subject "Canada's Second Century". The effort was well worth while, as some of my friends and supporters needed a bit of shoring up after the battering I had been getting in the press.

The media reaction to my "apology" to Landymore had been absolutely devastating. An editorial in the *Lethbridge Herald*, which had been a staunch supporter, was titled "Mr. Hellyer Goes Too Far". The final paragraph read: "The defence minister's arrogance and tactlessness makes it difficult to maintain confidence in him. In this latest episode he has damaged both himself and his cause."[27] A lead editorial in the *Daily Colonist*, a Victoria paper that acted as the admirals' advocate, was headed "Hellyer Must Go". It went on to say that my "apology" was not an apology, it was a retraction. Consequently, Landymore should be given the option of returning to his command. "But even this would not be enough. The only real thing that would meet the needs of the moment in the interests of justice, in the interest of morale in the armed forces, and in the interests of the nation, is Mr. Hellyer's resignation."[28] As I read these editorial missiles, I recalled Bill Lee's strategy of building a bank of favourable publicity at the outset, so we would have something to draw on when hard times came. Looking back, I reflected that there had been withdrawals almost every day for weeks, and I wondered if we were not, by then, overdrawn.

Late Sunday morning, my assistant Michael Barry phoned to say that Governor General Georges Vanier was dead. "I knelt in thanksgiving to God for a man who has set such a wonderful example for all and who displayed in his life the spiritual qualities which are so rare. I feel that I have lost a real friend. His shoes will be difficult to fill."[29]

On Monday cabinet agreed on seven days of mourning, comparable to the period for Lord Tweedsmuir in 1940. Parliament would meet briefly that afternoon, just long enough for party leaders to pay tribute, and then adjourn until Thursday afternoon. The funeral service would be held in the Ottawa Basilica Wednesday morning, after which the body would be moved by train to Quebec City for an interment service Thursday morning. "Burial would ultimately be in the chapel of the Citadel in Quebec City, in keeping with the G.G.'s request, but this wouldn't be possible immediately."[30]

Although Parliament was not meeting, the cabinet met again Tuesday morning, and George McIlraith underlined that, because of the loss of three days, the government would have to reconsider its entire legislative program for the remainder of the session. There were 110 items to be voted (supplementary estimates), covering forty-two departments and agencies, and a great deal would depend on the atmosphere in the House, particularly as it might be affected by the debates on the Bank Act and the Canadian Forces Reorganization Bill (C-243). This sounded like a signal to me that, despite cabinet's agreement in principle to proceed, my bill was likely to be dropped from the essential list. The PM observed that it was necessary to put the Bank Act through the Senate by March 31, and interim supply had to be dealt with by April.[31]

Allan MacEachen insisted that the unification bill not be brought back until all-party negotiations on new interim rules were completed. Meanwhile, George McIlraith made the unrealistic suggestion that he try to get Opposition agreement to resume consideration of Bill C-243 at the committee stage in the new session, rather than repeating first and second reading. The PM sidestepped the issue by saying that he would speak to McIlraith and me privately. At the same time he pointed out that the first part of the next session would be fully taken up with eight days on the Throne Speech, six days on the budget, eight days on supply, thirty days on estimates, and seven days on broadcasting, for a total of 59 days.[32] It seemed that the tide had gone out and I was left gasping on the beach.

All ministers attended the funeral mass on Wednesday, but only a handful were delegated to accompany the train to Quebec City. Ellen and I rode in the Pearsons' private railway car. Before dinner Mike and I retired to his bedroom for the private chat he had suggested in cabinet. I reviewed the situation in considerable detail, and supported Allard's view that uncertainty was our greatest enemy. In summation, I said that he was the boss, and he could do whatever he liked. But, if the completion of the unification bill were left for the next session of Parliament, he would have to find a new minister to finish it. "You're serious," he observed, to which I responded simply, "Yes." The debate had already been one of the longest and most difficult in memory, and living with the "enemy" of uncertainty, for heaven only knew how many more months, was more than I or the Forces could take.

I have always thought that this was the turning point. The PM didn't want to face a controversial resignation in Centennial year so, for once, he was the one caught between a rock and a hard place. When cabinet met the following evening, I deliberately referred to the earlier decision in principle and asked for confirmation that there had been no change. The PM noted that a final decision would only be appropriate after we could see what progress was made in the House the following week, but for the first time it was agreed to seriously consider completing the armed forces bill immediately after Easter. This would mean postponing prorogation beyond April 3 – and all was subject to certain conditions of cooperation on the part of the Opposition.[33]

The good news was always offset by bad, and I was both shocked and dismayed to read front-page headlines like "All-Party Agreement, Deal May Put Unification Bill on Shelf", which appeared in the *Montreal Star* of March 14, and about which I had known nothing. The assumption was that the Opposition would agree to reintroduction of the bill at some intermediate stage in the next session. I laughed at the naivety of those of my colleagues who thought that they could get unanimous agreement from the Conservative Opposition.

Cabinet's on-again-off-again attitude was understandable in the face of the Tories' relentless pressure. On Tuesday, March 14, Marcel Lambert raised a question of privilege concerning the defence estimates, alleging that their form anticipated passage of the unification bill and consequently constituted "a gross irregularity having regard to the law as it stands to-day".[34] The argument was strongly supported by Gordon Churchill, who led the Tory attackers.In reply I said that, except for the actual numbers, the format of the defence estimates was exactly the same as the previous year. My explanation was endorsed by Andrew Brewin (NDP, Greenwood). "As the Minister of National Defence pointed out, this form of presenting the estimates is perfectly appropriate whether or not the unification bill is passed. What has happened is that the estimated expenditures have been grouped under the different roles and commands which were set up under the legislation of 1964. In my view this method of presenting the estimates is an improvement over the previous method and in no way prejudges our determination on the unification issue."[35]

After listening to argument on both sides, the Speaker reserved judgment until Wednesday, when he ruled that, although the change was a valid point of debate, it did not constitute a *prima facie* question of privilege. Rebuffed, but still not satisfied, Churchill raised the subject again during Question Period. The war continued to be fought on many fronts.

The afternoon newspapers carried reports of Admiral Rayner's appearance before the Defence Committee the previous day. He had said that loss of the navy uniform would be "catastrophic". One headline put his concern succinctly: "Navy green? 'Queer Uniform' Makes Admiral See Red".[36] This was only a slight exaggeration of the Tory position, which emerged in the Commons again on March 21 when John Diefenbaker sardonically inquired if the green uniform, allegedly sighted on Parliament Hill a few days earlier, had been worn with the authority of the Minister of National Defence.

In reply I explained that some experimental uniforms were being tried out by various service personnel that summer, in order to gauge their suitability. For his part Gordon Churchill was interested in the cost of the project, but the symbol-conscious Diefenbaker zeroed in on the question of my sponsorship of the new uniforms, leading to one of the few humorous exchanges of the debate.

Mr. Diefenbaker: Mr. Speaker, perhaps the minister will come down from the high atmosphere and answer the question.

Were the soldiers on Parliament Hill on March 17 wearing a uniform which was authorized by him? That is the question!

Mr. Hellyer: There is an old saying which my Right Honourable Baptist friend will appreciate. "The better the day the better the deed." I think it was on St. Patrick's day when these uniforms were worn. Certainly at that time they were worn on the authorization of the Minister of National Defence and the chief of defence staff.

Mr. Diefenbaker: The reference to Baptists leads me to state that we Baptists would never abolish the navy.

Some hon. members: Oh, oh.

Mr. Macdonald (Rosedale): On a question of privilege, Mr. Speaker, speaking for at least my section of the Baptist church, I do not agree with the right honourable gentleman.[37]

The House rose for the Easter recess the following day, March 22, at 12:54 a.m. (actually it rose on the 23rd, but that is how the House keeps time – the day doesn't end until the adjournment). Most of the final days had been spent on the Bank Act, which passed and received Royal Assent that night, much to Mitchell Sharp's relief. He had been fighting his own battle in cabinet against the sustained opposition of Walter Gordon, who never quite accepted the fact that he was no longer Finance Minister and chief financial policy-maker for the government. I felt a little sorry for the PM, who had been adjudicating the Sharp–Gordon spat at the same time he was trying to reconcile the diverse interests over the unification bill.

The last items to clear the Commons were supplementary estimates and the ways-and-means motion piloted through by Edgar Benson. One of the "sups" related to defence, and the Tories couldn't resist firing a parting salvo just minutes before the traditional cease-fire. When it came, Jack Pickersgill, who was acting PM, said the usual words of praise for the Speaker and officers of the House and a kind word for the Opposition, to which Gordon Churchill, with the same combination of goodwill and tongue-in-cheek humour, replied. There was only one point of disagreement.

Mr. Churchill: I am afraid I cannot agree with the Acting Prime Minister, that the balance of this prolonged session will necessarily end very quickly following our return, because I note that the Minister of National Defence (Mr. Hellyer) is in moderate health and may wish to take part in a debate with us when we return after Easter. If in the interval, refreshed from a Caribbean cruise or some such vacation, he has a change of mind, the session will end very quickly. We will then be able to begin the long-awaited centennial session in the best of humour. I do not mind on this occasion, and this may not often be repeated, extending my congratulations to the government side of the House."[38]

I must have been in good health, although the fact eluded my consciousness at the time. I was so totally exhausted from the constant bombardment that, when Ellen and I reached Antigua for a few days' rest, my weary mind wondered if my eyes would actually open when dawn came. They did, and the brief exposure to sun and sea proved sufficient recharge to keep me mobile.

On my return to Ottawa I found that George Hees had been inspiring headlines like "Hellyer's Plan for Unification No Good – Hees".[39] The Tory leadership battle was in full tilt. John Diefenbaker, whose plans were uncertain at best, was calling for the reinstatement of Admiral Landymore. "It would only be fair," he told a CBC free-time TV audience.

Offsetting all this negativism was a report of a speech by Group Captain David Adamson, base commander at Canadian Forces Base, Trenton, Ontario. " 'Integration works – and Its Here To Stay,' Group Captain Tells Kiwanis . . . and Hees" read the head-line. The article continued: "Morale in the armed forces was high, the commander said, with several thousands returning to the forces after trying a stab at 'civie street'. 'But it's a long drawn out evolution. We need an organization which will meet the problems of the day . . . not the problems of the past.' "[40]

The same tone appeared in a feature article by Maj.-Gen. F. F. "Worthy" Worthington in the Toronto Telegram. Under the heading "The Straitjacket of Military Dogma", the general wrote:

In February and March the Parliamentary Defence Committee sat for six weeks hearing 23 high-level military "experts" on the integration and unification of Canada's armed forces. The testimony of most of them had a disturbingly familiar theme: What was good enough for the last war will be good enough for the next.

As one of Canada's oldest generals, I believe that at the end of any large war the existing generals should be thanked, decorated and pensioned off.

Put up statues if you like, but don't let them meddle with the future organization of the services. . . .

With the exception of a few great leaders of history, such as Alexander the Great, Genghis Khan and Marlborough, the army (along with the church) has always been rigidly bound by ritual and dogma.

Integration and unification offer a chance for Canada to escape from the straitjacket – if the traditionalists will let it.[41]

This kind of assessment was helpful with the open-minded, but had no effect on the traditionalists.

Whether morale in the forces was as good as Group Captain Adamson proclaimed in his speech is an arguable point, but one major factor in the improvement of morale for sailors was a reduction in sea-time. Before this, they had been pressed into excessive service in order to keep all the ships at sea. Cutting back a bit and working out long-range plans, so each sailor would know in advance what was expected of him, helped a lot. I found that problems of this nature, like the ratio of sea- to shore-time for sailors, or the length of the tour of duty in Cyprus or the Sinai for soldiers, had a more immediate effect on morale than the cut or colour of uniforms.

My own morale, however, took a beating when cabinet met for the first time after Easter on April 3 for the sole purpose of discussing House business. I was dismayed when the Acting PM, Paul Martin, advised that "most ministers appeared to have agreed that the best course would be to proceed that day with Rules of the House as a first item."[42] I was thunderstruck because I thought I had an iron-clad undertaking that my bill would have priority. I pointed out that, unless there was agreement on time allocation, it would be better to give priority to the defence bill. I had to go to Washington for a day at the end of the week and wouldn't be available then.

Jack Pickersgill said he had previously thought we should begin with the rules, but had changed his mind because it would be said that the PM was undercutting another of his ministers – which is exactly what would have been said. A debate raged between the rules proponents and those opposed. Finally Paul

Martin slipped out to phone the PM, who agreed we should proceed with the defence bill. Crisis "number 3729" resolved.

When the PM returned to cabinet the following day he said he had recommended to the Queen that Roland Michener, Canada's High Commissioner to India, be appointed Governor General. He was to be installed April 17. He further reported the resignations of Guy Favreau and Lucien Cardin. He expressed concern over Lucien's continuing ill health, which had required repeated hospitalization. Favreau, too, was no longer capable of taking an active part in political life, but could serve on the bench, to which he was subsequently appointed.[43]

Consequent on the resignations, he announced the following changes in the ministry. Two ministers without portfolio, Walter Gordon and John Turner, were to become President of the Privy Council and Registrar General, respectively. Pierre Trudeau was named Minister of Justice and Attorney General, while Jean Chrétien was to be minister without portfolio.[44] The new ministers attended their first meeting two days later, on April 6.

Although no one twigged at the time, these were events that would reshape Canadian politics. The potential impact of Trudeau's elevation was largely unrecognized, even though it meant that the second member of "The Three Wise Men" from Quebec, the triumvirate that had entered federal politics as comrades-in-arms, had been accepted into the inner circle. Gérard Pelletier, the third, was yet to have his day, but that would come. The press was more alert in recognizing the significance for another future leader. "Turner Facing Big Chance", the *Ottawa Journal* reported from a CP story.

> Rich, young, handsome, bilingual and politically ambitious, Mr. Turner could not hope to find a better job at a better time.
>
> Weeks before his promotion Tuesday from minister without portfolio, the decision had been made to transform the registrar-general's department to a department of consumer and corporate affairs.
>
> Now it is the Montreal lawyer who stands to gain credit for putting new strength into Ottawa's control over business in the service of the average shopper and investor.[45]

The same page of the same paper carried a feature story, "Verbal Flak Again Rakes Unification". The pounding continued without sign of let-up, and an article in the next day's Ottawa *Citizen*, headed "Commons Nerves Tattered", continued:

The Commons debate on armed forces unification goes into its fifth straight day to-day and already nerves are becoming tattered.

The bill to abolish the navy, army and air force and create a single service has 65 clauses and ostensibly the Commons is on clause-by-clause study.

But not a single clause has been approved.[46]

This was despite an impassioned plea by my associate for early passage on the grounds that morale was suffering from the indecision. The Ottawa *Citizen* reported: " 'I'm sure I speak for all servicemen when I say, let's get on with the decision,' said Mr. Cadieux, substituting for Mr. Hellyer who was in Washington.' [47]

I had been obliged to attend the NATO nuclear-planning committee meeting in the U.S. capital on April 5 and 6, even though it meant flying back and forth twice. At the meeting, McNamara informed the assembled defence ministers that the superpowers were making good progress towards an agreement not to proceed with counter-missile systems. That was good news. Canada had consistently declined the U.S. invitation to participate in its antiballistic missile installations, and we were never convinced of the advisability of the Americans proceeding with such a massive program.

At the end of the formal agenda, Robert McNamara invited NATO colleagues to a reception and buffet dinner at his home. During a private discussion in the garden, the U.S. defence chief and I exchanged experiences. I mentioned the constant battle to keep my colleagues on side and the difficulty of bringing the unification debate to a successful conclusion. My story acted like a lever opening a dam. McNamara revealed in intimate detail the kinds of abuse to which he had been subjected. Peaceniks, who considered him a hawk, labelled him a warmonger, while the extreme right accused him of being a communist whenever there was the least hint of an olive branch. Tears came into his eyes as he spoke of the extent to which opposition to him and to his policies had spilled over, second hand, onto his children at school. Though we were light-years apart in power and influence, we shared the unspoken bond of kindred spirits.

The controversy over unification had not diminished during my absence from Ottawa. Lord Mountbatten had been dragged back into the debate. From London he issued a "clarifying statement" in response to a message from Richard H. Gaunt, a retired Canadian naval officer, in which he stated that he was being quoted out of context as a supporter. The Mountbatten press release favoured integration of common services as "more efficient and economical", but underlined that in the British reorganization "great care had been taken to preserve morale and service tradition. . . . It has been accepted that to achieve this the three services must retain their uniforms and ranks with an identifiable professional head of their service."[48]

I was somewhat taken aback, because Lord Louis, or "Dickie", as his friends called him, had always assured me that he favoured "unification". His sole reservation had been the common uniform, which he considered unnecessary unless, as he said on more than one occasion, it was "navy blue with brass buttons". Even this was a limited caveat. He had proposed that all British officers of major-general equivalent and above be placed on a single promotion list and wear a common uniform. His recommendation for complete unification at the top, where it counted most, was rejected by the U.K. Ministry of Defence, and Mountbatten's change of heart followed the rebuff. Later, in the course of a Canadian speaking engagement in support of his "revised" position, he phoned to apologize. He alleged that he had allowed himself to be outmanoeuvred, but I got the impression that too many of his old comrades had been accusing him of desertion and that he was trying to recover their goodwill.

In the propaganda war we lost some battles and won others. Mountbatten's apparent defection made big waves because he had been a star witness for the affirmative. In his wake it was doubly courageous for Vice-Admiral R. L. "Spike" Hennessey to come to the rescue in a speech to the Navy League of Canada. "Unification Defended", the Montreal *Gazette* reported.[49]

The Fiftieth Anniversary of the Battle of Vimy Ridge on Sunday, April 9, provided an unofficial one-day truce in the war of words. Roger Teillet, Minister of Veterans' Affairs, hosted a dinner in the West Block, Parliament Buildings, and proposed the toast to Departed Comrades. Following a minute's silence, I proposed one to the Veterans of Vimy, which was responded to by a survivor of that famous battle, during which Canadians emerged from the cocoon of colonialism. Appropriately, the late General the Lord Byng's "Vimy" cigarette box was presented to

Secretary of State Judy LaMarsh for the National War Museum. The evening ended with an eloquent address by the Prime Minister – the lull before the cease-fire ended.

Monday's Toronto *Telegram* carried a column by Lubor Zink, entitled "Unification: Now's the Time for Closure". Lubor put the government's case succinctly:

> The less dogmatic opponents of Bill C–243 say: "Why gamble? Why not leave things as they are now?"
>
> The flaw in this argument – which of course is the age-old argument of all status quo defenders – is that the process of experimental change is well advanced.
>
> It has, in fact, already progressed through the approved integration stage to the point where, in the form of the new field command structure, the momentum of change requires completion of the whole cycle.
>
> The Government sees it as an organic growth, a sort of pregnancy which cannot be stopped except by abortion. To my mind the Opposition has even less public support for forcing an abortion in this case than it had in the flag debate.
>
> The Government shouldn't therefore, hesitate to use closure for bringing the issue to the final vote."[50]

At cabinet on April 11, it was clear that the PM was not yet ready to act on Zink's advice. George McIlraith indicated that John Diefenbaker would be speaking that day, followed by others, and that if the government intended to move on time allocation – a type of closure – it would be necessary to give notice on routine proceedings. The PM said "not yet" – until the leader of the Opposition had spoken. He would follow in the debate if time allocation proved to be necessary.[51]

When the House met, the session began on a high note as the Prime Minister announced that Madame Vanier was moving to Montreal, and that she was being appointed to the Privy Council for Canada, "the first woman, apart from Ministers of the Crown, to occupy that honourable place."[52]

The harmony with which the news was greeted soon gave way to discord when Diefenbaker began to speak on the unification bill. He accused General Allard of political ambition and suggested that this was the reason for his support of the government plan. This was a monstrous falsehood, so I rose to the general's defence. I knew Allard had been invited to enter political life at an earlier stage in his career, but I also knew he harboured no political ambition beyond making the armed forces more amenable to French-speaking Canadians. My heated exchange with the Opposition leader was reported in the *Globe and Mail* under the heading "Diefenbaker, Hellyer in Head-on Clash as Defence Debate Flares in Commons."[53]

The tenor of the debate made it painfully obvious that the Tory strategy was to force the use of closure, which they thought would embarass the government. I sensed that they were out of keeping with the public mood, so when cabinet met on April 13, I recommended that time allocation be applied under the new rule 15A. George McIlraith had already complained to cabinet about the poor attendance in the House, especially by ministers. This reflected a general lack of interest by all parties, except for the hard-liners. Cabinet accepted my proposal, and when the House convened, McIlraith gave notice of the application of Section 15A. That gave House leaders until the following Tuesday to make a deal. Should they fail, the government was in a position to introduce a further motion limiting debate to as little as three additional days.

At cabinet on Monday, McIlraith reported an Opposition offer to pass the bill, with the exception of clauses two and six – the two clauses that contained the essence of the legislation. I noted that the proposal was not helpful for that reason. The armed forces were still suffering from the verbal conflict and the uncertainty of the outcome of the debate. Cabinet, to its credit, agreed to reject the proposition and press on.[54] However, the subject came up again the next morning when McIlraith said the smaller parties would accept whatever the Government and Opposition could agree on; but the Opposition was adamant. The Prime Minister proposed that the Government give notice immediately for the allocation of the minimum time provided by the rules. That would mean two days for the committee stage and one for the third reading.[55]

Time allocation was on cabinet's agenda again on April 20. Press reaction to leaks of the Government's intentions had been generally matter-of-fact. The heading on the Toronto *Telgram*'s lead editorial of April 15, "The Guillotine – No!", appeared to take a firm stand, but the text was far less categorical. It really pleaded for a little more time. Then, if the Opposition didn't cooperate, the Government should act. The final paragraph provided the balance. "Needlessly delaying the passage of important legislation can be just as harmful as rushing it through before there has been adequate time to examine it carefully."[56] Another story in the Toronto *Star* was headed: "Tories Intransigent, Seven Days then Guillotine for Unification Debate". The subsequent article supported our case that the debate had gone on long enough. "The bill now getting detailed study, has elicited more than 3,000,000 words and 11,000 questions since October 31 when debate began in the House on interim supply.[57] Reassured by the tone of the press reaction, the cabinet stood firm.

Diefenbaker was adamant to the end, and accused the Government of using "brute force" to push the bill through. "They brought in a flag by closure. They're going to bring in unification by closure with the assistance of the third [minority] parties," he told the *Star*.[58]

The "Chief's" opposition was caused largely by the break with tradition. It was the change in symbolism that upset him. He wasn't alone in this regard. Angus MacLean, a decorated and distinguished RCAF veteran and future Premier of Prince Edward Island, made an impassioned plea not to drop the "royal" prefix for the navy and air force. This had been the subject of intensive internal debate in the department between proponents and opponents. It was agreed we would have only one name for the forces, and "royal" seemed to fit with the word "marines" when Royal Canadian Marines was mooted briefly. The idea had been quickly ruled out, because it sounded too much like both the British Royal Marines and the U.S. Marines. Attention was then focussed on something new and dramatic – not "Nairmy", as cartoonists had suggested in fun, but a word which would adequately denote the unity of land, sea, and air force. All attempts failed – ending usually in ridicule – and we finally fell back on the unimaginative but comprehensible Canadian Armed Forces. In that case the prefix "royal" couldn't be applied because the initials would be RCAF, and the army and navy would have none of that.

All of this was grist for the Annual Press Gallery dinner on April 22, at which I was lampooned in the lead song, entitled "Garbed, for Hellyer in the Green", which was probably written by Southam's Charles Lynch, a New Brunswick Tory who had been one of my vociferous critics. A star performer at these annual off-the-record bashes, he relished doggerel, which he always sang fortissimo.

Oh I'm a former admiral
And I'm an A.C.2;
But our blues are gone and so we don
A lovely shamrock hue.

Two other songs, one in English and one in French, assessed the lineup of hopefuls for Liberal and Conservative leadership. Neither of the eventual winners was mentioned.

The unification bill was considered in committee of the whole again on Monday afternoon, April 24. Under the threat of the guillotine, opposition collapsed, and all remaining clauses were passed before the dinner recess, which, by unanimous consent, was lengthened by one hour to give MPs a chance to celebrate or drown their sorrows as the case might be.

At cabinet the following morning, I reported that the previous evening Mr. Churchill, MP for Winnipeg South Centre, had requested that I ascertain whether the passage of Bill C-243 would affect the prerogative of the Crown, as titular head of the armed forces, and therefore require the consent of His Excellency, the Governor General before third reading. I read a letter from the Deputy Attorney General, whose advice I had sought, expressing the opinion that the bill in question did not affect the prerogative of the Crown. It was my intention to inform the House of this opinion as soon as it met.[59]

I so informed the House. A few minutes later, when the orders of the day were called, Gordon Churchill agreed to have the vote on third reading at once, without debate. I was as pleased as I was astonished. The formal count was 127 to 73. Support for the measure was quite general, except for the Tories. As Arthur Blakely reported in the *Gazette*: "Voting for the measure were 101 Liberals, 12 New Democrats, 8 Creditistes, 4 Socreds and 2 Independents. Four maverick New Democrats joined 69 Conservatives to vote against the measure."[60] Blakely continued:

The sudden and expedited end to the long debate on unification took most Members of Parliament by surprise.

Conservative strategists offered no explanation for the abrupt cessation of their attacks which made possible an afternoon vote, though observers noted the absence of John Diefenbaker, who had been filling a speaking engagement in the U.S. . . .

Defence Minister Paul Hellyer – who received a long burst of applause from jubilant Liberals when his bill passed yesterday – has indicated it will not be proclaimed before this fall, at the earliest.[61]

The release of months of pent-up emotion on our side of the House was really quite phenomenal. Behind the curtain Jim McNulty, MP for St. Catharines, said: "Hellyer, I would follow you through hell." He didn't, when the crunch came in the spring of 1968, but his bravado represented the mood of the moment.

With the bill passed, I had one free day to catch up on other matters before Expo '67 opened in Montreal on Thurdsay, April 27. What a wonderful day it was and what a magnificent tribute to the combined genius of Expo Ambassador, Pierre Dupuy, the irrepressible mayor of Montreal, Jean Drapeau, Col. Ed Churchill and Bob Shaw, who had been in charge of construction, and the thousands of others who had proved that Canada could pull off a project on this scale. It was an achievement that signalled our country's finest hour had arrived and we would all revel in it and bask in the reflected glory. I was in fine fettle when I flew to Toronto on Saturday to take the salute at the Air Cadets' Centennial Parade past the Old City Hall.

When cabinet met on May 2 the PM said that arrangements had been made to prorogue on Monday morning, May 8, and begin the new session that same day at 4:00 p.m. The address in reply to the Speech from the Throne would be moved by the new MP for Nicolet–Yamaska, Florian Côté, and seconded by the member for Burin–Burgeo, Don Jamieson.[62] This pleased me, because I knew them both. Don had worked closely with me during the Liberal rally of 1961, and I had squeezed out a day to campaign for Côté during the by-election to fill Lucien Cardin's vacant seat. We had visited a factory that made sunglasses for the armed forces. As they came off the assembly line they were put into three different cases – navy, light blue, and brown – and they would be packaged, stored, and distributed that way. It was one more little bit of nonsense soon to be eliminated.

On Friday, May 5, cabinet met to review a draft Speech from the Throne, and we agreed on a number of modifications. From my vantage point, the most significant thing was that, for the first time since the Pearson government was formed in 1963, the speech contained no reference to the armed forces. The war of words was over!

CHAPTER 13

CENTENNIAL YEAR
1967

T he year 1967 was very special. It marked the hundredth anniversary of the union of the provinces of Upper and Lower Canada, New Brunswick, and Nova Scotia, into one country – a union that subsequently expanded to ten provinces and two territories, extending from Newfoundland to British Columbia and from the Great Lakes to the Arctic Circle. The survival of the country alone was no mean feat, and called for a celebration unlike anything we had seen before. This was the perfect occasion for L. B. Pearson. No one could have been a more charming and gracious host to the parade of world leaders who came to salute our "coming out" party, and I was never prouder of him. The PM was ably supported by the minister responsible for protocol, the Secretary of State, Canada's one and only Judy LaMarsh.

One of my most intriguing assignments that year was to represent the Government of Canada at a gala soirée aboard the gargantuan S.S. *France*. One had to presume that the ship,

France's elegant and exciting state-of-the-art floating palace, was coming to Canada to pay tribute to the country on its centennial. I wondered, however, if the decision to berth the S.S. *France* at Wolfe's Cove, the launching point of the English invasion, had been made as a reminder to "New France" of glory lost, and of what might have been had the French chosen more wisely in negotiating the Treaty of Paris.

My instinct proved to be correct, and I was to be a participant in an incident that was to be a precursor of the only sour note to break the harmony of that memorable year – General Charles de Gaulle's now-famous visit to Quebec. On May 11 I escorted a planeload of invited guests to Quebec City, where the S.S. *France* lay alongside – every bit as impressive as I had been led to expect. I was taken to a lovely suite. Soon after I had my gear spread around the stateroom, someone came and said it was the wrong one – mine was a "grander" one. I declined to change, because I had already settled in and I was suspicious about the motive for the change.

Two minutes before dinner, the ambassador said there had been a terrible mix-up in the seating. Instead of my being the "invité d'honneur", this place was being afforded to The Honourable Hédard Robichaud, my cabinet colleague, and his wife. I was to sit at the second head table. He was very sorry, but had learned about it only a few minutes before. I was perfectly happy because I could now sit with my friends, but I knew the French well enough to feel that the "mix-up" was unlikely to have been accidental.

"Soon the plot was a little clearer. Premier and Mrs. Johnson occupied the places of honour. The Robichauds were two places down on the other side of the head table. The president of the steamship company and the ambassador spoke, as did Mr. Johnson. No federal rep. was invited to. It was a deliberate French snub of the feds."[1]

I found it interesting to note that during dinner the French minister argued the "states supremacy" theory of the constitution with Jean Marchand and Pierre Trudeau. It was also interesting to note that the CBC cameramen filmed only the provincial politicians – to the point of cutting a conversational group in half when taking a picture. "The 'cold war' is intensifying,"[2] I noted later. A fashion show, followed by dancing, continued until 4:00 a.m., but I didn't stay until the bitter end because I was leaving for Calgary at the crack of dawn.

The long sunrise flight gave me a chance to shift my mind from Canada–France relations to defence and domestic politics and to prepare for a jam-packed day visiting Calgary installations, including Currie Barracks, Sarcee, the mens' mess, the junior NCOs' training course, and the sergeants' mess. "In one hour of informal discussion with the Sgts not one question re unification. The problems were Pay Field III, etc."[3]

That evening provided one of the highlights of the year for me. One of the innumerable contributions of the forces to Canada's birthday bash was the *Armed Forces Tattoo*, written and directed by Major Ian Fraser. Men and women of the navy, army, and air force collaborated in one mammoth production that traced our military history from the days of the early French settlers. It was a fast-moving and thrilling spectacle, ending with a lone piper's plaintive and eye-moistening lament. The cast knew I was in the audience, and after they had moved out of the arena, to thundering applause, I became quite apprehensive about the unidentifiable sound I heard from off-stage. My relief was incalculable when I finally realized they were chanting – with increasing volume – "We want Paul." I was escorted backstage, where I told the assembled actors and musicians what a fantastically good job they had done and that it was one of the proudest occasions of my life to watch the show. They were great ambassadors for the armed forces. "When I finished they gave me three cheers. I must admit it brought a lump to my throat. The men who really count – the men of the future – are with me."[4]

The next morning I read the lesson at St. Giles Church and then lunched with Marc Favreau of my staff and David McDonald, who had agreed to head my campaign in Edmonton. Even while I was eating, David put me on the phone to various Liberals across the province, so that no opportunity to gather support would be lost. After lunch I addressed the graduating class at Mount Royal College and then dashed back to the hotel to meet Max Bell, the soft-spoken head of the FP Publishing empire. Max escorted me to a cocktail party, where we circulated briefly before going to his stately home for dinner *en famille*.

After dinner we had a long chat about the Liberal leadership. He had discussed the matter with several of his associates, including tycoon George Gardiner of Toronto, and had eliminated each of the other candidates one by one. They had been somewhat intrigued by John Turner, who had prepared himself both academically and linguistically, but concluded he lacked the maturity to lead the country at that time. The group's final position was that I was the best choice, and Max was willing and anxious to help – first by calling *Free Press* publisher Dick Malone and his closest adviser, the nationally syndicated columnist and former editor, Bruce Hutchison. This was to soften them up as a preliminary to getting the FP chain "on side" editorially. Bell's endorsement appeared to be a major breakthrough with the opinion-makers.

Monday morning I arrived back in Ottawa at 7:30 after about three hours' sleep. Max Bell phoned to say that he had spoken to Dick Malone, who would see me on May 27 – almost two weeks hence – when I was scheduled to be in Winnipeg. Max also reported on Malone's reservations about me. "Dick thinks I 'am going along with the Gordon line', a laugh if I ever heard one, 'and this is part of the reason for his opposition.' "[5] Max suggested that when I talked to Dick I should keep doors open. Later the four of us, Max, Bruce, Dick, and I would get together. There was little doubt that Max was sold and would do everything within his power, including some gentle arm-twisting, to convince the others.

On May 25, I flew to St. Mary's, Ontario, in response to an "irresistible" letter from Lorne Eedy, a Grade Ten student at St. Mary's District Collegiate and Vocational Institute. He had written in March to say that some of his fellow students were "running down" unification without knowing what it was all about, and he thought they should hear about it from the man who knew most about the subject.

At a press conference in London, en route, I said Canada considered the Gulf of Aqaba, which Egypt had closed to Israeli shipping, an international waterway. I also pointed out that, while Canadian troops on peacekeeping duty in the Gaza were not in any immediate danger, the two Canadian destroyers and the support ship *Provider*, which I had dispatched to the area, were on standby in case they were needed for evacuation, and were not for the purpose of helping to keep the gulf open to shipping. This was what the Egyptians privately feared. On the way back from St. Marys, Ellen and I stopped in London for a private reception and dinner sponsored by Bob and Barbara Rankin, John and Ann-Marie Harding, and Janice and Jim Steele – six of my core supporters.

The next morning, Friday, May 26, began with an in-depth briefing by the Director General, Intelligence, Brig. L. E. Kenyon. I listened intently and soon concluded that war in the Middle East was inevitable and that Canadian troops would be in physical jeopardy. Cabinet met later, and when the agenda was completed, I expressed concern for the members of the United Nations Emergency Force and said that it should be withdrawn immediately, as I could not, otherwise, accept responsibility for the safety of the Canadian contingent. If we waited for a phased withdrawal, our men would be the last out, because they were providing support services. They might easily be trapped if the Israelis bombed escape routes through Port Said and El Arish. Then the only alternative might be evacuation by helicopter to the Canadian ships, an operation that would be both painfully slow and risky. Not only did I think we should evacuate Canadian troops at once, I suggested that we should offer to help move the whole UNEF.

The Prime Minister agreed that we should act, and Paul Martin was given the responsibility of advising the UN Secretary General of our intentions. Frankly, I was flabbergasted, because it was so uncharacteristic of the PM to make a decision of that nature so quickly. This untypical behaviour remained a mystery to me for twenty years, until, when I was reading cabinet minutes, I noted that my colleagues had debated the question of Middle East instability on three occasions when I was absent – on May 18, May 23, and May 25. The conditioning had been completed, and the PM was psychologically prepared for a decision when I provided the final little push.

That evening I headed West on a rigorous three-day schedule that included my critically important session with *Free Press* publisher Dick Malone. After an early Saturday-morning breakfast with Saskatchewan Young Liberals in Regina, I doubled back to Winnipeg for a trooping of the colours by the Cameron Highlanders of Canada. It was an excellent presentation, and even the jaded Brigadier Malone was favourably impressed. We both attended the reception that followed, after which he took me to his attractive but unpretentious house for dinner.

I knew Dick quite well, because he and Bruce Hutchinson had bought me lunch several times in Ottawa, and had questioned me and others about the political pulse of the nation. Consequently,

I was sure that his suggestion to Max Bell that I was soft on the Gordon line, which Malone interpreted as excessive governmental interference in all aspects of business, was just a red herring. He knew better from innumerable other conversations. Our real difference was over unification, which he feared would leave Canada vulnerable to what he termed a "Man on Horseback" – the banana-republic-type military coup that Landymore had suggested was a possibility. It was a fear I considered utter rubbish, though I used politer language in his presence. Now, once more, we were to get it all out on the table in a seven-hour interview that began with drinks and extended through dinner, coffee in the drawing room – military style – and liqueurs.

I use the word "interview" with reservations, because for the first three or four hours Dick did nearly all the talking. He reviewed his wartime experience in minute detail, from the time he and Victor Sifton first arrived in Ottawa at the outset of the Second World War to straighten out the Department of National Defence. One of the first things they had had to do was to sell to the Mexicans warehouse lots of saddles from cavalry days to provide storage space for the new equipment that was essential to fight a contemporary war. As the story unfolded, and he related experiences similar to mine, I thought to myself that he should be an ally and should understand exactly what I was trying to do – and why.

Alas, this was not to be. When he finally got around to a discussion of unification, his mind was as inflexible as the World War I officers who had kept all those saddles in readiness. Dick was obsessed with the image of the Man on Horseback he had got from some book he had read, and he was not the slightest bit interested in the kind of rational argument the *Ottawa Journal* had published in response to the same outlandish concern from Admiral Landymore. I have never met a Canadian officer whom I suspected would join anyone in attempting a military coup. Our democratic roots go too deep. Still, Dick argued that the danger was real. In summing up his position, he said that all the senior officers had been against unification. They were professionals who knew their business, and I should have heeded their advice.

By then it was late, and I had only one more card to play. I had prepared myself with some advice from one of the professionals he was talking about – advice I was sure would upset him. I knew that Dick had a deep and reverent attachment to the regimental system, so I pulled the document from my briefcase that I thought would provoke a response. It was a memorandum from Lt.-Gen. W. A. B. Anderson, Commander of Mobile Command, recommending that the six infantry regiments on active service be combined and reduced to three. There were good and rational considerations given, but pressing the case for logic and efficiency meant that The Queens Own Rifles, The Royal Highland Regiment of Canada (Black Watch), and The Canadian Guards, all household names, would be retired to the Supplementary Order of Battle. One, the Queen's Own, was Dick's regiment.

I told him the document was classified, but I trusted him to keep the contents confidential, and I watched closely as he began to read. Soon his face turned pale pink and then the deep purple of a winter's sunset. He continued until he was in a near rage. "You can't let them do it!" He shouted. You can't let them do it! You have to overrule them," he insisted. "That's what ministers are for. You have to overrule the staff when they are wrong." To his dying day I don't think Dick recognized the basic contradiction in his position. In essence he wanted me to rubber-stamp staff recommendations he agreed with, and to overrule proposals that displeased him.

Sunday's activities included attendance at Knox United Church and a reception following the service in the morning, a strategy session with key supporters in the afternoon, and two evening meetings – the first with the Fort Garry Liberal Association and the second an address to the West Kildonan B'nai Brith. An even heavier schedule had been planned for Monday, but I had to cancel out and return to Ottawa when word came that the situation in the Middle East was critical.

Monday the evacuation of Canadian troops from the Gaza Strip began. Six Hercules aircraft – the ones that the RCAF had been reluctant to buy – flew personnel from El Arish to Pisa, the UN staging base in Europe. The first 360 personnel were transferred to Yukon aircraft at Pisa for the trip home to Trenton, Ontario. The evacuation plan put into effect called for all Canadian troops in UNEF to be out of the United Arab Republic by sunset May 30 – the deadline imposed by Colonel Nasser after he learned from the UN Secretary General of the Canadian intention to withdraw. His indignant ultimatum was a response to our plan to pull out, rather than the reason for it – as was reported at the time.

On June 2, in an address to the World Federation of Canada, I admitted "that the compulsory withdrawal of the United Nations Emergency Force had been a 'setback' to the cause of world peacekeeping . . . the ideals of the United Nations Charter have been frustrated by the unwillingness of member states to accept the restraints on the exercise of national sovereignty implicit in such a system. This will remain the case until replaced by international trust. In the meantime, we must expect slow progress and not be too surprised when setbacks to the concept – such as the current one in the Middle East – do occur."[6]

On June 3 I flew to St. Paul, Alberta, a bilingual community northeast of Edmonton. The brief visit proved to be both exciting and memorable. St. Paul boasted the largest number of centennial projects of any Canadian community, and I was showered with mementos ranging from imaginative computer printouts by school children to a cowhide bearing the signatures of the entire population. The *pièce de résistance* for me, however, was being able to preside at the dedication of the world's first Flying Saucer Landing Pad, erected by the citizens of St. Paul with a view to, as they put it, "extending the goodwill existing between the two linguistic groups who lived and worked side by side across the light-years separating earthlings from extraterrestrial visitors."

The next day war broke out in the Middle East. There were several casualties suffered by UNEF troops who had not yet been evacuated.

The following week I visited Mobile Command Headquarters for another performance of the *Armed Forces Tattoo*. None of the magic was lost in seeing it a second time. If anything, I found it even more enjoyable. The unique feature of the week, however, was the big naval review in Halifax – the most spectacular naval array ever assembled in Canadian waters. Forty warships from Canada and twelve from Commonwealth and foreign countries were reviewed by Governor General Roland Michener. As the big ships steamed past, I recalled that on two or three occasions, with a twinkle in his eye, the GG had asked when I was going to make him an admiral – presumably in accordance with the precedent set for General Vanier. I always assumed that he was kidding, though I was never completely certain.

When the festivities ended, the Prime Minister offered his nemesis, The Rt. Hon. John G. Diefenbaker, a lift back to Ottawa in a government plane. Later he told me that, en route, my name came into the conversation.

"I like that man Hellyer," said the Leader of the Opposition.
"You're joking," replied the PM.

"Oh no," said the Dief. "I have a lot of time for him. He's my kind of guy."

"How can you say that," Pearson demanded, "when in the House of Commons you have been cutting him mercilessly into little pieces?"

"Ah yes," responded the old Chief, "but that's politics."[7]

Friendship aside, the Chief was probably not as pleased with a nice boost I got from the Ottawa *Citizen* the final Tuesday of Canada's ninety-ninth year. A brief editorial, entitled "Anti-unifiers Please Note", read as follows:

> Armed Forces recruiting for the first five months of 1967 is up 73 percent over the same period of 1966. The month of May was the biggest recruiting month since 1962.
>
> Now what was all that about unification destroying morale?[8]

Cabinet's morale was shaken on June 29 by a portent of things to come on another front. The PM advised us that arrangements for the visit of General de Gaulle were leading to a number of awkward situations and that plans were being made to minimize any serious friction, either domestically or with France. The Governor General would greet the President on arrival, and would then turn him over to Premier Daniel Johnson of Quebec. He would be in the hands of Quebec authorities for the morning, and would then come back under the feds in the afternoon. There was some disagreement over the arrangements for the evening reception. Quebec wanted to host it, but the Canadian authorities were continuing to insist that it was the GG's prerogative, in keeping with the practice followed for other heads of state. At the same meeting there was discussion of a constitutional Bill of Rights. Cabinet had a memo from Pierre Trudeau proposing that, at the July 5 meeting with the premiers, the possibility of a Bill of Rights be explored.[9] Late that afternoon the Queen and the Duke of Edinburgh arrived at Uplands Airport and excitement increased as the countdown to July 1, and the official centennial birthday, continued.

Saturday, July 1, was a day to remember! For me it began in a most unexpected fashion. I was at my office early, taking advantage of a few quiet hours, when the phone rang. It was the irrepressible Premier of Newfoundland, Joey Smallwood, who seemed equally surprised and delighted that I was "on duty".

Coming quickly to the point he said fires in the Labrador forests were out of control, and forest rangers could no longer cope. Would I send help from the armed forces? "Yes," I replied, and the conversation ended. I called General Allard, and within hours an advance party was in the air. By early morning there were soldiers on the ground, fighting the fires shoulder-to-shoulder with the rangers. The story was to end happily a few smoke-filled, back-breaking days later, when the fires began to abate. Joey credited the armed forces with saving the forest industry that was so critical to the economy of Newfoundland.

The balance of the day was as pleasurable as it was memorable. Judy LaMarsh and her team at State had planned well. Nothing that might mar this special day had been left to chance. The lawn in front of the Parliament Buildings was packed when Her Majesty and Prince Philip arrived for the deeply moving ecumenical service. All doubt and pettiness was put aside when the Speakers of the Senate and the Commons each read a Loyal Address. The crowd was ecstatic when the royal couple walked to the Centennial Flame, smiling and chatting amiably as they went.

Ellen and I skipped the garden party in the afternoon, because we were part of a small group invited to dine with the royal party at 24 Sussex in advance of a *son-et-lumière* show on the story of Canada, which was scheduled for the evening. The party was much more informal than a State dinner, and consequently much more enjoyable. After dinner, in the mood of the moment, Prince Philip donned a lapel flower with a tiny bulb connected to a hidden battery. He moved from group to group, catching each by surprise as he pressed the button and flashed the light. It was time for us to leave, and Maryon Pearson was somewhat less than amused. "Oh for heaven's sake, stop playing with your flower and come on," she ordered the prince, in her own inimitable manner.

At Nepean Point, where the spectacle was to be held, we were seated directly behind the Pearsons and the royal party. The narrative in sound and light told the story of Canada from its early beginnings through to the day we were celebrating. Commenting on the Fathers of Confederation, a deep booming voice said: "I prefer Sir John A. Macdonald drunk to George Brown sober." With less than a second's interval Her Majesty turned to the Prime Minister to say: "We have a George Brown too, and he is seldom sober." It was a wistful comment about an English politician I came to admire for his many other endearing qualities.

When the performance ended, the fireworks began. An unbelievably dazzling display of pyrotechnics etched the gray stone Parliament Buildings and Peace Tower against the deep blue night. It was a thrilling spectacle that drew exclamations from the crowd – including some of us who are not known for expressions of emotion. Instead of subsiding with the flicker of the last barrage of rockets, the excitement actually intensified as we drove downtown and midnight approached. People waved and shouted, horns were blown incessantly, there was a general euphoria that resembled the celebrations at the end of a long war. The nationalistic binge was unlike anything I had seen before or am likely to see again.

However, the celebrations could not continue at that pitch, and soon it was back to work. On July 11 I flew to Newfoundland with my friend, Jack Pickersgill. In a brief interlude, pacing back and forth in front of his cottage, Jack confided that he planned to leave the government and accept a job as the first President of the Canadian Transport Commission, established by the legislation he had piloted through the House in 1966 and early 1967. My name, he said, was one of two he had mentioned to the Prime Minister as a suitable successor as Minister of Transport.

The next day, July 12, Guy Favreau died. It was a tragic end for one of the nicest men I have known in public life – his health completely broken on the altar of dedicated service to party and country. With responsibilities as Minister of Justice, Quebec lieutenant in charge of patronage, and Leader of the House, he had been badly overloaded. Any one of those jobs was enough to keep a man occupied full time; together, they required superhuman effort. Even then he might have survived had it not been for the royal commission on the Rivard case and the feeling that he had been betrayed. Guy's voluntary exile to the bench came too late to restore him to health. For me it was a deep personal loss, and my mind was filled with philosophical ramblings as the priest went through the ritual of thanksgiving for a life of dedication and service to Canada. We would all be poorer without him.

At noon on July 14 Ellen and I attended a luncheon Lionel Chevrier, our High Commissioner to London, held at the Montreal St. James's Club in honour of Lord Mountbatten. Our host seated me opposite the guest of honour, as we were well acquainted and had much of mutual interest to talk about. Inevitably unification became the main topic of conversation, and despite his publicly stated reservations about the uniform, Mountbatten was still very much in favour. As we talked, the exchange became more and more animated, until finally, in a burst of emotion and with that characteristic modesty for which he was noted, he slammed his fist on the table and said: "There are only two people who understand this; you over here and me over there." If only that declaration had been captured on film. It would have made a great endorsement.

Of the many centennial events, a few stand out for one reason or another. One was "sole-disturbing" in the literal sense – and probably the silliest crisis of my public career. Les Fusiliers du St-Laurent had chosen, as their centennial project, to retrace the route of the King's soldiers in the long Loyalist trek from Edmundston, New Brunswick, to Notre Dame du Portage on the St. Lawrence. They invited me to join them for the final mile, and I accepted. At bedtime the night before the event, I began to wonder if I could march a mile. In the rush of daily events there was always a car waiting to take me from one side of the street to the other, and I couldn't remember when I had last walked a mile – or if I could. So I got dressed, put on my moccasins, and marched around several blocks on a route I estimated to be about a mile. No problem!

In the middle of the night I awoke to find that my feet were so sore I couldn't stand on them. Only by putting on shoes, a painful exercise in the circumstances, could I walk as far as the bathroom. I was panic-stricken. I would have to cancel out at the last minute; and who would believe my excuse? It seemed as though dawn would never come, but when it did, Ellen insisted that I fulfil the assignment. "Even if it kills you," she added. I gathered up my courage, accompanied General Jean Allard to the rendezvous, and kept up with him and the troops for that final mile. My soles were burning as we crossed the finish line, and I thanked my guardian angel that it was one mile and not two.

It was more than ironic that, in a year when relations between French- and English-speaking Canadians appeared to reach an all-time high in the common celebration, trouble should come from abroad. The government had been nervous about General de Gaulle's visit and about persistent efforts by France and Quebec to bend protocol enough to establish a unique relationship between them. However, even given these warnings, no one was prepared for what did happen. De Gaulle's cry of "Vive le Québec Libre" during his speech in Montreal seemed an obscene gesture in the midst of a celebration of Canada's hundred years as a federation. The Prime Minister and members of cabinet were appalled and shaken. Worse, they had to decide how to react to the General's outburst at a time when he had not yet visited Canada's capital – and was still scheduled to do so.

I was in Saskatchewan at the time, which I consider a blessing because I was spared involvement in the protracted debate on how the Canadian government should respond. Almost every point of view was expressed. It was the consensus that the statement should not be allowed to go unnoticed or unchallenged, but at the same time the government couldn't just tell the General to leave Canada. There was a range of suggestions. Some felt the Prime Minister should refuse to see de Gaulle, while others thought things should proceed in a "frigid formal way".[10] Some ministers emphasized that what really mattered was the reaction of the French-speaking population, which, except for the separatists, did not seem favourable to the General. The PM noted that the government had to think of the reaction in other parts of the country as well. He had received several hundred telegrams, including some from Quebec, most of which were unfavourable to de Gaulle.[11]

After seemingly interminable argument, a watered-down press release was agreed upon. The invitation to visit Ottawa was not withdrawn, although there were some minor changes to the schedule, largely for security reasons. Nevertheless, mild as it was, the government's reaction could still be interpreted as a reprimand for a head of state.[12]

Cabinet must have been relieved when it met at 9:00 a.m. the following morning and Paul Martin reported that, in the middle of the night, the Canadian Ambassador to France, Jules Léger, had been informed by the Foreign Minister of France, Couve de Murville, that General de Gaulle had indicated he did not intend to come to Ottawa. Mr. Martin also said that he himself had spoken directly to the foreign minister, who had indicated that, in his judgment, pressing the matter with the General would not alter his decision, and the best course was to let him depart.[13]

The fallout from this incredible episode was not unlike that from an atomic explosion. It dissipated substantially over the years, but never completely disappeared. Argument raged as to whether the General acted deliberately or was merely carried away by the warmth and enthusiasm with which he had been greeted by the people of Quebec. In my view, based on the evidence, and influenced by my experience aboard the S.S. *France* and by subsequent events, it was a coldly calculated act. It was an escalation of French mischief, born in part of remorse at its centuries' of neglect of its former colony and a dream of turning back the clock.

While I could never condone de Gaulle's impertinence, I was more understanding than many of my colleagues. I recalled the resentment he held against Anglophones in general as a result of the second-class treatment afforded him by Churchill and Roosevelt during the war. Inevitably some of this would have spilled over on the Canadian establishment, and the feeling was probably reinforced by the shabby way we treated France when it wanted to buy our uranium. We had imposed restrictions that had not applied to the United States and Britain, and which were unacceptable to the French for that reason. This must have been a festering sore. So, apart from the historic relationship with New France, meddling in Canada's internal affairs was one way of getting even – with relish!

The week of August 6, cabinet considered items of interest to the Defence department. On August 8 I noted that it might be necessary to amend the Elections Act in order to integrate the armed-forces vote with other returns on election night. This was to eliminate a long-standing grievance. Traditionally the service vote had been taken at the same time as the civilian vote, but by the time it was counted and reported from the four corners of the world, about a week would pass. In some cases candidates didn't know, until the service vote was released, whether they had been elected or not. Worse, from the standpoint of members of the forces, the delay meant their vote was singled out for national attention, which they did not like.

For years the Chief Electoral Officer had insisted there was no solution to this vexatious anomaly. But as in numerous other cases where officials said something was impossible, once they were instructed to do it anyway, it became possible. As far as the service vote was concerned, the impasse was resolved by the simple expedient of taking it in advance, so the results could be unobtrusively melded with national returns on election night.

Another item on the cabinet agenda was a joint proposal from the Minister of Public Works, George McIlraith, and myself to build a new Defence Headquarters on Le Breton Flats, overlooking the majestic Ottawa River. Few projects that I have been privy to have been as carefully thought out. Freddie Johns, the thrice-retired Air Vice-Marshal in charge of everything, had researched it thoroughly. Offices and functional meeting rooms were arranged on the basis of traffic flows, all of which had been measured, in order to minimize the time lost en route from one room to the other. The final plan was a masterpiece of advance planning.[14] Pity it was never built.

A matter of even greater significance was decided when ministers met in an all-day session on August 11. We were considering estimates for the following year, and agreed on cuts of $622 million in total. The defence budget was slashed by $58 million, and that meant reducing the combined military and civilian establishment by nine to ten thousand. The reduction posed a major problem, but it might have been worse considering the financial mess we had drifted into.

A brief interlude in the discussion resulted in one of cabinet's lighter moments.

"Léo [Cadieux] told me a joke re de Gaulle.

"He has two churches on his estate.

"What is the reason for the second one?

"Reply: It is for God.

"When LBP heard this he said 'And I'll bet it is the smaller one too!' "[15]

On August 16 I presented cabinet with a family of flags for the armed forces: an ensign, embodying the CAF crest, a naval jack, and various modifications of the ensign that would provide identifying flags and pennants for commanders, senior officers, and officials of the Canadian Armed Forces. The Prime Minister said he had been under some pressure from naval personnel and Lord Mountbatten (apparently trying the direct approach after the indirect had failed) to preserve the tradition of the sea by adopting a naval jack displaying both the Maple Leaf and the George Cross, thus indicating the naval ancestry of Canadian ships. He had promised to raise the matter in cabinet. I said that while I preferred a jack designed in Canada, I would like further discussions with naval personnel before making a final recommendation. At the moment I wanted approval of the ensign only. After a discussion in which some ministers expressed their disapproval of flags for commanders, and questioned the desirability of having either an ensign or jack, cabinet approved the ensign as recommended.[16] The other flags were subsequently to be approved on the recommendation of my colleague Léo Cadieux after he became minister.

That night Léo and I co-hosted a performance of the *Armed Forces Tattoo* at Lansdowne Park. Almost everyone on the Ottawa protocol list had been invited as official guests, including the Prime Minister. Ellen was in Muskoka, so daughter Mary Elizabeth subbed as my date for the evening. It was a great night all round, because having seen the show twice, I relaxed totally in the assurance that the crowd would love it. I wasn't disappointed. The applause at the end, following the fading strains of the lament, was deafening – quite uncharacteristic of staid Ottawa audiences. The PM must have been favourably impressed, because in my diary I recorded that he was "moved", not surprising in view of the deeply stirring performance.

The following morning I flew to British Columbia where I was to spend some time with the army cadets at Camp Vernon. On the return flight the passenger list included George Van Roggen from Vancouver and David McDonald of Edmonton, two members of my national campaign committee, who were joining me and some other top members of my team for a weekend strategy session at Arundel Lodge. As soon as we were airborne, I had the captain radio ahead to the Lodge to ask my wife to meet us at Muskoka Airport, since I was anxious to give my guests the VIP treatment.

You can imagine my dismay when we touched down three hours later and Ellen was nowhere in sight. Instead, she had sent Ian Mahon, our garbage boy, to pick us up in the truck. Worse, the so-and-so – here I guard my language carefully – hadn't even bothered to take the garbage cans out of the back of the truck, so, although there was room for the two VIPs in the cab with him, I would be stashed between, if not actually in, one of the cans in the back. We presented a strange sight as the air-force officers saluted smartly and prepared to take off. Frankly, I was not in my best humour.

At that precise moment, Ellen and the whole gang from Arundel poked their heads up from behind the hedge along the asphalt, where they had been having great difficulty stifling their amusement. Toronto Liberal lawyer David Greenspan had a "Moshe Dyan" patch over one eye to add to the conspiratorial nature of the prank, and the whole group broke into raucous laughter, which eventually erased the solemn frowns on the hapless victims. Good-nature returned by the time we all loaded into the five or six cars that were waiting in the driveway. As I suspected, they had encountered great difficulty in persuading the gentle and ever-proper Ian Mahon, son of a retired naval officer, to go along with the gag, and it had taken Ellen's guarantee of clemency to accomplish it.

That night there was a full moon, and I took my guests for a ride in our cedar-strip outboard down the lake to the Muskoka Sands Hotel and back. Fifteen years later George Van Roggen, then Senator Van Roggen, admitted I almost lost his support that night. "The man is mad," he had thought to himself as we breezed along at a cooling thirty knots per hour. He expected that any moment we would plough into a submerged log lurking beneath the surface, such as one might expect in the ocean off Vancouver. Had he shared his concern, I might have explained that the absence of "deadheads" is one of the delights of lakes like Muskoka.

When I got back to Ottawa, after the weekend in Muskoka, I received a nice psychological boost from the *Ottawa Journal* in an article headed "Wants It as Quickly as Possible: Canada's NATO Forces Stirred by New Uniform" by Maj.-Gen. F. F. Worthington, Special Journal Correspondent. "Worthy", who was Colonel-Commandant of the Royal Canadian Armoured Corps, had been invited overseas to present the annual trophy for the best tank gunnery among the NATO forces. He travelled in the new green uniform – the first Canadian to wear it in Europe.

As he wrote:

> It was a curious sensation. I admit I felt somewhat like a little green man from Mars at times, but the reaction among all ranks was one of outright enthusiasm to get it.
>
> Perhaps even more surprising was the enthusiasm of our NATO allies. The Germans especially seemed keen on it.

"Now you Canadians will be recognizable – now you can look like yourselves and not like the British" was the comment I heard over and over from Germans, Dutch and Belgian officers."[17]

The unofficial leadership race was always there, just beneath the surface. Earlier that week David McDonald had reported from Edmonton that he had lined up a number of prominent Edmonton Liberals. Alan Edwards was for me, as was Alan Wachowich, who "would work hard". Dr. Herb Meltzer and his wife, Jean, were on board, as well as Tevi Miller and Bill Sinclair. In Calgary Harry Hays, Nick Taylor, Harry Rowbottom, Reg Gibbs, and Jim Anderson all signed in. David suggested that I ask Max Bell about a money man for Alberta. An embryo organization was also taking form in Ontario. Jim Service agreed to write policy papers, which was his forte. Gordon Edick and Dave Greenspan decided to set up shop in the Muir Park Hotel, with one bedroom, two telephone lines, and one secretary two days a week. The hotel would use her services the other three days.

The Tory leadership convention provided a dry-run of pitfalls to watch for in a campaign. In Ottawa Bill Lee attended as an observer and joined the "Youth for Dief" demonstration. In Toronto we accepted an invitation from Marlene and Elvio Del Zotto to a TV-watching party in their home. In addition to giving us a chance to witness the Conservative countdown, the party provided an opportunity for some of my friends and supporters to meet others for the first time and to be assured they were not alone. My eyes were glued to the television. The drama was almost unbelievable as the old Chief was subjected to a terrible humiliation. I couldn't help but feel sorry for him and Mrs. Diefenbaker. Robert Stanfield finally won on the fifth ballot, following a speech which was uninspiring at best. However, he was well organized and had performed ably at the policy sessions the previous day. That was enough to see him through to victory.

As soon as the tumult and the shouting of the convention subsided, and the story was known, Ellen told me that her mother had taken ill. She died early the next morning. I can honestly say that no one could have been a better mother-in-law! She was great.

Monday afternoon "George Van Roggen phoned to say that Bob Winters told Alec Walton that I would be going to Transport and the reason why. The PM implied as much. I am the only one in the dark."[18] Not long after, Mike phoned to tell me that I would be moving from Defence to Transport. We didn't discuss the succession in Defence because I just assumed Léo Cadieux would move up. I should have known that nothing can be taken for granted in politics and should not have been surprised when the grapevine telegraphed a whiff of uncertainty. My curiosity aroused, I phoned the PM Saturday morning, September 16, to get the straight goods. I could scarcely believe my ears when he said he was going to appoint Léo "acting minister". Knowing Léo's strong feelings about the division of senior portfolios, I was certain that this wouldn't be acceptable, and I said so. I also assured him that Léo was perfectly capable and probably better than anyone else, because he had been involved in the unification process and understood it. It was only logical that he should finish the job. "After a few minutes he said, 'Why don't I just call him and say I am going to appoint him.' I agreed and said, 'You're wonderful.' To have done otherwise would have driven poor old Léo right up the wall – and rightly so."[19]

Sunday was sunny and warm – summer in September. I attended the Battle of Britain ceremony for the last time, and then went to Toronto for a meeting of my national campaign committee. It was a good meeting: "Not as orderly as the last one – but worthwhile. The situation seems to be improving in all provinces from Ontario west.

"I told the boys at the airport that this would likely be my last trip as MND. They seemed genuinely sorry. Group Captain Boland [Commanding Officer of Canadian Forces Base, Downsview] said I would be missed. He wished me well and said that he hoped I became leader of the country and that quite a few chaps at the base agreed."[20]

At cabinet on Monday, the PM announced his intention to appoint me as Minister of Transport and Léo Cadieux as Minister of National Defence. At the same time Jack Pickersgill was appointed president of the new Canadian Transport Commission. The PM told Jack that he took with him the good wishes of all his colleagues.[21]

Tuesday, Defence Council met to consider the proposed cuts in defence expenditures. It was my final meeting. "I told Council how much I had enjoyed working with them and wished them well. I asked them to support the new minister and said I had confidence in them. Elgin Armstrong said some nice things about me and that it had been stimulating working under my imaginative brain. He was very kind.

"Léo said some nice things and asked for support, etc.

"We then went to Government House to be sworn in at 3:00 p.m. A glass of champagne with His Ex., a few pictures and it was all over.

"Back at the ranch a few of the faithful dropped in for a farewell toast. Some of them will miss me – they said with some feeling."[22]

Wednesday was moving day. I started at 8:30 a.m. picking out the books I wanted and reviewing the files that were piled on my desk. With the wonderful cooperation of the staff, who did the equivalent of three days' work in one, everything was cleared by 6:00 p.m. The safe was empty, except for a few "special" documents that I left for Léo, such as those that had to wait for General Allard's return to Ottawa. "The walls are bare and I take a last long look from the window. The die is cast and there is no turning back. Tomorrow starts a new chapter in my life. I am sure it will be interesting."[23]

CHAPTER 14

THE RACE IS ON

T he first day in my new office, Thursday, September 21, 1967, was a wipeout as far as departmental matters were concerned. Cabinet met early to discuss the financial crisis and the mess we had gotten ourselves into. Inflation was running ahead of the United States, at four percent, and unemployment had risen to four percent, which was considered excessive. We also learned that H. A. "Bud" Olson, the Social Credit MP for Medicine Hat, would be joining the Liberal caucus that day. I had to leave cabinet early to fly to Newfoundland, where I would be attending a state dinner in honour of my predecessor, Jack Pickersgill. My role, officially, was to bring greetings from the Government of Canada. My real function was to provide transport for Jack and Margaret Pickersgill. When he was Minister of Transport he had been charge of one of the government's two fleets of VIP aircraft; but after his resignation and appointment as president of the Canadian Transport Commission, he was dependent on others, and I was the most convenient helpmate. I was happy to oblige because Jack was one of my favourite colleagues. (I learned some years later that his delightful wife, Margaret, was a distant cousin on my mother's side.) In addition, my new deputy, John Baldwin, would be going with us, and I would have the opportunity for a good private chat on the return trip.

The dinner, vintage Smallwood 1967, was quite a show. After we were seated at the head table, before the banquet began, Joey hove to behind me and asked me to speak for three to five minutes. He would speak for fifteen minutes, he informed me, and Jack twelve to fifteen. He had scarcely finished the sentence before upping the ante. I would speak five to eight minutes, his introduction of Jack would last eighteen to twenty minutes, and Jack's response would be in the order of fifteen to eighteen. A final rapid-fire, across-the-board escalation raised my allotment to the eight- to ten-minute range. "It would be good for a Mainlander to say something," he said.

When the food and wine were finally consumed, Joey began his marathon eulogy, laced with travelogue. It lasted one hour and ten minutes. Jack's reply to the well-deserved tribute took just under forty minutes, and the big clock at the back of the hall was on the home stretch to midnight when Joey called on me to bring greetings from Ottawa. I took less than ten minutes and was greatly relieved to note that no-one was sleeping when I finished who had not nodded off before I had begun. "Joey was elated. He said (to others) such things as 'Here is our answer to Stanfield right here,' and to John Baldwin, 'How soon can you bring him back again?' I was lucky."[1]

On the way home John Baldwin was able to brief me on the more urgent problems I had inherited. The stickiest wicket, of course, was a controversial proposal to move Channel 3–TV from Palgrave (Barrie), Ontario, to Toronto. It had ceased to be an immediate problem, however, thanks to Jack Pickersgill putting everything on hold. Also, there was little likelihood of either a rail or an air strike in the near future; and the Canadian Transport Commission would probably accept primary responsibility for branch-line abandonment, which was as emotional an issue with western farmers as Channel-3 fever was in Toronto. On the other hand, Baldwin foresaw the possibility of some problems with the longshoremen and perhaps some tension with the provinces concerning jurisdiction over interprovincial and international trucking. Furthermore, I might get caught in a nutcracker if Premier W. A. C. Bennett of British Columbia insisted on building his own port facility to handle bulk coal shipments to Japan; and the choice of a successor for Gordon McGregor as president of Air Canada would pose a tricky problem. We discussed only the principal concerns and, not surprisingly since the two men had collaborated, it was almost the identical list that Pickersgill's executive assistant, Sandy Morrison, had given me in a memo when my move to Transport was first mooted.

When we landed in Ottawa, we ramped at the air-force terminal, because the VIP #412 Transport Squadron had a farewell presentation for me. The men with whom I had flown so often for so long gave me a refreshment box with the squadron crest on it. It was a poignant gesture and deeply appreciated.

When I got back to my new office, confusion reigned. Sandy Morrison had agreed to stay as my executive assistant, but some of Pickersgill's other key people had gone to the CTC with him, or had other plans. My two key people, Bill Lee and Marg Bulger, had moved with me, but soon found there was no ministerial staff to do letters. I asked Léo Cadieux if he would allow Marg Ryan and Alice Goodwin, two of my most faithful assistants, to transfer from Defence, and he agreed. We were back in business. The two days were equally profitable politically. Eric Facey, a Newfoundlander who had worked in Jack's office, agreed to support me in the leadership race, as did Senator Syd Smith from British Columbia, a powerful figure in the Interior.

Sunday morning the Liberals held a special weekend caucus. "It is obvious that [my] move to Transport has had a favourable impact on the MPs. It is also obvious that although I still have quite a few friends – and some very new ones – the total isn't as great as it was last fall. It is also obvious that the MPs have lots of problems in the Transport dept. I am going to be busy."[2]

As days flew past, I felt like a juggler in a circus keeping umpteen balls in the air at one time. There were my parliamentary duties during the week, the necessity of learning about my new department and solving some of the knotty problems Jack had left behind, as well as the inevitable Wednesday-night and weekend forays into various parts of the wider Canadian constituency. On October 4 I addressed a meeting organized by Ted Glista, our candidate in the new riding of Peel South, and two days later, on the Friday night, another one on behalf of Wally Zimmerman, candidate in Wentworth North. Both men became staunch Hellyer supporters.

On October 12 I took time out for a farewell mess dinner in my honour, sponsored by the service and civilian officers at National Defence Headquarters. It was a grand and memorable affair, where the superb dinner was followed by entertainment that was sardonic and funny without being cutting. I could tell that the senior officers were on my side. They presented me with two handsome gifts: a beautifully inscribed copy of *The Oxford Dictionary of Quotations*, which proved invaluable during my subsequent career as a newspaper columnist, and the first casting of the Canadian Armed Forces crest, which still hangs proudly in my study.

The following morning I received a memo from Bill Lee regarding Toronto supporters. It read as follows: "Call from Joe Goldenberg. 1) What time will you be available this Sat. afternoon for 'street-walking' with Bill Bassell. 2) Bring $1500, situation desperate! 'Hmmm'." This was a portent of things to come. One of the major problems associated with any leadership campaign is raising money. Another is controlling expenditures. Of the two, I am not sure which is the more difficult.

I had asked John Aird to be my chief fund-raiser, but he declined on the grounds that he had undertaken that same function for the party, and he was concerned about a potential conflict of interest. It was a point well taken. As an alternative he recruited a former roommate, John Grant, Sr., Q.C., to take on the job. John didn't know me from a hole in the ground, but on Aird's say-so he signed on. I was most grateful for his all-out and very effective effort on my behalf.

I hadn't been in Transport long before I began to chew away at some of the seemingly intractable problems. High on the list was a new deep-water super-port facility to handle B.C. coal destined for Japan. There had been a total stand-off between the federal and provincial governments concerning the site of the port, to the point where Premier W. A. C. Bennett threatened to build his own – a prospect which drove the National Harbours Board up the proverbial wall. I found that one trip to the coast was enough to break the ice and reach a tentative agreement with the province. The newspaper of that name wrote a laudatory editorial titled "A Handshake All Round for Roberts Bank . . ." The lead paragraph read:

> New Transport Minister Paul Hellyer has brought a new meaning to that controversial word "integration". From now on it should mean, out here, a sensible co-operation between federal and provincial governments on harbor development, particularly in relation to Roberts Bank and the proposed bulk-loading port there.[3]

The resolution of another extremely thorny impasse, this time between Air Canada and the government, over the question of the airline's maintenance facility in Winnipeg, was enough to persuade even the *Free Press* and my old friend Dick Malone to say a few nice things about me. In the 1965 election, Prime Minister Pearson had promised that the base would remain in Winnipeg and not be consolidated with the one in Montreal, as mooted. But the president of the airline, Gordon McGregor, was adamant. He wanted a single operation and said he didn't care a hoot what the government had promised. It was left to me to work out a compromise solution, under which the Winnipeg facility would be sold to a private company with guarantees of maintenance contracts from Air Canada, the Department of National Defence, and other government departments, sufficient to make the operation viable. It took a lot of head-knocking, but a deal was finally struck that was generally acceptable to all the parties. On October 27 an editorial headed "Brighter Prospects" began: "In Winnipeg's eyes Paul Hellyer has made an auspicious start in his new job as minister of transport."[4]

Even more surprising were a few kind words from the Halifax *Chronicle-Herald*, which had been noted for its spirited defence of the status quo in my previous portfolio. Transportation costs that seemed, and were in fact, excessive had long been a Maritimes grievance, and I decided that the exercise of a little "moral suasion" with the railways might result in some amelioration, which it did. In its lead editorial of November 1, entitled "Mr. Hellyer's Move", the *Chronicle-Herald* began:

> Transport Minister Hellyer has told the House of Commons that he has discussed with the CNR and CPR a proposal which, if implemented, would ease the impact of higher less-than-carload rates recently announced by the railways.

The final paragraph read:

The sometimes obscure language of the new National Transportation Act does not appear to give to the minister of transport any discretionary power to alter tariffs. Presumably, therefore, Mr. Hellyer is setting out to exercise his talents of persuasion which, history shows, can be considerable on occasion. We wish him every success.[5]

By early November the unofficial leadership race had gained considerable momentum. While departmental matters occupied most of my time, the extracurricular campaigning continued unabated, and there was no attempt to kid anyone about the ultimate aim of the game. Martin, Sharp, and Turner were every bit as active – and visible. So when we all planned to attend a provincial party convention in Edmonton, the press made an issue of it. An article in the Toronto *Telegram* by Gary Oakes was headed "Heirs to Pearson Start Their Leadership Moves".[6]

The publicity upset the PM. Once before when we planned to attend a convention in Quebec City, he had asked us to tone things down, and we cancelled out at the last minute. This time he blew the whistle on us. A story in the *Ottawa Journal* by Richard Jackson was captioned: "Campaigning Irks PM–Grit Hopefuls Get Orders To Ease Off". Jackson said the crackdown was described by an official spokesman from the Prime Minister's office as "a request that all members of the cabinet 'be available' – as it was carefully phrased – 'in Ottawa this weekend.' "[7]

I could understand the boss's discomfiture, but in a sense he was the author of the situation by suggesting that he intended to step down sooner rather than later and by encouraging us to do some discreet organizing. Once begun, the campaign eventually reached the stage where it was difficult to differentiate between what was discreet and what was not. I can't speak for the others, but I had been invited to Edmonton in August and had accepted in September. To cancel in November was most embarrassing, and Alberta Liberals were not pleased by the PM's interference. In any event, like good turtles, we pulled our heads into our shells for the time being.

On November 21 François Boulais joined my staff. He was the brother-in-law of Jacques Tremblay, MP, and was highly recommended for the kind of administrative tasks, including translation, that were crying out for attention. That evening I had dinner with Jean Marchand. "He will not be a candidate for leader. He may not stay if Pearson doesn't resign soon. He no longer considers M. Sharp a serious candidate. He couldn't support Paul Martin other than interim (4-5 months) and doesn't think he would quit once he got it. Beyond that his mind is not made up. We will meet again."[8]

On Sunday, November 27, we held a national campaign meeting. It was the first time the venerable Montreal organizer René Lagarde had been with us, and my aide Bob McDowall was invited to sit in as well. Reports from British Columbia and the Western provinces indicated little change in support, which was good from my perspective. Ontario and Quebec seemed to be moving along quite satisfactorily as well. Apart from the Maritimes, about the only area of weakness was with the young Liberals, where David Smith, Turner's executive assistant, was doing a good job of switching my supporters to his boss's camp.

Monday I had lunch with Marcel Inkel, former executive assistant to the Hon. Hugues "Bobby" Lapointe. Marcel impressed me greatly and became a very staunch supporter. On the same day, the "Conference of Tomorrow", which had been the brainchild of Ontario Premier John Robarts, opened in Toronto. The federal government had been very skittish about participating in any way, but finally agreed to send an observer when it was made clear that it would be billed as a meeting of provincial premiers rather than a full-blown constitutional conference. I noted in my diary: "There is deep division in the country on constitutional issues."[9]

Saturday morning, December 2, three hours after returning from a very successful two-day speaking tour in Manitoba and Saskatchewan, I headed for Montreal en route to St. Jérôme to attend a testimonial dinner for my friend Léo Cadieux. François Boulais took me in tow, stopping at the St. Jérôme City Hall long enough for the customary book-signing ceremony, and then on to the Hôtel Lapointe for the reception and dinner. It was Léo's night. How proud the "militants" (rabid political supporters) were to celebrate the accession of their friend as the first French-speaking Minister of Defence. It was a proud night for me, too, as I rose to pay homage to a man for whom I had great respect and considerable affection. When I finished, the crowd stood and sang "Il a gagné ses épaulettes", which was their way of saying I was okay.

On Wednesday, December 6, after Orders of the Day, I met with the PM to talk about estimates. The belt had to be tightened just a little bit more. It had already passed the point where it hurt, but I agreed to cooperate. He told me that he planned to announce his retirement the following Wednesday. But no-one knew – not even his office staff.

On Sunday "Bill came over at 4:30 for a pow wow. He doesn't think either Gord [Edick] or Keith [Davey] can be campaign manager, and I agree with him. They don't think he [Bill] can be, and I agree with that too. He is just too busy and I need him for other things. Bill has a brilliant suggestion – Royce Frith. He would be great. Bill is a little hurt, I think, but he shouldn't be because he is carrying too heavy a load and it will get worse."[10]

Earlier Keith had seemed like a natural for the campaign-manager's job, but in addition to the instinctive rivalry between Keith and Bill, some of my key Western supporters had put the "nix" on Davey. If he got the job, they explained, in language too explicit to repeat, they would walk out. They left no room for compromise on that score. Top organizer Gord Edick's forte was Ontario, and it didn't seem to make sense to move him to the wider field. Neither of them was content to work under Bill, who was popular in the West – and hence the stalemate.

"I phoned Royce and he is willing to talk, Tuesday. I hope he will say yes.

"The going gets very tough. The family are unsympathetic and I find it difficult to carry on – but I must."[11]

On Monday the Federal–Provincial Conference on Housing, for which I had spent most of the previous day preparing, got under way in a blaze of lights. The Prime Minister's opening statement was good, but not earth-shaking, and the debate that followed was, on balance, pretty dull. I tried to put the cat among the pigeons by suggesting that one of the biggest impediments to the provision of affordable housing was government rules and regulations – a truism I had learned from bitter experience. I gave a number of examples I was thoroughly familiar with. My intervention may not have been welcomed by everyone, but it did have the effect of livening things up and getting the discussion back to earth.

I ducked out of the conference for an hour to walk with the troops at General Worthington's funeral. I had great respect for "Worthy" and the outstanding leadership he had shown in developing the Royal Canadian Armoured Corps almost from scratch. His outspoken support of unification raised him even further in my esteem. There was no opportunity to extend my sympathy to the family that day, but I sensed they would know I was there.

What they didn't know, and what the old general never knew, was that I was responsible for him being granted his heart's desire – the right to be buried at Camp Borden, close to his beloved tanks. Actually it was my wife, Ellen, who provided the key to Worthy's "heaven". Months earlier I had arrived home from work late at night. Ellen was just finishing the book she had been reading – "*Worthy*", written by his wife, Larry.

"Isn't that nice," she said. "General Worthington is going to be buried at Camp Borden, close to the things that have been important to him all his adult life."

"I've got news for you," I responded. "He isn't."

She gave me one of those sceptical looks I always got when my opinion conflicted with something she had read, and the latter was assumed to be authentic. Nevertheless I was able to convince her that I had privileged and more-up-to-date information. That very day, during one of our routine working sessons, the Chief of Defence Staff had shown me such a request from the Armoured Corps Association on the general's behalf. It had been turned down because burials at military bases were against regulations. Ellen didn't think that was a good enough reason, so at my next meeting with CDS I suggested he have the association reapply. He got the message, and the next time the matter appeared on my desk, Worthy's request was recommended for approval.

When I returned to the Federal–Provincial Conference on Housing after the funeral, I took advantage of the opportunity to do a little campaigning on the side. I had lunch with P.E.I. premier Alex Campbell, who was primarily interested in things affecting his island. He was still uncommitted for the leadership, but added that federal Liberals were so unpopular in P.E.I. that he didn't dare admit any association. At dinner my guest was New Brunswick Premier Louis Robichaud, who let me know that he was interested in the leadership himself. It was obvious that the two of us thought alike on quite a few things, but I got the impression he had decided to support someone other than me in the event he didn't run himself.

Wednesday morning, Newfoundland premier Joey Smallwood spent three-quarters of an hour in my office pacing back and forth, as was his wont when he was expressing himself. He wanted me to go ahead with the Churchill Falls airport in Labrador, and also suggested that the federal government should put up $1 billion for secondary education in Canada in increments of $250 million annually.

"He told me that if Bob Winters doesn't run he will support me and organize for me. He is not certain what he will do if Bob does run – depends on how hard he runs.

"Well! He's [Pearson's] done it again – changed his mind that is. Today was to have been the day of announcement, but LBP changed his mind again."[12]

Thursday, December 14: "I did him a great injustice. He didn't really change his mind but probably waited till today in order to advise his cabinet colleagues in advance of the announcement.

"At cabinet, just before noon, LBP announced that he would have to go, but first he wanted to read a letter he had written to Senator Nichol [President of the Liberal Party]. He then said he had made up his mind, the subject was not debatable and would we excuse him because he had a press conference at 12:30. Art Laing protested, but LBP was off. Cabinet carried on for about an hour discussing the thing. The general reaction was shocked amazement. Marchand was visibly shaken."[13] Nearly everyone had hoped for a change of leadership, but seemed unprepared for Mike's surprise anouncement.

After cabinet, I had lunch with Keith Davey. Everyone could feel the excitement now that the race had become official. Of the many things we discussed, the most urgent, the number-one priority was someone to act as campaign-manager. Our friend Royce Frith, who had seemed to be on the verge of saying, yes, had said no, so we were back to square one. Bill Lee had given us an appealing new name to add to the list – Bob Andras, MP for Port Arthur – and it was decided Bill should approach him formally.

One other problem was the amount of time Keith would have available for the campaign. He was just buying into an advertising business that required considerable attention, and this did not bode well for the kind of all-out participation we had both taken for granted.

On Friday, December 15, my diary reflected on the progress of the leadership race: "House of Commons in a good humour. The papers are full of the Pearson resignation and speculative stories of possible successors.

"Toronto *Tely* and *Toronto Star* reported me in the lead in Ontario. They are correct but I am not happy to see it in print. The lineup of MPPs, however, is disappointing. Mostly Turner, Sharp, and Martin.

"Ian Wahn phoned and signed in. Also Don Walkinshaw and Senator Arthur Roebuck. That is good.

"Bill had lunch with Bob Andras. There is some hope.

"I am most concerned with Marchand and Trudeau. They are key.

"Everything else going quite nicely."[14]

On Saturday a small crisis arose concerning Bill Lee's plan to have a film made of the Hellyer family in their natural habitat. In retrospect it was not one of Bill's most productive suggestions, but it seemed quite sensible at the time. The idea was to portray me as a nice, congenial family man and to distribute the film to supporters across the country to prove that I was not the cold, aloof, arrogant s.o.b. I was so often alleged to be. The crisis began when Ellen learned that the film crew would be arriving at our house on Sunday. She was livid. To her our home was our sanctuary, and the intrusion of crass politics, no matter how well-intentioned, was an unwelcome and unacceptable sacrilege. She was so distressed that she was about ready to take off for Toronto, but she finally decided to stick with the ship.

When we got home from church, media personality Warner Troyer and his crew were waiting. We had bought hot dogs enough for everyone, and the cameras rolled as we ate our lunch. Of the family, only David acted naturally; the rest of us were so self-conscious that the film was bound to give a negative impression in more ways than one. The intrusion of the cameras continued throughout the day and into the evening, and I suspect that some of our muted unhappiness was captured on film.

The TV news at 11:00 p.m. should have been a welcome relief from our ordeal, but it was full of bad news. It confirmed that Australian Prime Minister Holt had been drowned and later announced that the Liberal Convention would be held on April 4, 5, and 6. The movie-making continued through much of Monday and Tuesday, but I found it distracting, and it was difficult to concentrate on anything important with the crew always in the background.

Tuesday evening Pierre Trudeau came to my office for dinner. Early in the conversation he told me that his aide, Eddie Rubin, would like to work for me, though he didn't understand why. Nor did I, though he would have been most welcome had there been an opening available. Pierre wondered whether I didn't think it would be desirable to have a French-speaking candidate on the list, and I agreed that yes, in principle, I thought it would be. That's what I really believed, although I was fully aware that it would complicate my agenda. I noted in my diary: "He *is* very bright. Obviously he isn't running – says there are only three serious candidates. He said he liked the way I handled cabinet when in the chair; but, had the line about me being a conservative – grace à WLG. A very useful talk."[15]

It wasn't just imagination at work when I attributed much of my alleged "conservative" image to Walter Gordon. Not only had it come to me from several sources that he was responsible; I had seen him in action. Midway through a group discussion he would poke me in the ribs with his elbow and say, "We can't all be conservative like you, can we, Paul?" The paper would burn if I recalled what I really thought of this devastating technique. My fury was all the more intense because there was no effective way to combat it.

The attack seemed doubly unfair because earlier that year there had been a concerted, if somewhat amusing, effort to slot me at the other end of the ideological spectrum. In a *Globe and Mail* column headed "Problem of the Evil Nuts" George Bain wrote:

> Somewhere in Ottawa there's a nut with a mimeograph ma-chine who has taken to sending out what he calls special bul-letins to alert people – me for one – to the coup d'état that the Jewish-Communist Minister of National Defence, Paul Hellyer, is starting."[16]

Bain quoted from a series of bulletins in the same vein, and there was some consolation in being lumped in with "William Maurice Lee" and General J. V. Allard. Every cloud has a silver lining, and in this case it was a very funny exchange of letters with Phil

Givens, former mayor of Toronto, who admitted he had always been "suspicious" about me, welcomed me to the clan, and offered, in the event I wanted to join Beth Tzedec, to get it for me wholesale.[17]

My discomfort in both instances lay in the fact that I perceived myself as neither left- nor right-wing but about midway between the two extremes, and certainly on the cutting edge of innovation and reform on matters as diverse as pensions, housing, pollution control, urban design, and military organization – not to mention my life-time obsession concerning the elimination of the twin evils of inflation and unemployment. Regrettably, the reality I believed in was slowly but effectively being blotted out by the perception Walter worked so hard to create in the hearts and minds of potential supporters as well as in the press.

After we finished dinner, Pierre left, and it was back to the filming crew, which was waiting in a nearby room. The story was to end with a powerful and dramatic speech written by Warner Troyer. The material was first class, and consequently had to be letter-perfect in the delivery. "Filmed speech until 1:30 a.m. Repetition, repetition, etc. but the crew were patient and satisfied with the result!"[18] Thank goodness someone was pleased. Supporters across the country, who were supposed to use myriad copies of the film, apparently were not. Perhaps it was just too cumbersome to use, but it was rarely shown, and as far as I know, though it was one of the most expensive projects of the entire campaign, it didn't produce a single vote. The time would have been better spent talking to potential delegates and resting in between.

Wednesday, December 20: "Saw André Ouellet. He said he is on my side *but* the Quebec caucus this a.m. was almost directed by Marchand not to take any position before their January convention. Some of them are angry *but*, and this is the interesting thing, most of them will go along. If Marchand decides to run, he will get an almost unanimous Quebec vote plus some from outside. Formidable. It is a very interesting phenomenon."[19]

Thursday, December 21: "I saw René Lagarde. He is worried about Marchand's position. On the other hand the general reaction is still good. But he, René, is considered old guard. This is a problem.

"Jacques Tremblay reported on his meeting with Mitchell Sharp. Mitchell says I am a 'doer', but I may not be able to manage provincial premiers.

"Dined with Marchand who explained his position. He will make up his mind in January."[20]

Friday, December 22: "Doug Everett phoned to see if I had heard from Rod McIsaac [both prominent Winnipeg liberals]. I had and I am delighted. He has also seen Gil [Molgat – Manitoba Liberal leader] and thinks he has him lined up for Hellyer – but he doesn't want his name used yet. He [Gil] wanted to be reassured that I had support in Quebec. Doug told him that I did and I confirmed.

"The nature of the question, however, and its wording indicates a plant – probably by Maurice Sauvé. There really is a battle royal shaping up.

"Doug and Rod are ready to make their announcement after Jan. 22nd. This should be good timing!"[21]

Saturday, December 23: "Spent the day in Toronto and took a room at the Park Plaza to interview several people. Barney Danson came down to tell me about the meeting planned for Jan. 11th [the tentative date of the launch of my leadership campaign]. It sounds pretty good. They have a list of about forty names of prominent Liberals around town who are going on the invitation. It is a little weak on MPs and MPPs, but still very impressive."[22]

We spent Christmas at home in Waterford with the Races, and on Boxing Day my brother-in-law John invited prospective Norfolk County delegates to the Hellyer farm for coffee, Christmas cake, and a chat. "After an hour or so everyone loosened up a bit and I thought we parted good friends. I hope they will support me. This kind of encounter is good, but it takes time and there is so little of it."[23] The meeting must have been a success, because John persuaded the entire Norfolk contingent to join the Hellyer camp.

At the crack of dawn on Wednesday I was headed back to Ottawa. "By the time I got to cabinet, it was half over. It proves that seven ministers can do the same amount of work in half the time. The Government should be organized along these lines."[24]

It was New Year's Eve and Ellen and I were headed to Hawaii, the exotic group of islands we had only dreamed about. We had no way of knowing that on another airplane a cabinet colleague was on his way to Tahiti to swim and relax. While musing and surveying the stars in distant galaxies, he would reach a decision that would change the course of Canadian history.

CHAPTER 15

IT'S TRUDEAU ON
THE FOURTH BALLOT

A week in Hawaii provided a pleasant change of pace, but it wasn't long enough to recharge my batteries; it simply kept them from going completely dead. Even the partial charge was largely offset by the six-hour time difference. We had just nicely adjusted in one direction when it was time to reverse the clocks and begin the process all over again.

When we got home, the political situation appeared very much as we had left it. I had good solid support in Toronto and across southwestern Ontario. The prospects were equally bright in the West, especially in Manitoba, Alberta, and British Columbia, where I had strong local leadership. Saskatchewan had potential, but nearly everyone was sitting on the fence until Premier Ross Thatcher gave them the nod, and he was waiting for the final word from business tycoon Bob Winters.

To the East, the Maritimes were difficult turf. My connections had been excellent when we were in Opposition and I made frequent visits to the university clubs. After five years, however, contacts were widely dispersed, and I had been too busy with the defence reorganization to cultivate new ones. This relative inattention, plus the fallout from the long war of unification, took its toll across the three provinces. My only hope was Newfoundland, where Joey Smallwood had promised to support me, but from whence there had been an ominous silence. In Quebec I had good backing from MPs and veteran organizers, but again things were tentative until the question of Marchand or some other French-speaking candidate had been settled.

This was the situation when my team decided to officially launch our campaign on January 11, 1968. Editorial reaction to my candidacy was generally, though not universally, favourable. Under the head "Mr. Hellyer Wants To Be PM" the Toronto *Telegram* was quite laudatory, and played down the damage done by the unification debate.[1] The *Globe and Mail*, while admitting some of my strengths, was less than complimentary. "He may not be arrogant, but his cold, ruthless treatment of the admirals during the dispute over unification of the armed forces and his aloof manner, not infrequently, in answering questions in the House, have painted an image which will sit uneasily with those who reject the arbitrary."[2] The editorial went on to list some of my strengths, including youth and experience, and it may have been considered a "balanced" piece, but the tone was surly and made no attempt to mask editor Richard J. Doyle's bias as a former naval officer. The *Globe*'s broadside was a far cry from the endorsation Max Bell had planned for this, his flagship newspaper, but he had fallen ill soon after giving me his support.

It was a bad omen as I took off for Halifax and the annual meeting of the Nova Scotia Liberal Association. Many of my colleagues who were potential candidates had been reluctant to go to Halifax because it was Allan MacEachan's turf. I particularly didn't want to go, because I wasn't prepared either physically or psychologically. I was still tired from a combination of the after-effects of jet lag and the hectic events of my first week back on the job. In addition, the extended two-and-a-half-year pounding I had been given by the Halifax press over unification had created intense hostility in its readership area. With this in mind I needed time to psych myself up. My team urged me to run with the pack, because all the other hopefuls, with the exception of John Turner, had agreed to go. Finally I agreed as well, and my performance was dismal – one of my worst. I would have been much better off to have stayed home and taken the weekend off, especially when I was still a front-runner and had little to gain by pressing my luck.

An invitation to the crucially important Western Liberal Conference, which was being held at the Marlborough Hotel in Winnipeg, provided a golden opportunity for me to recover momentum. Alas, the best laid plans of mice and men can come to naught. Burning the candle at both ends finally caught up with me, and a totally debilitating bout of the flu had me flat on my back. This was a serious blow, because key Liberals from across the West were there, and George Wither, one of my top strategists, had reported the rumour that Manitoba Liberal leader Gil Molgat and his entire caucus planned to use the occasion to endorse me as their choice – a move that would have been psychological dynamite. Whether that possibility really existed or was just a pipe dream couldn't be tested in my absence. One thing is certain, it didn't happen. Worse, my opponents circulated the rumour that my real reason for not attending was indifference rather than illness. The snipers took full advantage of my lost opportunity and, according to newspaper reports, my colleague Mitchell Sharp made substantial gains in delegate support.

I was still leading in my own province, including rural Ontario, and while my position vis-à-vis Sharp and Martin appeared to be quite satisfactory, the prospect of a French-Canadian "star" taking to the field became more likely. One of Peter C. Newman's columns titled "Professors, Writers, Support Trudeau" reported a straw in the wind.

> A Toronto Committee for Trudeau has been set up by Professors Ramsay Cook, Bill Kilbourn, and John Saywell, three of the Canadian academic community's brightest young political scientists. They are circulating a petition in Canadian universities, hoping by January 22 to enlist at least 150 professors in their crusade to persuade the Minister of Justice to stand for the leadership.[3]

Later a column by Douglas Fisher and Harry Crowe captioned "Helping the Trudeau Buildup", began: "It is our hunch shared with many, that Pierre Trudeau, Minister of Justice, will become Quebec candidate for the Liberal leadership and the co-favourite with Paul Hellyer."[4]

The blizzard of intriguing and predominantly favourable publicity gained added force with Pierre's whirlwind tour of provincial capitals to discuss the federal position with the premiers in advance of the federal-provincial constitutional conference scheduled for early February. The reaction of the first ministers ranged from enthusiasm on the part of British Columbia's W. A. C. Bennett to near adulation from Joey Smallwood. A caption under a CP wire photo of Trudeau and the Newfoundland premier read "Justice Minister Pierre Trudeau ran into a flood of praise from premier Joseph Smallwood when he visited Newfoundland yesterday. Premier described him as 'the perfect Canadian' and 'the most brilliant of MPs'."[5]

It was a tough battle. Trudeau's every move seemed like part of a brilliantly orchestrated buildup, the next step of which was proclaimed in a *Toronto Star* headline: "Quebec Liberal Meeting Is Tailored To Launch Trudeau." The article added that, although no announcement was expected before the constitutional conference, "everything at the Montreal meeting has been stage-managed to enhance Trudeau's stature as a leadership candidate and ensure him a solid bloc of votes at the Ottawa convention next April."[6]

Indeed it was. The actual event was every bit as bad, and probably worse, than the advance billing – at least from the standpoint of the other leadership hopefuls. Marchand, who was really in charge of the Quebec Liberal conclave, forbade us to entertain while the policy sessions were taking place, which was almost all of the time. We were not allowed to participate, only to watch. The entire conference was a spectacle designed for the ascendancy of one star only, and the rest of us were used as extras – props as it were – to underscore the superiority and unique qualities of the main player.

Jean Marchand's symphony in Pierre major continued through the closing banquet on Saturday night. The Minister of Justice was the only potential candidate at the head table. The rest of us were dispersed throughout the hall and were introduced at such a rapid-fire tempo that the names and applause melded into a slur and the spotlight operator gave up any attempt to keep in sync. Those few jarring notes accomplished, Marchand's score returned to the melody composed to suit his chosen soloist.

With the Quebec Liberal meeting over, the constitutional conference got under way in Ottawa on February 5. The federal delegation was led by the Prime Minister and included Senator Connolly and ministers Martin, Sharp, Laing, MacEachen, Marchand, and Trudeau. It was obvious, and understood from the beginning, that it would be Trudeau, the junior minister who had written the government's position, who would be featured front and centre. As the debate developed, Premier Johnson elaborated his hopes and aspirations for a distinct Quebec, endowed with powers additional to those already recognized. In rebuttal Pierre Trudeau took him on head to head. Not only did Trudeau reject the concept of distinct status, or of two nations, as some people interpreted it, he gave the impression that Johnson was a very bad boy and that the kind of Quebec Johnson was describing deserved a good swift kick in the *derrière*. He didn't say that, of course, which was and remains his genius. He can create an impression that is not borne out by the text when it is examined. But in politics, perception is reality, and Pierre gave English-speaking Canadians the strong impression that he was their champion, someone who would resist the "unreasonable" demands coming from nationalists in his own province. By the time the conference ended, Trudeau had become a household word. English-speaking Canadians were dazzled by this tough, articulate champion of their rights; and so was the press.

The week that followed the televized debate must have been one of intense activity for Trudeau's underground supporters. It was learned that one of them, a secret "Mr. X", had made all of the necessary convention arrangements for Trudeau's candidacy. Bryce Mackasey was appointed to the cabinet for the specific purpose, as he explained later, of helping Pierre Trudeau win the leadership of the party. This was thanks to the Prime Minister, whose fine hand could also be seen in the choice of Richard Stanbury to succeed John Nichol as party president. Dick had been one of my loyal supporters, and although his appointment was not scheduled to occur until the leadership convention was held, he felt obliged to sit on the sidelines. One of my most respected lieutenants had been effectively neutralized. His wife, Marg, stuck with the Hellyer team, but losing Dick was a blow – as the PM must have known it would be.

Finally, the other shoe dropped. The Toronto *Telegram* of February 15, 1968, announced that Jean Marchand would be resigning as Quebec leader of the federal Liberals to be campaign manager for Justice Minister Pierre Trudeau, who was expected to announce his candidacy at a press conference at 10 a.m. the following morning. The article discussed the possibility of block voting by Quebec delegates, and added: "This would cut sharply into delegates who might otherwise have supported External Affairs Minister Paul Martin and Transport Minister Paul Hellyer."[7]

At his press conference, Pierre read a letter he had just sent to Senator John Nichol, president of the Liberal Federation, telling him he would be a candidate for the leadership. Although he said he had made his decision just the previous night, following a meeting with friends, a handsome and meticulously prepared brochure was circulated before the press conference had ended. "I guess somebody worked all night. My, isn't this awful," he commented with some embarrassment.[8]

Press reaction to Pierre's announcement was primarily positive, but not without reservations. The *Windsor Star* listed a number of attributes "which make him an attractive candidate", but went on to say they were not all "total blessings".[9] The *Toronto Star* was quite laudatory while entering a note of caution: "If the Liberals make Pierre Elliott Trudeau their leader and prime minister, they will be gambling on intelligence and fresh thought – and also on political inexperience and tactlessness. Are they, and is Canada, ready for a philosopher – King?"[10]

When reporters caught up with me to get my reaction to the latest entry, I said I thought his candidacy had been inevitable because of the intense pressure brought to bear on Mr. Trudeau, not only from Quebec but also from other parts of the country. His participation would make the race more interesting and I welcomed him as "a man of quality."[11] To the best of my recollection, I was being totally sincere. I might have been less enthusiastic had my heart not overruled my head. I probably believed that anyone of such limited experience, who had been a member of the Liberal Party for less than three years, could not possibly win.

An event of near-catastrophic proportions would soon tarnish the image of all the mainline candidates. On the evening of February 18 the government was defeated on third reading of a tax bill. It was one of those silly things that shouldn't have happened, but it did. In brief, it was a setup. The Tories had flown in four MPs whose presence was not known to the Liberals; they had been hiding behind the curtains. Their votes tipped the balance, to the acute embarrassment of those of us on the government side. If the vote had been on second reading, we would have had no choice but to resign, but on third reading the precedents were less compelling, so we introduced, and won, a vote of confidence. On the Tory side Diefenbaker was furious, and never forgave Bob Stanfield for letting us get away with it. On our side there is little doubt that Mitchell Sharp, whose bill it was, suffered most, but in the public mind there was a strong element of collective responsibility, so that all of us were hurt as a result.

There was little doubt that Bob Winters's late entry into the race that weekend was an important factor. He was very popular in the Maritimes, and had he thrown his hat into the ring sooner, he would have had support from many delegates who had pledged to Allan MacEachen in the meantime. Whether Bob's delay resulted from a genuine reluctance to run or was a strategic move, I never knew. I do know it cost him delegate support in the Atlantic region, including Newfoundland, where Joey Smallwood defected first to me and then to Trudeau while Bob was out of the race.

The month of March was spent criss-crossing the country when the House wasn't sitting. I was still doing well close to home. The first weekend Ellen and I, accompanied by my executive assistant Sandy Morrison, took off for the Prairie provinces in one of the most gruelling marathons of the campaign. It involved three days of constant hopping from one city to the next in a search for votes. Perhaps it was inevitable, but in Lethbridge my itinerary overlapped Trudeau's – or vice versa – not just once, but twice. It was a time for putting on a bold face, as opposed to being genuinely delighted. As Tony Westell reported in the *Globe and Mail*: "The two ministers played the game, congratulating each other, and there were broad grins and handshakes when they met again at the airport here on Saturday night. Mr. Hellyer had just arrived from Calgary to attend a reception in Edmonton, Mr. Trudeau had met the Edmonton Liberals and was travelling on to Calgary."[12]

On March 12 an article by Peter Regenstreif in the *Toronto Star* said that I was leading with a first-ballot edge over Winters and Martin in the Sarnia, London, Kitchener, and Barrie areas. There was more good news the next day when Léo Cadieux agreed to be my campaign co-chairman and said some very nice things about me at a press conference.

That weekend saw a whirlwind trip through Northern Ontario. Although the number of committed delegates was disappointing, the quality was exceptional. The hard-core Hellyerites included George Nixon, the wonderful veteran Algoma East MP, Saul Laskin, highly respected mayor of Port Arthur, Carl Legault, the industrious MP from North Bay, and the irrepressible Jo Ann Gosselin, his riding president.

An article by Peter Worthington, on March 18, provided a summary of the plans for that week. "To-night he dashes in and out of Montreal for a meeting, then at the end of the week, he's off again on one of those Hellyer-hoppers to Newfoundland, Nova Scotia, Prince Edward Island, and Quebec – all in four days."[13] The day the article appeared, Marcel Prud'homme, the smooth-talking and charming MP for Montreal–Saint Denis came aboard. He was an important addition to the team and complemented fellow Montrealers John J. Pepper, Philippe Roberge, and Jean Langelier, who had been fighting an uphill battle in the metropolis.

It was a day that gave my campaign a big boost. Not only did Marcel Prud'homme contribute mightily to a very successful debut in Montreal that night, it was the day the one and only Judy LaMarsh re-enlisted in the Hellyer forces. She had been a long-time friend and supporter and had sent me numerous notes in cabinet addressed "My Leader". Often she had been a useful source of information. At the crucial moment, however, she had defected. She was influenced by Walter Gordon, whom she adored, and soon found herself on the Trudeau side, even though she had not been one of his great admirers. The timing was critical, because she had tremendous influence in three Niagara-area ridings. These ridings chose eighteen delegates for Trudeau during the time she was in his camp. What might have been a clean sweep for Hellyer became a goose egg.

Judy's return to my camp was triggered by an altercation with the Minister of Justice over the appointment of a county court judge. He rejected her candidate, someone she had known for years, in favour of someone she had never heard of. She was livid! Disillusioned with Pierre, she came back to me, where she really felt more comfortable. However she brought only one vote – her own – instead of the nineteen that might have been.

My eastern swing was surprisingly upbeat. I got a warm reception in St. John's where Joey Smallwood introduced me as a man "for whom I have tremendous admiration and respect."[14] He denied point-blank that he had committed himself to anybody, despite a special and unprecedented invitation to Pierre to address the legislature the following Monday. " 'As God is my judge, Mr. Hellyer,' he said, 'we are committed to no one. We in Newfoundland have kept our powder dry despite many strong temptations.' "[15] I tried to believe him because it was a time for grasping at straws.

A quick stop at Charlottetown held no fear for me, but Halifax did. I had bombed a few weeks earlier at the Nova Scotia Liberal Association meeting, and I didn't really want to go back. We joked on the airplane that I might be met by a picket line of admirals. That didn't happen, and there was, in fact, no mention of unification. The visit was a minor triumph and went to prove the unpredictability of politics. The *Toronto Star* reported, "Former defence minister Hellyer visited this home of the admirals' revolt last night and was given two standing ovations by delegates to next month's Liberal leadership convention."[16] The *Telegram* story included a number of heartwarming comments. "Gerald Regan, leader of the Liberal opposition in the province said: 'His was by far the best presentation of any candidate we've heard. My first vote is committed to MacEachen, but if he fails, no one looks better than Paul.' J. H. Dickey, former parliamentary secretary to the late C. D. Howe, said: 'The best impression anyone's made.' "[17] It was heady stuff, but – there were no first-ballot votes.

Meanwhile the uncommitted kingmakers were placing their bets. Bud Drury, Jean-Luc Pepin, and Jean Chrétien lined up with Sharp. Maurice Sauvé announced for Martin. Former Justice Minister Lucien Cardin, Labour Minister Jack Nicholson, and Veterans' Affairs Minister Roger Teillet went public for me. Walter Gordon told questioners on the CBC television show *Front Page Challenge*: "I've made up my mind. It's Pierre Elliott Trudeau."[18] Even more significant in terms of votes and potential impact, "Joey Smallwood all but promised Trudeau the support of Newfoundland's 84 delegates to the April 4-6 leadership convention" before the Justice Minister left St. John's following his address to the legislature.[19]

Although I had a number of real successes, like an excellent TV interview with Pierre Berton, there was no doubt Trudeau had moved into a strong first place in delegate support. He was also capturing the hearts of Canadians and rapidly overtaking Paul Martin as the people's choice. The press loved him because he was fresh and different. We had to do something, my team argued, to shore up support in the most populous centres. I was cajoled into two last-minute meetings in Toronto and Montreal.

On the surface each seemed to be a smashing success, which made us think that the change in plans had been good. The downside, which would soon become apparent, was devastating. I had gone into the campaign with battle fatigue resulting from one of the longest and most acrimonious political wars on record, and then, since early January, I had been working double shifts seven days a week. I had needed that last-minute bit of time off to build up my strength for the sprint to the finish line. Instead I found myself mentally inert, which was hardly the condition best suited to four days of frenetic activity.

My ability to keep tabs on changing loyalties was pretty good, thanks to an excellent headquarters organization operating under Bill Lee's ever-watchful eye. Brother-in-law John Race had moved in early, as had Colin – now Senator – Kenny, Elaine Downing, and Hope Picard from Calgary, along with others. As the critical four days approached, these stalwarts were reinforced by the key people from the provinces. We had committees in charge of entertainment, demonstrations, hospitality, and the candidate's itinerary. Everything was organized to the highest degree when delegates began to arrive in Ottawa for the April 4 to 6 leadership convention. At that point, there were ten names on the slate: Greene, Henderson, Hellyer, Kierans, MacEachen, Martin, Sharp, Trudeau, Turner, and Winters.

It was difficult to gauge the state of Trudeau's organization, but it was producing some highly visible results. When Joey Smallwood arrived, he announced that the entire Newfoundland delegation of eighty-four, with only about five exceptions, was supporting Trudeau. That wasn't too surprising when it was learned that Joey had virtually made such support a condition for anyone desiring free transportation on the chartered aircraft paid for from one of the party's slush funds. Three of the exceptions – Andy Chatwood and Eric Facey, who had worked for Jack Pickersgill when he was Transport Minister, and MP James Tucker – voted for me. Each subsequently paid a high price for his independence of mind.

Another major break for Trudeau was a prime-time interview arranged by Roy Faibish, an executive at CJOH-TV and one of the Justice Minister's private army of promoters. In a one-on-one interview with Patrick Watson, the front-runner sparkled like the evening star. It was a public-relations person's dream come true. "When I think of music I think of Beethoven," Trudeau opined in response to Patrick's in-depth probing. It wasn't that his musical preference was unique or different from some of the rest of us; it was the way he said it – as if it were the authentic word from the top of Mt. Olympus. The effect was electric, as delegates' eyes remained glued to the television monitors that were everywhere at the convention.

Of all the plums that seemed to be falling into Trudeau's lap, none was greater than Mitchell Sharp's withdrawal from the race and declaration in favour of Pierre. The rest of us were thunderstruck – especially in light of some of the things that Mitchell had been saying about Trudeau in private as he attempted to win MPs' votes. It didn't add up, and yet it was a fact. Many of Mitchell's committed delegates deserted him in the move, but of the four ministers in his camp, only Senator John Connolly refused to move with him. The others – Drury, Pepin, and Chrétien – moved to Trudeau, and the resulting media hype was enormous.

Paul Martin, in particular, was upset by this unexpected development. He suggested that three of us agree to an arrangement under which the one with the most votes on the first ballot would automatically receive the support of the other two. My instinct told me his proposition was born of the belief that he was number two, next to Trudeau. That's what a poll published by the Montreal *Gazette* had indicated. But I knew that this was not correct, and I felt it would be unfair to make an arrangement that was based on a false assumption. Meanwhile Paul met with Winters, who rejected the idea outright and told the press he would have no part of a deal. The idea died without further consideration.

On April 3 the influential Montreal daily *Le Devoir* gave me its stamp of approval. The endorsement was reported in the Ottawa *Citizen* as follows:

> In an editorial signed by publisher Claude Ryan, the independent daily says the logical choice is between Mr. Hellyer and

Justice Minister Trudeau, a superior man to Mr. Hellyer in the field of intellectual ability.

However, Mr. Hellyer is a more accomplished man of action. He is a man of decision. He knows how to administer and to delegate authority.

Le Devoir also refers to the differences between the two on the subject of Quebec nationalism and describes Mr. Trudeau's position as "rigid and too often negative".

Mr. Hellyer would be more inclined . . . to seek solutions acceptable to both sides rather than defend absolutely inflexible principles.[20]

On April 4 the front-page headline in the Montreal *Star* read: "Leadership Race Developing into Trudeau–Hellyer Battle".[21] That was good news, and confirmed our private polling. The campaign seemed to be building momentum. I did quite well at the policy sessions that day, and the luncheon Ellen and I hosted at noon for women delegates and delegates' wives was a fantastic success. My brief address was extemporaneous, passionate, and convincing. Attendance at our evening reception stretched the capacity of the Château Laurier's Adam Room, and there was a whiff of victory in the air.

Friday morning was for visiting caucuses. It was largely an exercise in futility – especially in the caucuses of those provinces that were supporting a local son. That afternoon was set aside for the big speeches. I had no quarrel with the place I had drawn near the middle of the list; the problem was my speech. Several people had submitted texts, including some that arrived too late to be of any assistance. The one I had chosen was written by Toronto lawyer Bill Macdonald, a longtime friend and associate. The content was solid, but certainly not sparkling, and somehow I had convinced myself that this didn't matter. The previous fall, at the Tory convention, Stanfield had consolidated his support with a workmanlike performance at the policy sessions and had gone on to win the convention with a flat, boring speech. Somehow I must have believed that history would repeat itself. I couldn't have been more wrong!

Worse than the content was my decision to read the speech. I seldom read my speeches because, invariably, that puts people to sleep, and I can't fathom why I thought this time would be an exception. The sound-system provided a further handicap. I had to stand in a fixed position in relation to the microphones in order to be heard. When I stood up straight, or leaned back to eyeball the crowd, the sound faded in the cacophony of extraneous noises in the hall. Within minutes I had lost the audience. Loss of control contributed to loss of composure as I stuck my nose between the microphones and glued my eyes to the text. The result was disastrous! If a speech is judged ten percent on content, thirty-five percent on delivery, and fifty-five percent on body language, I had just forfeited any hope of a passing grade. The audience reaction when I finished told the story.

The negative effect of my performance was compounded by the fact that Joe Greene was next. He had "bombed" at the workshops the previous day – so badly that some of his managers actually wondered if he shouldn't drop out of the race. That idea was abandoned when one of his key supporters, Lloyd Francis, discovered the root of the problem. It was the microphones. Joe simply wasn't being heard. Lloyd got one of those little mikes that clips on the lapel, so Joe could move and turn at will on the big night. It wasn't as much what he had to say as the way he said it. The speech was described as "Lincolnesque" as he damned the Tories and praised motherhood with every muscle of his body to earn an A-plus for delivery and body language. The crowd roared its approval.

The only other memorable performance was Trudeau's. It began with his walk to the platform and ascent to the podium. There were no blaring bands nor orchestrated hoopla to detract from the centrality of the figure all eyes were focussed on. He walked like the "Quebec Messiah" Liberals were hoping for. When he spoke he was sensitive enough to mention Martin Luther King's tragic death earlier in the day. As I listened, I wished that I had had the presence of mind to be the first candidate to pay tribute to the incalculable contribution of the American civil-rights patriot. Trudeau went on to talk about Canadian unity and a just society. It wasn't a great speech by historical standards, but in the hush of the great cavernous hall, he sounded the right notes for Liberal ears. When he finished, young people in the upper seats of every section sprang to their feet, chanting and waving Trudeau signs. The effect was electrifying, and this seemingly spontaneous demonstration ringed the auditorium in living witness to a kind of collective movement. No matter that we learned weeks later that the whole demonstration had been stage-managed at Pierre's suggestion and involved hundreds of non-voting "instant Liberals". They had used the guest passes Walter Gordon had purchased – to the exclusion of all other candidates' representatives. The net effect was a tremendous psychological boost that created a media storm for Trudeau and consolidated hundreds of second- and third-ballot commitments.

Moods are quickly transmitted in politics, and my feeling that this had been my personal Black Friday was confirmed when I dropped in to our reception at the Château Laurier that night. The room was the same, and the crowd was still big – but not quite as large as the night before – and the mood was more subdued. I had the same feeling one gets standing on a beach when the tide turns. Thursday, the waves had been getting higher. Friday, the flood tide of support was ebbing – gently, perhaps, but ebbing.

The unease was real though unspoken on Saturday morning as my team discussed floor strategy before proceeding to the hall. Tension mounted as we took our places and saw the solid phalanx of Quebec and Newfoundland delegates lined up behind Trudeau. No one doubted Pierre's commanding lead; but was my second-place position still strong enough to ensure that I would be a rallying point? We voted and returned to our places to suffer through what felt like eternity before the result was announced. The vacuum was filled with the kind of banal banter appropriate to a haunted house in the dead of night. Finally John Nichol read the numbers: Trudeau 752, Hellyer 330, Winters 293, Martin and Turner 277 each, with Greene, MacEachen, and Kierans far behind with 169, 165, and 103 respectively. Rev. Lloyd Henderson drew a zero. I felt as if I had been kicked in the stomach by a wayward bull. I was in second place all right, but the number of votes was abysmal. Until Friday we had expected something in the 450 to 500 range, and had informed the press accordingly. Now the credibility of that prediction lay in tatters.

Martin Goldfarb, who was cutting his polling teeth on my campaign, had sampled delegates on the way in to hear the speeches on Friday and on their way out afterwards. He had estimated that we had lost 130 first-ballot votes as a result of the speeches, but this vital information wasn't relayed to me. Consequently I was ill-prepared for the magnitude of the slippage, and I am afraid that my face reflected the shock. Seconds later I had relocated my "all is well" mask.

Paul Martin must have been even more devastated. He and Kierans dropped out after the first ballot, and the rest of us descended on them like a flock of vultures. Both Bob Winters and I talked to Paul personally, but he decided to sit tight and release his delegates. I felt deeply for him. Few men had given so much to the Liberal Party. Now he was retiring from the race with great and admirable dignity.

Standing in line for the second ballot, I had person after person lean over to say, "Don't worry, Paul. I'll be back with you on the next ballot. I'm just giving Joe Greene one more vote in appreciation of his outstanding speech." At least fifteen to twenty individuals said something to that effect, and these were just the ones within a radius close enough to speak. The news was heartwarming, but, alas, another development would intervene.

Allan MacEachen announced to his supporters that he was withdrawing after the first ballot, although official notice reached the chairman too late to remove his name from the list. His delegates were free to switch their allegiance, and for many Nova Scotians that meant voting for their other favourite son, Bob Winters. When the result was announced it was Trudeau 964, Winters 473, Hellyer 465, Turner 347, Greene 104, and MacEachen 11. Bob Winters had moved into second place – 8 votes ahead of me.

At this point the lobbying became frenetic. Bob wanted me to move at once, and Judy LaMarsh made her immortal plea to me to stop Trudeau. But I really couldn't move when the difference was so small. The majority of my supporters wouldn't understand – nor would my family, who had been so wonderfully loyal throughout. Ellen urged me to stay in, and I may have been further influenced by the faint dream that some of those delegates who had promised to come back on the third ballot still would. I decided to sit tight as the temperature – and the pressure – in the arena rose even further.

One humorous incident broke the tension as we waited for the results of the third ballot. The CBC's intrepid reporter Larry Zolf stuck a microphone in Ellen's face and demanded:

"How are you bearing up, Mrs. Winters?"

"As well as you are, I think," she replied with her usual unflappable composure.

The results of the third ballot were Trudeau 1,054, Winters 621, Hellyer 377, Turner 279. There was no remaining doubt about the polarization, so I decided to move to Winters. It was a heart-wrenching and emotional moment. Neither before nor since have I seen so many grown men cry unashamedly. It was a scene beyond the comprehension of anyone who hasn't lived through a similar experience. My twelve-year-old son David captured the essence of the emotional turmoil when he said: "One minute we are shouting 'Go Paul Go', and the next minute it's 'Winters, Winters'. Tears continued to stream down exhausted faces as loyal supporters stowed their Hellyer paraphernalia under their seats and donned Winters garb.

Although the majority followed me to Winters, there were a number who couldn't. Whereas I represented the middle of the political spectrum, which was the first choice of people like Keith Davey and Barney Danson, for example, Winters was too far right. So they took a walk across the floor. Keith now says that he moved to Trudeau on the second ballot, but there was no visible evidence at the time, since he remained in my section until the fourth ballot, when he and Barney joined Trudeau's "orange" brigade.

Bob Winters welcomed me with open arms, and the two of us trekked off to see John Turner in an effort to make it a threesome. Our entreaties were in vain; Turner couldn't be moved. Perhaps he was thinking ahead to "next time" and his place in history. Or he may not have been in full control of his own destiny, because many of his supporters were young and, had he dropped out, it is likely that Trudeau rather than Winters would have been the principal beneficiary. In any event, he decided to hang on.

The die was cast, and the fourth ballot merely confirmed what everyone expected as John Nichol went to the podium and announced: "The new leader of the Liberal Party and next Prime Minister of Canada is . . . Pierre Elliott Trudeau." Pandemonium broke loose as the fifty-one percent of delegates who had voted for the winner jumped, cheered, waved placards, and chanted TRU–DEAU, TRU–DEAU. Bob turned to me and said "Come on, Paul", as we began the long walk through the crushing mob to the platform to demonstrate solidarity with our new chief.

Although the majority of Liberals were pleased with the convention's choice, there were some who were not. I was accused then, and on and off throughout the years (as late as the Liberal convention in Windsor in March 1988), of being a traitor to the Liberal Party and to Canada for not going to Winters on the third rather than the fourth ballot. The inference was that he then would have won. This is fantasy born of wishful thinking. Bill Macdonald and his partner Joe Duffy, publishers of *Hi News*, a paper for high-school students, had done an extensive poll of delegates' intentions. The questions included not only first and second preferences, but also their last choice – the person they would not vote for under any circumstances.

The poll showed that there were more delegates who did not want Trudeau than who did not want me. Consequently, had I been ahead on the second ballot and in the race to the showdown, I would have won by a narrow margin. But there were more delegates who did not want Winters than who did not want Trudeau. So as soon as Bob pulled ahead of me, it was all over for both of us, and there was nothing that anyone could do about it. Bob's error was in pulling out of the unofficial race and saying that he did not intend to run. Had he been in from the beginning, he might have held the allegiance of people like Joey Smallwood and Bob Andras. It might just have made the difference. But he didn't opt in soon enough, and he didn't win!

Naturally I was disappointed that the decision had turned on so few votes – just eight on the second ballot. It was especially frustrating since Bill Lee could list so many "what ifs" – not just one or two, but more than a dozen. What if I had attended the Western Liberal Conference in January? What if Allan Mac-Eachen had stayed in for one more ballot to hold the Nova Scotians intact? But most significant and devastating of all was, what if I hadn't read my speech?

Sunday morning I opened an envelope Bill Lee had left on the music cabinet in the hall at our house. It contained a fresh and punchy speech written by ad-man Gerry Goodis. Bill's note said he preferred it to the one by Bill Macdonald, but it was my decision. He only pleaded that, whatever my choice, I should not read it. Years later, when I was cleaning my desk at Transport, I found a note I had made at an Ontario Liberal Convention against the eventuality I might someday run for federal leader. It mentioned the size of sign that was best for maximum impact without blocking people's view, the necessity of loading the seats that would be picked up automatically by the TV cameras, and the third point was not to read my speech, underlined three times!

Apart from the immediate hurt, I really concluded that the convention had made the right choice. Pierre was so fresh, so different, so representative of the restless sixties. He seemed just right for the times. I never doubted that experience was important and that I was much better qualified to run the Canadian economy. But then there was Quebec. The seeds of revolution and possible separation had been obvious for some time. It seemed to me that any unrest in Quebec might be attributed to the fact of an English-speaking leader, even if the assessment was quite unfair. It would be one more instance of perception becoming reality. With a Quebecer like Pierre in the hot seat, people would be less likely to confuse cause and effect.

My spirit was calm when Ellen and I left for church on Sunday. We had told the press we would be attending, which was our custom, whether we won or lost. Though bone-weary, we drew on our inner reserves during the service, and everything was under control when we left the church by the front door. About halfway to our car we were stopped by a lady – no doubt well-intentioned, but not well versed in the fine art of sensitivity – who had watched the entire convention proceedings on TV and said: "My, you must have had fun." That did it! Ellen, who had been an absolute brick throughout the long, excruciating ordeal, couldn't hold back the tears any longer. We turned and fled for the anonymity of car and home.

NOTES

Throughout the notes HP/PAC is used to indicate material with the Hellyer Papers in the Public Archives of Canada. HP/T indicates material in the author's private papers. PAC indicates the Public Archives of Canada. The Hellyer diaries are all in the private papers.

Chapter 1: Early Days and Politics

1. Letter to Mitchell Sharp, October 7, 1960. (HP/PAC)
2. Letter from Mitchell Sharp, October 11, 1960. (HP/PAC)
3. Letter from Walter L. Gordon, January 16, 1961. (HP/PAC)
4. Paul Hellyer, "The Task of the Liberal Democratic State" (An address to the Young Liberals National Convention, Banff, Alberta, September 21, 1961), p. 13. (HP/PAC)
5. Both the fact that Gordon wasn't consulted and the quote itself were confirmed in a telephone interview, June 24, 1985.
6. Canada, Cabinet Minutes, June 18, 1963.
7. Lester B. Pearson, *Mike: The Memoirs of the Rt. Hon. Lester B. Pearson*, eds. John A. Munro and Alex I. Inglis, vol. 3 (Toronto: University of Toronto Press), p. 107.

Chapter 2: The White Paper on Defence

1. Copy of draft of White Paper returned to me by A. H. Zimmerman, Chairman of the Defence Research Board, with his note of December 20, 1963. (HP/PAC)
2. Top Secret and Strictly Personal letter to the Rt. Hon. L. B. Pearson, from the High Commissioner for Canada, Canada House, London, S.W. 1, October 8, 1963. (HP/PAC)
3. Strictly Personal and Confidential for Personal Use Only letter from Prime Minister Pearson to the Honourable George Drew, High Commissioner for Canada, Canada House, London S.W. 1, October 14, 1963. (HP/PAC)

4. Department of National Defence, *Report of the Ad Hoc Committee on Defence Policy*, September 30, 1963, para. 35, p. 34.

5. House of Commons, *Debates*, August 5, 1960, p. 7602.

6. J. G. Forth, "Unification – Why, How, When", *Canadian Army Staff College Journal, 1959-1961.* (HP/PAC)

7. Personal and Confidential letter from General Charles Foulkes, Victoria, B.C., June 13, 1963. (HP/PAC)

8. General Charles Foulkes, "The Case for One Service", 1961, p. 2.

9. *Ibid.*

10. *Ibid.* pp. 3-15.

11. *Ibid.* p. 23.

12. *Weekend* magazine, September 22, 1956, p. 2.

13. *Ibid.*

14. *Ibid.*, p. 3.

15. Postscript to a letter from a Mr. Justice Donald Keith of the Superior Court of Ontario, Osgoode Hall, Toronto, December 17, 1980.

16. Paul T. Hellyer, *The White Paper on Defence* (Ottawa: Department of National Defence), March 1964, p. 19.

17. Note from Bill Lee, December 20, 1963. (HP/PAC)

18. Letter from Vice-Admiral H. S. Rayner, December 20, 1963. (HP/PAC)

19. Memorandum from Air Chief Marshal F. R. Miller, Chairman, Chiefs of Staff, December 20, 1963. (HP/PAC)

20. Memorandum from Air Marshal, C. R. Dunlap, Chief of the Air Staff, December 20, 1963. (HP/PAC)

21. Undated memorandum from Derry Dwyer, Chief of Parliamentary Returns. (HP/PAC)

22. Undated memorandum, initialled by Elgin B. Armstrong, Deputy Minister of National Defence. (HP/PAC)

23. Hellyer diary, February 7, 1964.

24. *Ibid.*, February 8, 1964.

25. *Ibid.*, February 10, 1964.

26. *Ibid.*, February 12, 1964.

27. *Ibid.*

28. *Ibid.*, February 21, 1964.

29. *Ibid.*, March 24, 1964.

30. *Ibid.*, March 26, 1964.

31. *Toronto Star*, "Sensible Defence to a Point", March 28, 1964.
32. *Ibid.*, March 28, 1963, p. 7.
33. "Defense for a Decade Ahead", *Time* magazine, April 3, 1964, pp. 11-12.
34. "A Force To Fit Canada's Needs", *Montreal Star*, March 30, 1964.
35. "Nothing but Praise for Defence Minister Hellyer", *Canadian Aviation*, vol. 37, no. 5, May 1964.
36. Lubor J. Zink, "Clear Thinking on Our Defense", Toronto *Telegram*, March 30, 1964, p. 7.

Chapter 3: Home on the Rideau

1. James Plomer, "*The Gold-braid Mind Is Destroying Our Navy*", *Maclean's* magazine, September 7, 1963.
2. *Ibid.*
3. *Ibid.*
4. Jeffry V. Brock, *The Thunder and the Sunshine*, vol. 2 of *With Many Voices: Memoirs of a Sailor* (Toronto: McClelland & Stewart, 1983), pp. 131-3.
5. Canda, House of Commons, *Debates*, February 21, 1964, p. 81.
6. Hellyer diary, February 3, 1964.
7. Canada, House of Commons, *Debates*, February 24, 1964, p. 129.
8. *Ibid.*
9. Hellyer diary, February 25, 1964.
10. Paul Martin, *A Very Public Life*, vol. 2, (Toronto: Deneau, 1985), pp. 547-8.
11. Lester B. Pearson, *Mike: The Memoirs of the Rt. Hon. Lester B. Pearson*, ed. John A. Munro and Alex I. Inglis, vol. 3, (Toronto: Univeristy of Toronto Press, 1975), p. 135.

Chapter 4: Reprieve

1. Hellyer diary, February 24, 1964.
2. *Ibid.*, March 7, 1964.
3. *Ibid.*, April 9, 1964.
4. *Ibid.*, April 13, 1964.

5.   *Ibid.*
6.   *Ibid.*, April 14, 1964.
7.   Judy LaMarsh, *Memoirs of a Bird in a Gilded Cage* (Toronto: McClelland & Stewart, 1968), p. 91.
8.   *Ibid.*
9.   *Ibid.*
10. Hellyer diary, May 6, 1964.
11. Letter from Graham Towers, Rockcliffe Park, Ottawa, April 12, 1964. (HP/T)
12. *Ibid.*
13. Hellyer diary, February 23, 1964.
14. *Ibid.*, February 29, 1964.
15. *Ibid.*
16. *Ibid.*, June 6, 1964.
17. *Ibid.*, June 8, 1964.
18. *Ibid.*, June 9, 1964.
19. *Ibid.*, June 14, 1964.
20. *Ibid.*, June 17, 1964.
21. *Ibid.*, June 19, 1964.
22. *Ibid.*

Chapter 5: Troubled Waters

1.   William Manchester, *The Last Lion: Winston Spencer Churchill* (New York: Dell, 1984), p. 34.
2.   Canada, Department of National Defence, *Defence Council Minutes*, January 21, 1963.
3.   Hellyer diary, August 5, 1964.
4.   Jeffry B. Brock, *The Thunder and the Sunshine*, vol. 2 of *With Many Voices: Memoirs of a Sailor* (Toronto: McClelland & Stewart, 1983), pp. 167-8.
5.   Letter from P. T. Hellyer to Air Chief Marshal (Ret.) Frank Miller, Toronto, July 18, 1985. (HP/T)
6.   Letter to P. T. Hellyer from Frank Miller, Charlottesville, Virginia, July 27, 1985. (HP/T)
7.   Hellyer diary, August 28, 1964.
8.   Canada, Cabinet, *Minutes*, September 29, 1964.
9.   Hellyer diary, September 29, 1964.
10. *Ibid.*, September 30, 1964.
11. *Ibid.*, October 3, 1964.
12. *Ibid.*

13. *Ibid.*, October 6, 1964.
14. *Ibid.*, October 7, 1964.
15. *Ibid.*, October 9, 1964.
16. *Ibid.*, October 10, 1964.
17. *Ibid.*
18. *Ibid.*, October 13, 1964.
19. *Ibid.*, October 15, 1964.
20. *Ibid.*, October 16, 1964.
21. Charles Lynch, "The Wonder Boy Carves His Niche", Hamilton *Spectator*, January 11, 1964.
22. Editorial from the Calgary *Albertan*, as reprinted in the Kingston *Whig-Standard*, March 24, 1964.
23. Ron Collister, "Pearson's Star System Blinks Out", Toronto *Telegram*, May 8, 1964.
24. Five articles by C. W. Borklund in *Armed Forces Management*, June 1964, p. 45-77.

Chapter 6: Reserves, Rumbles, and Reorganization

1. Peter C. Newman, *True North Not Strong and Free* (Toronto: McClelland & Stewart, 1983), p. 36.
2. An undated memo from Marg Bulger attached to a message from Esmond Butler, Private Secretary to the Governor General. (HP/PAC)
3. Editorial, "Shillelaghs for the Minister", *Star Weekly* (Toronto), December 12, 1964.
4. *Ibid.*
5. Lester B. Pearson, *Mike: The Memoirs of The Right Honourable Lester B. Pearson*, vol. 3, eds. John A. Munro and A. Inglis, (Toronto: University of Toronto Press, 1975), p. 151.
6. *Ibid.*, p. 152.
7. Canada, House of Commons, *Debates*, November 24, 1964, p. 10429.
8. Pearson, *Mike*, vol. 3, p. 151.
9. Richard Gwyn, *The Shape of Scandal*, (Toronto: Clarke Irwin, 1965), p. 48.
10. Canada, Cabinet, *Minutes*, December 17, 1964.
11. Editorial, "Pearson Fiddled While Favreau Burned", Brantford *Expositor*, October 8, 1965.
12. Richard Gwyn, *The Shape of Scandal*, p. 49.

13. Letter from J. W. Pickersgill, Ottawa, November 2, 1985. (HP/T)
14. Hellyer diary, October 21, 1964.
15. *Ibid.*, October 27, 1964.
16. *Ibid.*, October 21, 1964.
17. *Ibid.*, October 26, 1964.
18. Canada, Department of National Defence, *Defence Council Minutes*, November 9, 1964.
19. Hellyer diary, December 2, 1964.
20. Canada, Cabinet, *Minutes*, December 8, 1964.
21. *Ibid.*
22. *Ibid.*
23. *Ibid.*, December 10, 1964.
24. Hellyer diary, November 20, 1964.
25. *Ibid.*, December 29, 1964.
26. *Ibid.*, December 30, 1964.
27. *Ibid.*, December 31, 1964.

Chapter 7: The Maple Leaf Forever

1. Canada, Cabinet, *Minutes*, May 19, 1964.
2. *Ibid.* May 21, 1964.
3. *Ibid.* May 25, 1964.
4. *Ibid.* May 26, 1964.
5. Canada, *Defence Council Minutes*, July 20, 1964.
6. Canada, Cabinet, *Minutes*, January 20, 1965.
7. Jim Rae, "Ten Thousand Cheer Raising of New Flag," Ottawa *Citizen*, February 16, 1965.
8. Canada, Cabinet, *Minutes*, February 16, 1965.
9. Memorandum to the Deputy Minister, January 9, 1965. (HP/PAC)
10. Memorandum to the Deputy Minister Elgin Armstrong entitled "Systems Analysis", from J. S. Hodgson, Assistant Deputy Minister (Finance), Feb. 5, 1965. (HP/PAC)
11. Hellyer diary, March 31, 1965.
12. Staff memo to Minister of National Defence, May 10, 1965. (HP/PAC)
13. Letter to Paul T. Hellyer from Air Commodore Frank Ball, Commandant RCAF Staff College, Armour Heights, Toronto, May 11, 1965. (HP/PAC)
14. Hellyer diary, May 18, 1965.

15. *Ibid.* May 21, 1965.
16. *Ibid.* June 7, 1965.
17. *Ibid.* June 8, 1965.
18. Canada, *Defence Council Minutes*, November 9, 1964.
19. Canada, Cabinet, *Minutes*, December 8, 1964.

Chapter 8: Another Minority

1. Canada, Cabinet *Minutes*, January 26, 1965.
2. *Maclean's* magazine, January 3, 1965 p. 7-11.
3. Walter Gordon, *A Political Memoir* (Toronto: Mc-Clelland & Stewart, 1977), p. 98.
4. Canada, Cabinet, *Minutes*, July 16, 1965.
5. Paul Martin, *A Very Public Life*, vol. 2, (Toronto: Deneau, 1985), p. 491.
6. Hellyer diary, November 4, 1965.
7. *Ibid.*, November 8, 1965.
8. *Ibid.*, November 9, 1965.
9. *Ibid.*, November 10, 1965.
10. *Ibid.*, November 11, 1965.
11. *Ibid.*, November 13, 1965.
12. Walter Gordon, *A Political Memoir*, p. 233.
13. Hellyer diary, December 9, 1965.
14. Walter Gordon, *A Political Memoir*, p. 233.
15. Hellyer diary, November 14, 1965.
16. *Ibid.*, November 15, 1965.
17. *Ibid.*, December 8, 1965.
18. *Ibid.*, December 10, 1965.
19. *Ibid.*, December 13, 1965.
20. *Ibid.*, December 18, 1965.
21. *Ibid.*, December 20, 1965.
22. *Ibid.*, December 21, 1965.
23. *Ibid.*
24. *Ibid.*, December 29, 1965.

Chapter 9: Damn The Torpedoes

1. Letter to Paul T. Hellyer from Keith Davey, National Organizer, Liberal Party of Canada, Ottawa, January 31, 1966. (HP/PAC)
2. Letter to the Minister of National Defence from the Prime Minister, February 7, 1966. (PAC)

3.   *Ibid.*
4.   John Bird, "Who's Leading the Field as Pearson's Successor?" *Financial Post*, February 26, 1966, p. 22.
5.   *Toronto Star*, Saturday, March 26, 1966, p. 7.
6.   Kenneth Bagnell, "The Churchman Who Could Be Our Next Prime Minister", *United Church Observer*, new series vol. 27, no. 24, March 15, 1966, p. 12.
7.   Douglas Fisher, Inside Politics "A Handicapper Sizes Up the Liberal Leadership Race", Toronto *Telegram*, March 5, 1966.
8.   *Newsweek*, March 21, 1966.
9.   Canada, Standing Committee on National Defence, *Minutes of Proceedings and Evidence*, no. 12, Thursday, June 23, 1966, p. 334.
10. Bill Lee, Memo to Minister of National Defence, March 24, 1966. (HP/PAC)
11. Surgeon Rear-Admiral W. J. Elliot, Personal & Confidential memo, January 28, 1965. (HP/PAC)
12. Henry L. Stimson and McGeorge Bundy, *On Active Service in Peace and War* (New York: Harper, 1948) p. 507, quoted in Demetrios Caraley, *The Politics of Military Unification* (New York: Columbia University Press, 1966), p. 26.
13. [Edmonton – Special to the *Star*], "Hellyer Stakes His Job Against Ousted Admiral", *Toronto Star*, July 16, 1966.
14. Hellyer diary, July 18, 1966.
15. *Ibid.*, July 19, 1966.
16. *Ibid.*, July 20, 1966.
17. Canada, Cabinet, *Minutes*, July 20, 1966.
18. Toronto *Globe and Mail* [Ottawa Bureau], "No Penalty for Landymore – Hellyer Says Integration To Proceed Full Speed Ahead", July 20, 1966, p. 1.
19. Greg Connolley, " 'Full Speed Ahead', Hellyer Order after Admirals Revolt." Ottawa *Citizen*, Wednesday, July 20, 1966, p. 1.
20. *Ibid.*
21. Hellyer diary, July 21, 1966.
22. Canada, Cabinet, *Minutes*, June 14, 1966.
23. *Ibid.*, June 16, 1966.
24. *Ibid.*

Chapter 10: The Landymore Affair

1. Hellyer diary, August 2, 1966.
2. Bob McCleave, "Stormy Session ahead for Hellyer", *Dartmouth Free Press*, August 4, 1966.
3. Hellyer diary, August 9.
4. *Ibid.*, August 10.
5. Canada, Cabinet, *Minutes*, August 10, 1966.
6. Hellyer diary, August 12, 1966.
7. Canadian Press, "On Unification – Ex-Officers May Get Chance to Sound Off", *Ottawa Journal*, August 17, 1966.
8. Canadian Press, "Harkness Urges Halt to Unification Move", Saint John *Telegraph-Journal*, August 20, 1966.
9. Memorandum to the Hon. P. T. Hellyer from the Prime Minister, August 26, 1966. (HP/PAC)
10. Canadian Press, "Harkness Urges Hald to Unification Movement", Saint John *Telegraph-Journal*, August 20, 1966.
11. Canadian Press, "Hellyer Repeats Plan To Introduce Unification Bill", *London Free Press*, August 30, 1966.
12. "Two Retired Generals Add Voices to Chorus Protesting Unification", Toronto *Globe and Mail*, September 1, 1966.
13. *Ibid.*
14. Canadian Press, "Allard Branded 'Propagandist' for Unification" [Port Arthur *News Chronicle*], "MP's Question Allard's Role" [Regina *Leader-Post*], September 7, 1966.
15. Duart Farquharson, "CNE Speech – Hellyer Defends Service Chief", Ottawa *Citizen*, September 7, 1966.
16. Canadian Press, "In Forces Unification – Opposition Accuses Hellyer of Contempt", *Victoria Daily Times*, September 8, 1966.
17. Chris Morgan and David Langford, *Facts and Fallacies* (London: Webb Bower, 1981), p. 145, cited in Christopher Cerf and Victor Navasky, *The Experts Speak* (New York: Pantheon Books, 1984), p. 242.
18. *Ibid.*
19. *Ibid.*, p. 243.
20. Maréchal Ferdinand Foch, *Coronet*, August 1914, quoted in Cerf and Navasky, *The Experts Speak*, p. 246.

21.   "Boos or Cheers for Hellyer? Sailors Disagree", Toronto *Globe and Mail*, September 22, 1966, p. 27.

22.   Canadian Press, "Row Flares Over Diefenbaker Leadership", *Simcoe Reformer*, September 22, 1966, p. 1.

23.   "Hees Raps Unification" – 'Forces' Morale at Stake' ", *Vancouver Sun*, September 13, 1966.

24.   Headlines in the Vancouver *Province* and Toronto *Globe and Mail*, September 14, 1966.

25.   Ron Collister, "Pound for Pound, It's Perfect," Toronto *Telegram*, October 6, 1966.

26.   Hellyer diary, September 28, 1966.

27.   *Ibid.*, September 29, 1966.

28.   "Leegram" dated September 30, 1966. (HP/PAC)

29.   Hellyer diary, October 1, 1966.

30.   Walter Gordon, *A Political Memoir* (Toronto: Mc-Clelland & Stewart), 1977, p. 250.

31.   *Ibid.*

32.   Canada, House of Commons, *Debates*, October 12, 1966, p. 8569.

33.   *Ibid.*

34.   Canada, House of Commons, *Debates*, October 12, 1966, p. 8572.

35.   *Ibid.*, p. 8578.

36.   *Ibid.*, October 13, 1966, p. 8597.

37.   *Ibid.*, p. 8598.

38.   *Ibid.*, p. 8601.

39.   Victor J. Mackie, " 'Tampering' Charge May Shelve Motion, Nugent Hints", *Ottawa Journal*, October 15, 1966, p. 1.

40.   Canada, House of Commons, *Debates*, October 20, 1966, p. 8890.

41.   *Ibid.*, p. 8889.

42.   *Ibid.*, October 24, 1966, p. 8997.

43.   *Ibid.*, October 28, 1966, p. 9223.

44.   John Grant explained what happened and accepted responsibility for the changes in a memo dated October 20, 1966. (HP/PAC)

45.   David P. Burke, Lt.-Col., USAF, *The Unification of the Canadian Armed Forces: The Politics of Defence in the Pearson Administration* (Ph.D. diss. Naval Postgraduate

School, Monterey, California), Department of National Security Affairs (56BQ), p. 257.

46. *Ibid.*
47. Canada, House of Commons, *Debates*, October 31, 1966, p. 9353.
48. *Ibid.*
49. Eric Dennis, "What Happened? Forrestall 'Perplexed' by Ottawa Cold Shoulder", Halifax *Mail-Star*, November 3, 1966, p. 1.

Chapter 11: Bill C–243, 1966-67

1. Draft letter from Paul T. Hellyer to Scott Young, November 3, 1966, and Bill Lee's notation. (HP/PAC)
2. Canada, Cabinet, *Minutes*, October 18, 1966.
3. Canada, House of Commons, *Debates*, November 4, 1966, p. 9538.
4. *Ibid.*
5. *Ibid.*, p. 9540.
6. Hellyer diary, November 9, 1966.
7. *Ibid.*, November 10, 1966.
8. Editorial, "Call Diefenbaker's Bluff on Unification", *Toronto Star*, Thursday, November 10, 1966.
9. *Calgary Herald*, July 25, 1966.
10. Toronto *Globe and Mail*, August 27, 1966.
11. *Ibid.*, September 17, 1966.
12. *Ottawa Journal*, November 11, 1966.
13. Hellyer diary, November 11, 1966.
14. *Ibid.*, November 12, 1966.
15. Letter to Paul Hellyer from Patrick Watson, Toronto, Ontario, February 8, 1966. (HP/PAC).
16. Hellyer diary, November 14, 1966.
17. *Ibid.*, December 5, 1966.
18. *Ibid.*, December 7, 1966.
19. *Ibid.*, December 8, 1966.
20. "Mr. Hellyer's Gallant Gesture", Ottawa *Citizen*, January 9, 1967.
21. "Mr. Hellyer Saves the Ballet", *Toronto Star*, January 4, 1967.
22. "Abuse of Ministerial Responsibility", *Edmonton Journal*, January 10, 1987.

23.   Hellyer diary, January 3, 1967.
24.   *Ibid.*, January 4, 1967.
25.   *Ibid.*, January 5, 1967.
26.   *Ibid.*, January 9, 1967.
27.   *Ibid.*, January 11, 1967.
28.   *Ibid.*, January 26, 1967.
29.   Canada, House of Commons, *Debates*, January 31, 1967, p. 12477.
30.   *Ibid.*, January 31, 1967, p. 12489.
31.   *Ibid.*, February 1, 1967, p. 12533.
32.   *Ibid.*, February 2, 1967, pp. 12607-8.

Chapter 12: The War of Words Is Over

1.   The initial members of the Standing Committee on Defence when it met on February 7, 1967, were Robert Andras, F. Andrew Brewin, James Brown, Gordon Churchill, Grant Deachman, Frank J. W. Fane, Walter Foy, David W. Groos, Douglas S. Harkness, Leonard Hopkins, Marcel Lambert, Paul Langlois (Chicoutimi), Raymond C. Langlois (Mégantic), Gérald Laniel, H. Pit Lessard, J. Angus Maclean (Queen's), J. Chester MacRae, John R. Matheson, James C. McNulty, George E. Nixon, Heber Smith, Eric Stefanson, Raymond Rock, and Harold Winch. Source: Canada House of Commons, *National Defence Volume CXIII, 1966-67*, p. 103.
2.   *Minutes of Standing Committee on Defence*, February 14, 1967, p. 959.
3.   Hellyer diary, February 16, 1967.
4.   *Ottawa Journal*, Monday February 20, 1967.
5.   *The Times* (London, England), February 18, 1967.
6.   Letter from Jean I. Hall, Dominium, Pura, Ticino, Switzerland, February 21, 1967. (HP/PAC)
7.   Hellyer diary, February 16, 1967.
8.   *Minutes of Standing Committee on Defence*, February 16, 1967, p. 1228.
9.   *Ibid.*, February 17, 1967, pp. 1244-1292.
10.   Hellyer diary, February 17, 1967.
11.   *Ibid.*, February 18, 1967.
12.   *Ibid.*, February 20, 1967.
13.   *Ibid.*

14. *Minutes of Standing Committee on Defence*, February 20, 1967, p. 1312.
15. Hellyer diary, February 23, 1967.
16. *Ibid.*, February 24, 1967.
17. *Ibid.*, February 25, 1967.
18. *Ibid.*, February 26, 1967.
19. *Ibid.*, February 27, 1967.
20. Memorandum to the Minister of National Defence from the Judge Advocate General, Feb. 16, 1967. (HP/PAC)
21. Hellyer diary, February 28, 1967.
22. *Quebec Chronicle-Telegraph*, March 1, 1967.
23. Hellyer diary, March 1, 1967.
24. *Ibid.*, March 2, 1967.
25. Canada, Cabinet, *Minutes*, March 2, 1967.
26. Hellyer diary, March 4, 1967.
27. *Lethbridge Herald*, March 2, 1967.
28. Victoria *Daily Colonist*, March 2, 1967.
29. Hellyer diary, March 5, 1967.
30. Canada, Cabinet, *Minutes*, March 6, 1967.
31. *Ibid.*, March 7, 1967.
32. *Ibid.*
33. Canada, Cabinet, *Minutes*, March 7, 1967.
34. Canada, House of Commons, *Debates*, March 14, 1967, p. 13951.
35. *Ibid.*, p. 13959.
36. Ottawa *Citizen*, March 14, 1967.
37. Canada, House of Commons, *Debates*, March 21, 1967, p. 14258.
38. *Ibid.*, March 22, 1967, p. 14405.
39. Montreal *Gazette*, March 28, 1967.
40. *Intelligencer* (Belleville, Ontario), March 31, 1967.
41. Toronto *Telegram*, March 31, 1967.
42. Canada, Cabinet, *Minutes*, April 3, 1967.
43. *Ibid.*, April 4, 1967.
44. *Ibid.*
45. Ottawa *Journal*, April 6, 1967.
46. Ottawa *Citizen*, April 7, 1967.
47. *Ibid.*
48. Montreal *Gazette*, April 8, 1967.
49. *Ibid.*

50.   Toronto *Telegram*, Monday, April 10, 1967.
51.   Canada, Cabinet, *Minutes*, April 11, 1967.
52.   Canada, House of Commons, *Debates*, April 11, 1967, p. 14759.
53.   Toronto *Globe and Mail*, April 12, 1967.
54.   Canada, Cabinet, *Minutes*, April 17, 1967.
55.   *Ibid.*, April 18, 1967.
56.   Toronto *Telegram*, April 15, 1967.
57.   *Toronto Star*, April 19, 1967.
58.   *Ibid.*
59.   Canada, Cabinet, *Minutes*, April 25, 1967.
60.   Montreal *Gazette*, April 26, 1967.
61.   *Ibid.*
62.   Canada, Cabinet, *Minutes*, May 2, 1967.

Chapter 13: Centennial Year – 1967

1.   Hellyer diary, May 11, 1967.
2.   *Ibid.*
3.   *Ibid.*, May 12, 1967.
4.   *Ibid.*
5.   *Ibid.*, May 15, 1967.
6.   Montreal *Gazette*, June 2, 1967.
7.   Story as recounted by Prime Minister Pearson.
8.   Ottawa *Citizen*, June 27, 1967.
9.   Canada, Cabinet, *Minutes*, June 29, 1967.
10.   *Ibid.*, July 25, 1967.
11.   *Ibid.*
12.   *Ibid.*
13.   *Ibid.*, July 26, 1967.
14.   *Ibid.*, August 9, 1967.
15.   Hellyer diary, August 11, 1967.
16.   Canada, Cabinet, *Minutes*, August 16, 1967.
17.   *Ottawa Journal*, August 22, 1967.
18.   Hellyer diary, September 11, 1967.
19.   *Ibid.*, September 16, 1967.
20.   *Ibid.*, September 17, 1967.
21.   Canada, Cabinet, *Minutes*, September 18, 1967.
22.   Hellyer diary, September 19, 1967.
23.   *Ibid.*, September 20, 1967.

Chapter 14: The Race Is On

1. Hellyer diary, September 21, 1967.
2. *Ibid.*, September 24, 1967.
3. "A handshake all round for Roberts Bank", Vancouver *Province*, October 21, 1967.
4. "Brighter Prospects", *Winnipeg Free Press*, October 27, 1967.
5. "Mr. Hellyer's Move", Halifax *Chronicle-Herald*, November 1, 1967.
6. Gary Oakes, "Heirs to Pearson Start Their Leadership Moves", Toronto *Telegram*, November 9, 1967.
7. Richard Jackson, "Campaigning Irks PM–Grit Hopefuls Get Orders to Ease Off", Ottawa *Journal*, November 10, 1967.
8. Hellyer diary, November 21, 1967.
9. *Ibid.*, November 27, 1967.
10. *Ibid.*, December 10, 1967.
11. *Ibid.*
12. *Ibid.*, December 13, 1967.
13. *Ibid.*, December 14, 1967.
14. *Ibid.*, December 15, 1967.
15. *Ibid.*, December 19, 1967.
16. George Bain, "Problem of the Evil Nuts", Toronto *Globe and Mail*, April 21, 1967.
17. Letter from Philip G. Givens, Toronto, Canada, April 21, 1967.
18. Hellyer diary, December 19, 1967.
19. *Ibid.*, December 20, 1967.
20. *Ibid.*, December 21, 1967.
21. *Ibid.*, December 22, 1967.
22. *Ibid.*, December 23, 1967.
23. *Ibid.*, December 26, 1967.
24. *Ibid.*, December 27, 1967.

Chapter 15: It's Trudeau on The Fourth Ballot

1. Toronto *Telegram*, January 12, 1968.
2. Toronto *Globe and Mail*, January 12, 1968.
3. Peter C. Newman in the *Ottawa Journal*, January 13, 1968.

4. Douglas Fisher and Harry Crowe in the Toronto *Telegram*, January 20, 1968.
5. Toronto *Globe and Mail*, January 26, 1968.
6. *Toronto Star*, January 26, 1968.
7. Toronto *Telegram*, February 15, 1968.
8. Ottawa *Citizen*, February 16, 1968.
9. *Windsor Star*, February 17, 1968.
10. *Toronto Star*, February 17, 1968.
11. As reported in the *Winnipeg Free Press*, February 17, 1968.
12. Toronto *Globe and Mail*, March 11, 1968.
13. Toronto *Telegram*, March 18, 1968.
14. *Toronto Star*, March 22, 1968.
15. *Ibid.*
16. *Ibid.*
17. Toronto *Telegram*, March 22, 1968.
18. *Toronto Star*, March 26, 1968.
19. *Ibid.*
20. Ottawa *Citizen*, April 4, 1968.
21. *Montreal Star*, April 4, 1968.

INDEX